GIVE YOUR C

Bruce Kemble is a passionate supporter of parents in their battles with hostile teachers and local authority officials. He confesses his prejudice in favour of parents.

Born in South-East London in 1938, he was educated at the local primary school. He won a place to Dulwich College and after two years doing odd jobs, he went to Downing College, Cambridge. Married with two children, he has been Education Reporter on the *Daily Express* for the past six years and *Give Your Child A Chance* is the fifth education book he has been associated with. In *Looking Forward To The Seventies*, published in 1967, he wrote a long, controversial chapter attacking the streaming of children as early as the age of seven, and in *Crisis in The Classroom* he challenged the Government's policy in slowing down the expansion of education spending. Kemble acted as the 'midwife' for *Careers For The Unqualified*, published in 1970 and edited *Fit to Teach* (1971), a survey on teacher training.

CONDITIONS OF SALE

This book shall not, by way of trade or otherwise, be lent, re-sold, hired out or otherwise circulated without the publisher's prior consent in any form of binding or cover other than that in which it is published and without a similar condition including this condition being imposed on the subsequent purchaser. The book is published at a net price, and is supplied subject to the Publishers Association Standard Conditions of Sale registered under the Restrictive Trade Practices Act, 1956.

GIVE YOUR CHILD A CHANCE

Bruce Kemble

REVISED AND UPDATED

PAN BOOKS LTD : LONDON

First published 1970 by W. H. Allen and Co Ltd.
This edition published 1972 by Pan Books Ltd,
33 Tothill Street, London SW1.

ISBN 0 330 02930 4

© Bruce Kemble 1970, 1972

*Printed and bound in England by
Hazell Watson & Viney Ltd,
Aylesbury, Bucks*

Contents

	Acknowledgements	vii
	Foreword	ix
	Introduction	xi
1	Parents as Teachers	1
	SUGGESTED READING	11
2	The Vital Years – Birth to Five	12
	SUGGESTED READING	56
3	Nursery Schools and Play-Groups	58
	SUGGESTED READING	72
4	The Most Important Lesson – Learning to Read	73
	SUGGESTED READING	95
5	How to Choose a School	109
	SUGGESTED READING	132
6	Educating Girls	133
	SUGGESTED READING	144
7	Sex Education – Why, When, Where, Who, and How?	145
	SUGGESTED READING	175
8	Some School Questions Answered	176
	GLOSSARY OF EDUCATIONAL TERMS	199
	SUGGESTED READING	205
9	Education After School – Job Prospects	206
	SUGGESTED READING	220
10	Could Your Child Go to University?	221
	FURTHER SOURCES OF SUBJECT INFORMATION	244
	Organizations Mentioned Throughout the Book	246
	Index	249

One night, I sat down on a chair and said: 'I am St Peter at the Golden Gate. You are to be folks trying to get in. Carry on.'

They came up with all sorts of reasons for getting in. One girl even came from the opposite direction and pleaded to get out!

But the star turned out to be a boy of fourteen who went by me whistling, hands in his pockets.

'Hi!' I cried, 'you can't go in there!'

He turned and looked at me. 'Oh,' he said, 'you are a new man on the job, aren't you?'

'What do you mean?' I asked.

'You don't know who I am, do you?'

'Who are you?' I asked.

'God,' he said, and went whistling into heaven.

(A. S. Neill, *Summerhill*)

Give me a child who is normally healthy, and who has good relations with its mother for the first few months of its life – and I will educate that child to any level you like.
(Prof A. R. Luria, one of the world's greatest brain surgeons and psychologists)

Acknowledgements

I am deeply grateful to the following for their encouragement and advice :

Anne Allen, Roger Beard, Lord Boyle, Ronald Deadman, Iris Grender, Joan Cass, Roy Nash, the late Sir John Newsom, and, of course, the entire staff of the Advisory Centre for Education at Cambridge, where Richard Freeman and Richard Blake displayed great patience when dealing with my frequent inquiries.

Without their support I would not have found the courage (some would say the impertinence) to embark on this book.

B.K.

Foreword

Like Bruce Kemble, I came from a working-class home in which the twin educational forces were a hot-tempered, ambitious but affectionate mother, without much learning but with a voracious appetite for library books, and an easygoing, good-natured father who I can never recollect correcting me, who was very well read and extremely knowledgeable about politics and current affairs generally. These were the negative and positive terminals which produced the current to make me what I am educationally as well as genetically.

My elder sister was a teacher and she brought a succession of books into the home which made me aware of a broader world in space and time than the medieval squire-dominated village in which I lived. John Richard Green's *Short History of the English People* was a magical book to me. I have it still and its magic remains.

I read the *Children's Newspaper* each week (what a pity it disappeared) and *Bubbles* – both from a very early age. I still look back with tingling pleasure on the weekly cliff-hanging instalment of 'Jack and Jill' on the back page of *Bubbles*.

Another source of reading was a magazine club run by the local women's institute. The members, of whom my mother was one, purchased a magazine and circulated it. I became familiar from infancy with mystical journals such as *The Review of Reviews*, which I could not understand but which certainly provided an incentive for me to find out more about the exciting world which lay over the mountains which encompassed my village.

By today's standards I suppose I did not have much reading material as a child, but from what I had I, like Bruce

Kemble, acquired a vocabulary and a tremendous ambition to use it and to master the skill of reading which, at quite an early age, I realized was the highway to that other world of which I had only had vicarious glimpses. Of course I often came a cropper in using new words. I went to a Revival service at the local Wesleyan chapel at the age of about nine or ten. I had sat stubbornly with my father in our seats when the preacher had appealed to all who were saved – or wanted to be – to stand. At the end of the service the preacher at the door asked me why I had remained seated and I replied, 'Sorry, but I am an Angelican.' Later my father told me gently about my mistake and for years afterwards I blushed at the thought of it. But I never forgot the word Anglican.

Bruce Kemble has done a great service to education in this book. In his unpompous but extremely well-informed way he has told parents how they can and should become involved in the education of their children. Parental interest is probably the most important influence in a child's educational progress. What is needed is not the neurotic nagging interest – the over-anxiety with which so many middle-class parents ruin their children's education – but a genuine desire to be involved in the educational process both at school and at home. And they are equally important. Bruce Kemble's book is an excellent guide to sensible and helpful parental involvement.

EDWARD SHORT
Secretary of State for Education and Science, 1968–70

Introduction

My mother stood ironing in a back room of our South London home. My six-year-old sister, Ann, was reading to me. I was four.

Suddenly I anticipated a word and then read on in a book I had not seen before. The family rejoiced at this triumph – *I could read*.

This moment is part of our family history. It is a sort of incident we recall at the Christmas table when we have a rare reunion. Many of my childhood memories are about books, and being read to. I was lucky to have parents who surrounded us with magazines and books, and who had the patience to read our favourite stories over and over again.

Every Sunday afternoon, my father would take his newspaper – usually *The People* – into a back room on the ground floor, put his feet up on the sofa and settle down to an after-lunch nap. But my sister and I were restlessly prowling about with our copy of *Sunny Stories* which arrived with the paper every Sunday. Eventually we would creep into the room and sit on either side of our sleeping father. However hard we thought we were trying to keep quiet, we always woke him. Then he would hide his understandable annoyance and calmly begin reading the simple stories for us.

I also remember his infectious enthusiasm for *Treasure Island*. I have always associated this book most closely with him. I think it is because his home town was Plymouth, and he related his own nostalgic memories of childhood haunts around this ancient city to our knowledge of Drake, Hawkins, Raleigh, and to Stevenson's fictional pirates.

Our other main source of entertainment at home was the

radio. You can imagine my excitement when the BBC dramatized *Treasure Island*. I had lain awake at night thinking of the horrifying tap-tap-tap of Blind Pew's stick. Now I would be able to *hear* this dreadful sound.

My mother tells me my thirst for reading was so strong that at the age of about seven I used to read *A Short History of England*. It was the sort of account which takes children from the Roman invasion to the death of Queen Victoria, and covers Alfred and the cakes at the same length as the Crimean War.

I must have read this battered, green volume at least twenty times – restarting it almost as soon as I had finished.

At the age of nine I tackled *Oliver Twist*. It was a large Collins edition with sixteen photographs from a stage production. These pictures fascinated me. For some reason the actor who played Mr Brownlow (a far less memorable character than Bill Sikes or the Artful Dodger) made the biggest impression on my mind. When I was asked to draw at school I was always trying to reproduce this silver-haired man in a top hat and bottle-green coat.

My grandfather also played a major part in my early learning. After leaving school at thirteen, he made great efforts to broaden his vocabulary to help him make speeches at Trade Union meetings, or to cope with legal arguments when business opponents took him to court. He always impressed on me the importance of collecting words. While other boys worried about the names of cars or the numbers of trains, I carried a tiny, grubby notebook in my pocket and scribbled down every new word I heard – the more exotic or complicated it sounded, the better I liked it.

I remember the pleasure with which I acquired the adjective 'miscellaneous'. I was determined to use it to maximum effect and my great chance came in the eleven-plus examination. I looked at the essay questions in the English paper and selected the title 'Birds of London'. My main motive for this choice was that I could begin : 'Miscellaneous types of birds can be found in London . . .'

Sometimes this useful hobby led me astray. I learned the

word 'curtilage' (the area attached to a house) from my father, who was a policeman and had heard it used in court. I used it instead of 'garden', and annoyed my English teacher.

These incidents are important to me, and central to the theme of this book. When I see, or hear of, children from a background in which a book is almost as rare as a diamond, I realize how fortunate I was to have parents who valued reading and felt strongly about our learning.

At least seven out of ten parents today leave education to teachers. This majority of mothers and fathers are not *really* uninterested in their children's future, not *entirely* apathetic about education. In most cases they feel that 'it's no good my trying to get involved in my child's schooling – the teachers are either too busy or too snooty to see me, and it's *their* job after all'.

The majority of parents left school as early as possible, and in many cases they left an education system which had rejected them as early as the age of *seven* when they were placed in the lower 'streams' : the classes for pupils thought to be incapable of academic achievement. It is not surprising, when the system failed them in this way, that these parents cannot convey enthusiasm to their children about education.

These are the parents whose children leave school at fifteen. These are the parents who rarely visit a school, except to complain. These are the mothers and fathers who are resigned to the fact that our society is arranged for the benefit of the one child in five who will have a 'career', with the rest finishing up in 'boring' jobs.

Most children leaving secondary-modern schools go straight into jobs, and receive no further education. Of the pupils who leave grammar schools as soon as they can, the majority come from working-class homes. It has been estimated by Dr J. W. B. Douglas, in his book *All Our Future*, that 30,000 working-class school-leavers take up manual jobs each year when they are bright enough to become lawyers, doctors or teachers.

I have tried to avoid making this book the kind of 'advice

to mothers and fathers' guide which many parents have rejected in the past as being too full of theories and too weak on *practical advice*.

Parents need concrete information. They want to be told simply, briefly and honestly the best ways to help their children at each stage of schooling. When most mothers and fathers realize they can help 'educate' their young from the time they are born until the moment they start work, graduate from a university or finish a technical-college course, our society will be happier and more productive.

I have tried wherever possible to provide names, addresses and facts so that parents, and parents' organizations, can have, in a handy form, the vital ammunition they need when they have to talk to teachers or to battle with local-authority bureaucracy.

Some readers may wonder at my use of words such as 'working class' or 'middle class', but *some* terms of social description have to be used, and these are as accurate as any such definition can be. They are labels which are used meaningfully in the census statistics and without which social commentators and educationists would be severely handicapped.

CHAPTER ONE

Parents as Teachers

Research relevant to the theme in this chapter was carried out by Prof Basil Bernstein of the Sociology of Education Department of the University of London. I first discovered his findings in an invaluable supplement on toys compiled by ACE (Advisory Centre for Education). He attempted to indicate the different attitudes parents have towards their children's toys and play.

Bernstein's team interviewed 360 mothers of children under five. The women came from both working- and middle-class groups, but in no sense could it be said that these mothers were representative of the middle and working classes in society as a whole.

The mothers were asked what they thought toys were for, and what benefit children gained from play. It was found that only 121 of the 360 mothers mentioned, without prompting, that play was 'a good thing' and 'important'. Of these 121, 55 per cent were middle class, 27 per cent working class and 22 per cent were of the group described as 'in between'. Bernstein discovered that only 75 of the mothers said play had some educational value – and 64 per cent of these were middle class.

He said: 'In terms of the whole sample, however, this means that nearly one out of every two middle-class mothers saw that play had some educational value – compared with one out of every ten of the working-class sample'.

The survey also revealed that working-class mothers were less worried than the rest about their children playing 'too much' at school. They were also less aware of the need to choose toys carefully so they suited a child's age, sex and mental development. Working-class parents were found to be unsure whether play was meant 'to keep children amused' or 'to help them find out about things'.

But Prof Bernstein sensibly pointed out that middle-class mothers were not beyond reproach in their attitude to education:

> Many middle-class mothers think their child gets enough 'play' at home; at school he should learn the basic skills so that he can proudly take his place in the 'A' stream. Some are aghast if their children are not 'early' readers, and upset if their children cannot docilely repeat the tables.
>
> In the coffee groups of the suburbs they complain to each other of their children's apparent lack of progress. They go to see the teacher frequently in order to discuss their children's failure to master mechanical skills, pointing out how young *they* were when they could accomplish more than their child.
>
> Some middle-class homes are pseudo-educational pressure-cookers, forcing-houses for skills thought to be of examination rather than education relevance.

In view of such harmful attitudes found at this social level, Prof Bernstein says both middle- and working-class parents can be at odds with the primary school for very different reasons:

> On the one hand we are faced with the bewilderment and lack of involvement of many working-class mothers, and on the other hand the anxious, over-zealous, comparative and competitive, demanding middle-class mothers. The working-class child is trying to make sense of the world at school so different from his world at home; the middle-class child is struggling with the demands and aspirations of his parents, exposed to the parents' checks on where he is up to, while at school he acquires an understanding of principles, skills and sensitivities which may not be appropriately valued by his parents.

Both groups of children are inadequately prepared for many of our infant schools. Our problem is often to get working-class parents involved, interested in the school and to make the school a focal growing point for the community. Our problem with many middle-class mothers is to see that they have the *right* concern. This may well take the form of trusting rather than plaguing the teacher, stopping judging the children in terms of their 'A' stream or grammar-school chances: trying to understand what lies behind the informal, but considered, freedoms which are being developed within the primary school.

These findings, published in *Where* magazine in December 1967, must be related to the main message of the educational reports and books which have appeared since the Second World War. Academics know this research, and the thinking which results from it, but most parents and teachers have neither the time nor the energy to read the works. I hope in this book to provide, in an acceptable form, the guts of the message these surveys give us.

The essential fact to establish first is the *crucial educational role of parents* in their children's lives. (I have tried to show this in the account of my own childhood, and in the extracts from Prof Bernstein.) The importance of their role can best be realized when we consider the research of Prof Benjamin S. Bloom of the University of Chicago. In his book *Stability and Change in Human Characteristics*, published in 1964, Bloom estimated that *half the intelligence of a sixteen-year-old is acquired by the age of four, and a further third by the age of eight*. This kind of assertion may be difficult to prove convincingly, but it certainly makes us think about the importance of the pre-school period of a child's life. It also provides a strong argument in favour of swift Government action to set up more nursery schools, especially in slum areas. In 1969 the Minister of Education, Mr Edward Short, said the provision of nursery schools was his top educational priority. But only one child in ten is able to get a nursery-school place today.

We are lucky in Britain that our children start school at the age of five. In most other countries – where the provision of nursery-school places is equally poor or much worse – children are greatly handicapped by being unable to begin their education until they are six or seven years old. In recent years, however, because of the shortage of resources and teachers, there has been some talk that we in Britain should raise the school-starting age or consider part-time schooling for five-year-olds. Both these suggestions are unthinkable if we accept the impressive evidence (from such men as Prof Bloom) that these early years are crucial in a child's life.

It is in these years that some children gain a head's start over their contemporaries. Some begin to talk about the time of their first birthday, walk soon afterwards, and learn to read before they are five. A few are lucky enough to have multi-lingual parents or relatives, and these children are speaking several foreign languages before they go to school.

But thousands of pupils (especially those born in the summer and living in the centre of large cities) do not start school until it is already too late to retrieve a tendency towards slow learning, caused by poor home background; and when they do begin school the classes are overcrowded and their teachers come and go with alarming frequency.

The handicap of being born in the summer is an important one because there is strong evidence that pupils with birthdays between May and August often do less well than winter-born children.

The Plowden report pointed out that children who are born in the summer, who are younger and have a shorter time at school than their classmates before they are promoted to the junior school, tend to be placed in the 'C' stream. In one county borough it was found that six out of ten children who passed the eleven-plus examination were born in the first half of the year. According to a 1967 survey (by G. E. Bookbinder) of children in classes for the educationally subnormal, one in three children born in the summer months now in classes for backward children *would not be there had they been born eight months earlier.*

Teachers and local education authorities are becoming more conscious of this birth-factor in schooling. They are trying to prevent children from being treated as though they are dim or lazy when the real cause of their backwardness is that their birthday prevents them from having another year in the infant classes.

But, whether a child has the maximum time in the infant school or not, *all* parents must become aware of the importance of their role in the education of their children. A major campaign to enlist the help of parents is essential for the future of the nation. The Home and School Council, founded in 1967, plays one big part in this campaign; published literature plays another.

The Home and School Council was formed to bring parents and teachers closer together. It was organized from offices at York University and it held its first National Day in October 1968. Since then it has encouraged schools to start parent–teacher organizations that allow mothers and fathers to be welcome visitors to the classroom.

Two years and four months after the publication in 1967 of the Plowden report, which gave massive support to the campaign for parent–teacher cooperation, headteachers were still reluctant to open their schools to parents. In May 1969 six out of ten headteachers – at a conference in Blackpool of the 15,000-strong National Association of Headteachers – supported a motion expressing concern at the growth of 'Parent Power'. Mrs E. McMillan, a Liverpool primary-school head with twenty years' experience, proposed the motion. She said: 'Parents will think they have a right to interfere in the running of the school. I am tired of people claiming their rights. I prefer to return to the old idea of parents feeling a little *honoured* to be invited into the school. The operative word is "invited".' Mrs McMillan was warmly applauded when she went on to say that the movement to give parents a say in their own children's education could become a Frankenstein's monster which could harm pupils.

Obviously, with unlimited interference from over-bossy parents, the teacher's job could become very difficult indeed.

But this is not the idea. The idea is for both sides to respect one another's roles, and to cooperate. Tact, common-sense and discretion must be used by both parents and teachers. If teachers recognize that there are some things only a parent knows about a child, they also realize that cooperation with mothers and fathers can make their classroom tasks easier.

Some teachers may not know that many parents are *frightened* of them – indeed when some adults enter a school, their childhood memories, often unpleasant ones, come flooding back to them. On the parents' side, there should also be an understanding that teachers are *trained* to carry out their job. They should also realize that many young teachers with no children of their own are often nervous of meeting mothers, and afraid they will make some embarrassing mistake. But parents can meet all kinds of prejudice and opposition from teachers, and the following example indicates what you may encounter.

A village primary school had a flourishing parent–teacher association. Parents helped the school not only with the usual fund-raising projects, but also with more direct efforts. Fathers constructed extra furniture and equipment. Both working-class and middle-class parents attended meetings, at most of which about half the total parents turned up. Then the school changed its headteacher. The new headmaster was suspicious of the PTA from the moment he arrived. He kept referring to some unpleasant incidents at his previous school, but never explained what had made him hostile to parents. He said repeatedly he would never have created the PTA if one had not existed. Suggestions for cooperative activities, such as Saturday football, a recorder group, country dancing, and the making of a long-jump pit, were all turned down. Attendances at PTA meetings declined so that only ten per cent of parents were represented. The Association stopped being a vital force in the life of the school.

A survey carried out in 1969 by the CASE (Confederation for the Advancement of State Education) showed how common this kind of conflict is. It revealed how far we have to go before parents are welcomed into schools – as they are in most other countries. It quoted an infant-school parent who said:

> At the first interview, the only thing that concerned the headmistress was that we should not forget to send dinner-money on Mondays. Nothing else. Once a year parents received a notice to attend an hour-long meeting; it was to remind us about dinner-money, marking clothes and to discuss how to raise a few pounds for the school. There was no communication between parents and teachers. Parents were discouraged from entering the school, except when invited, and the school is still not in the phone book. They do not want to be bothered by us.

Another incident (this time in Scotland) from this survey shows how Ministry officials can be equally contemptuous of parents. Parents in Dundee were battling to keep open a popular school which was used as a demonstration school by the local teacher-training college. It was the policy of the Scottish Education Office to close down these schools, which usually charged parents a small fee. The Dundee school was, however, free. It had had an active PTA for forty years, and it had a fine reputation for its liberal, happy atmosphere. It was the only school in the area without corporal punishment. Parents wanted their children to go on learning free from fear of the strap. They wrote to the Secretary of State for Scotland asking for the school to be reprieved. For five months there was no reply. Then an official wrote saying the Minister did not consider any useful purpose would be served either by his meeting the parents, or by arranging for one of his representatives to do so.

This struggle to save a much-loved school is still going on at the time of writing. But my point here is the implication behind the official reply. The Ministers in charge of education in Scotland and England pay lip-service to the idea of parent–teacher cooperation. This reply gives heart to those teachers who oppose parents out of prejudice and unfounded fears. It is also depressing because the Dundee parents had the backing of CASE – a well-established organization, which aims to improve home–school relations.

My advice to any big PTA or CASE group which encounters difficulties of this nature is to use any influential parent to write to the local and national Press to expose the shortcomings of the school or the unreasonableness of the education authority. Questions asked in council meetings, reports and letters in the newspapers, can maintain pressure when teachers or councillors ignore the legitimate and reasonable wishes of parents.

Although the Dundee parents were fobbed off, in spite of having powerful backing, you should remember there is usually strength in numbers. If you ensure that ninety per cent of parents belong to your PTA, and if you get organizations such as CASE or ACE behind you, you will be less apprehensive that individual pupils will be victimized by your actions. If you have access to these groups you can always learn of examples of effective parent–teacher cooperation at other schools, and then you can ask: 'Why can't this happen here?'

But parents can do an enormous amount for their toddlers before they start in the infant school. In the late 1960s several new guides for parents were published. In 1968 at least four appeared with titles such as *Give Your Child a Superior Mind* by Siegfried and Thérèse Engelmann, and *How to Raise a Brighter Child* by Joan Beck. The sight of these works on the bookstalls was a symptom of the growth of the campaign to make parents recognize their role as 'teachers'. Many parents and teachers are suspicious of titles like these, because they dislike their brashness and superficiality, but these books do contain much good sense and, if treated with caution and mature scepticism, can be very helpful. The important point is that any book which arouses positive interest and action on the part of the parent is to be welcomed.

In America they talk of 'drop-outs' – teenagers who fall out of the academic race. But in Britain we need to think in terms of 'drop-outs' at the age of five. Consider a summer-born child from a large, working-class family, living in a slum area. If he is placed at the age of seven in a 'D' stream the chances are that his future will be decided at this tender age. Most primary schools 'stream' pupils in some way. Many of them have no consistent criteria for placing a child in one class rather than another. It is often the case that Mary, who wears bright new shoes and a well-ironed dress, is picked for the 'A' class, while Sam, with his grubby plimsolls and tattered cardigan, is shunted into a 'D' class cul-de-sac. To add to Sam's problems, it is usually true that the lowest 'streams' tend to get the worst teachers.

A child faced with these factors (confronted at birth with the *accidents* of heredity, geography and wealth) has very little chance, through no fault of his own, of competing with pupils from middle-class families living in, say, the suburbs of the affluent South-East of England.

Deprived youngsters become the forgotten *majority* who leave school as quickly as possible. As the late Sir John Newsom's committee said in 1963, when it studied children aged 13–16, of average, or below-average ability, they must not be neglected either for their own, or for the nation's, sake. The Newsom report said:

> Our anxiety is lest the relatively unspectacular needs of the boys and girls, with whom we have been concerned, should be overlooked. They have had *more than their fair share* of thoroughly unsatisfactory buildings and desperately unsettling changes of staff. *Given the opportunities*, we have no doubt they will rise to the challenge which a rapidly-developing economy offers no less to them than to their abler brothers and sisters. But there is no time to waste. *Half our future is in their hands. We must see it is in good hands.*

Parents can rarely persuade a headteacher to reverse a decision to place a child in a 'D' stream. A lively, well-informed PTA could perhaps point out to the head that all known evidence shows that 'streaming' is harmful, and that children 'live down to the reputation they are given'. If your school 'streams', you could get all the necessary information on this from a pamphlet compiled by ACE. You might convert the staff to sounder methods of dividing the pupils.

But if you take the advice provided in this book, your child is unlikely to be placed in the lower classes of his primary school for he will be able to read before he is in danger of being condemned to the 'D' stream. The age at which a child learns to read is absolutely crucial to his educational progress. 'A child's reading attainment and progress at the age of eight is fundamental to his whole future' (Brian Cane, senior research officer of the National Foundation for Educational Research).

It cannot be proclaimed too loudly that every parent with a child aged under five should try to *arouse his enthusiasm for reading from the moment when he first responds to words and ideas, and do everything possible to make books an important part of his life.*

Above all, we should never forget the reason why children need love, attention and help from their parents. It is *not* merely a question of giving them a start in the academic race. It is *not* just so that they can pass their exam hurdles and get a good, well-paid job after leaving school or college. It is primarily because a bored, depressed child is usually a naughty child. There are few discipline problems in a well-run infant school – the pupils are far too absorbed in various exciting activities to need smacking or scolding. The same applies at home: your toddler will be much happier and closer to you if you play and learn together from the cradle to the day he starts school. Begin your lessons in the home with love and a sense of fun and your child will be happy and respond intelligently. No parent need think that because his own school record was poor his child hasn't got a chance. Remember that all healthy children are intelligent. Use this book wisely and *give your child a chance.*

SUGGESTED READING

Bander, Peter, *Looking Forward to the Seventies*. Smythe: London, 1968.

Beck, Joan, *How To Raise a Brighter Child*. Trident: New York, 1967.

Bloom, B. S., *Stability and Change in Human Characteristics*. Wiley: New York, 1964.

Bookbinder, G. E., *The Preponderance of Summer-born Children in ESN Classes: Which is Responsible, Age or Length of Infant Schooling?* Educational Research Vol 9, No 3, National Foundation for Educational Research: London, 1967.

Castle, E. B., *A Parents' Guide to Education*. Penguin: London, 1968.

Green, Lawrence, *Parents and Teachers*. Allen & Unwin: London, 1968.

Jerman, Betty, *Do Something!* Garnstone Press: London, 1971.

McGeeney, Patrick, *Parents are Welcome*. Longmans: London, 1969.

Smart, Nicholas (ed), *Crisis in the Classroom*. The Hamlyn Group: London, 1968.

CHAPTER TWO

The Vital Years— Birth to Five

Betty went to school in Rochester, New York. She was six when she started. At this school, lessons were held only once or twice a week, and they lasted only fifteen minutes. Betty's mother attended classes with her. When she went to her first lesson the teacher taught her mother, and it was not until later that Betty was allowed to try what her mother had mastered.

The school showed Betty's mother how to play variations on 'Twinkle, Twinkle, Little Star' on the violin. After five months of watching her mother play, listening to her practise at home, and hearing gramophone records of violin music, Betty asked to be allowed to hold her own child-sized violin and to try for herself. Now she is nine years old, and can play Vivaldi and Handel with a proficiency many adult amateur violinists envy.

If she had not been lucky enough to go to the Eastman School of Music, and to have a mother who was able to cope with the lessons, she would probably have been only an average child at school. She might even have been considered below-average. There was certainly nothing in her family history or home background to suggest she was 'gifted' in any way.

She was taught by teachers trained in the ideas and methods of Dr Shinichi Suzuki, the Japanese violinist and educationist. Dr Suzuki once wrote:

One day about 30 years ago, I made a discovery which

overwhelmed me with astonishment. I discovered that all children throughout the world are educated to speak their native language with the utmost fluency. This education in their native language enables them to develop their linguistic abilities to an extremely high level.

This discovery made me realize that any child will be able to display highly superior abilities if only the correct methods are used in training and developing these abilities. The method of education I have been using is nothing but this method of education in the native language applied without any essential modifications to musical education.

His approach has been equally successful in teaching children to play the piano and to learn mathematics. In Japan toddlers starting at the age of three have achieved quite a proficiency on the violin by the age of five.

We may not agree with Suzuki that *all* children learn to speak with 'the utmost fluency' – there are deprived, slow-learning and handicapped children of all ages who are inarticulate – but we cannot deny that he has achieved something remarkable and worthwhile. He has taught *us* a lesson we must not forget.

His recognition of the crucial role of linguistic ability in a child's educational progress, and his belief that 'every child can be educated', or given a proficiency of skill in an art such as music, must make all parents think hard about their own responsibility in their child's education.

The lessons at the Eastman School have aroused predictable hostility among many teachers (who find it very different from anything they have encountered before), and among parents who at first resented the demands made on their patience. Some of them previously thought music lessons were a way of keeping children out of their hair.

But the implications of the work at this school are exciting and relevant to our study of the best ways in which parents can help their children and become involved in the life of the school.

An English primary-school teacher reporting on the Eastman School's achievements said:

> If ordinary unmusical mothers can master such an unfamiliar technique as violin-playing, and enable their children to make such dramatic progress, what might be the effect on our education system if we fully involved them in *all* their children's schooling?

Parents in the United States are already willing, and able, on a much wider scale than ours, to cooperate with teachers in the education of their children. Most of the 78,000 elementary schools – those for children under twelve – have parent–teacher associations, and the National Congress of Parents and Teachers has eleven million members.

We in Britain can unleash the enormous untapped resources among working-class boys, and girls of all social classes, if we convince parents of the importance of the years from birth to five. We must enlist the aid of parents so that they can act as 'teachers' before children reach the classroom.

There are many examples in history of determined parents who have embarked on a systematic course with their tiny children in order to make them learn *at the age when they learn most easily*. Many of them have been outstandingly successful.

For example, a nineteenth-century maths master in Belfast named James Thomson trained his four boys along lines suggested by the Austrian clergyman, Karl Witte. Two of Thomson's sons went to Glasgow University at the ages of ten and twelve. His two other boys were also distinguished: one became an expert engineer, and the other was to become Lord Kelvin – perhaps the greatest physicist of his age. Karl Witte himself showed that his ideas were not merely impractical theory. He told teachers who opposed him (they claimed the crucial part of intelligence is inherited and not acquired):

> If God grants me a son, and if he, in your own opinion, is

not to be called stupid – which Heaven forfend – I have long ago decided to educate him to be a superior man, without knowing in advance what his aptitudes may be.

His son was born in 1800 and Witte began instructing him from the cradle. His wife told him his efforts were a waste of time. Although the child was a slow infant and a normal four-year-old, he became a remarkable six-year-old and an exceptional nine-year-old. At the age of twenty-three young Karl became a professor at the University of Breslau, with a great reputation as a teacher and scholar.

Many people attacked both Thomson and Witte for their efforts to train and educate their children at such an early age. Both men were told such treatment would sap a toddler's energies and strain their brains. But both Lord Kelvin and the younger Witte lived to be eighty-three and had lively minds to the end.

Not many parents today will want to acquire a copy of the 1,000-page account of how Witte taught his son, nor will they feel *such* an emphasis on intellectual effort at this age is necessary. I confess I find John Stuart Mill's account of how his father taught him Greek at the age of three quite alarming. He tells us in his *Autobiography* how he was made to study the inflexions of nouns and verbs, and to memorize what his father called 'vocables'.

But men like Mill, Witte and Thomson do point the right direction for us today. People who say : 'I don't worry about my child's education – there's plenty of time for that when he goes to school', forget, or do not realize, how much a child can learn in his earliest years. Glenn Doman, in his controversial book *Teach Your Baby to Read*, tells of a nine-year-old boy he met in Brazil. The boy was of only average intelligence but he could understand, read and write *nine* languages.

He had been born in Cairo where he heard French, Arabic and English. His Turkish grandfather lived with him. When he was four his family moved to Israel, where his Spanish grandmother joined them. There he learned three more languages : Hebrew, German and Yiddish. At the age of six he moved to Brazil and picked up Portuguese. It is significant that his parents were no match for their son when it came to speaking, writing and understanding English and Portuguese. They were not as lucky as he, for they learned these languages as adults.

Winifred Sackville Stonar, in a book called *Natural Education*, published in 1914, tells how her daughter could speak in eight languages by the age of five.

But it was not until the 1960s that the full potential of the pre-school child was more generally recognized in Britain and America. The overwhelming majority of parents and teachers firmly believed it was wrong to 'educate' children at this stage. Intelligence was supposed to be fixed at birth, and only emotional factors could tamper with its automatic development. Deliberate stimulation or guidance of the intellect in the pre-school years was believed to be useless or harmful. Parents were praised for the financial or emotional security they gave their young and not for their skill as 'teachers'.

But, as Maya Pines says in her book *Revolution in Learning*, teachers began in the 1950s explaining how eagerly toddlers responded to teaching in the home. These teachers pointed out how very young children feel a passionate urge to make sense of the world. Toddlers and infants are, according to Mrs Pines, the most original scientists, the cleverest linguists – in fact the most intellectually alert of all human beings. Unfortunately, adults often stifle these talents instead of developing them.

Mrs Pines puts the whole convincing case for pre-school learning in this way. She says :

> According to the cognitive psychologists, an individual's achievement in life *depends very largely on what he has been helped to learn before the age of four*. If this startling theory is correct, it requires a radical change in society's approach to the years before a child enters school. It implies reversing the present pattern in which we spend the

bulk of our educational resources on more advanced students, and concentrating instead on children during their earliest years.

It seems clear from the evidence which has mounted in the last two decades that children who are deprived of early intellectual stimulation will never reach their true potential. Some authorities on special education, such as Samuel A. Kirk of Illinois University, believe only the outer limits of a person's intelligence are fixed at birth. A normal IQ is 100 and someone with an IQ of 120 should go to university. In Kirk's view, a given individual may have an IQ of 80 with a poor environment, or 120 with a good environment. Benjamin Bloom is less optimistic than this. He believes that a favourable environment can improve an IQ by 20 points. This could mean the difference between a place in a class for the educationally sub-normal and a position in a higher form providing an academic education and good job prospects. It could also mean the difference between a professional career, and an occupation at the semi-skilled or unskilled level.

Mrs Pines has surveyed the evidence on the question of how much good parents can do to their child's education. She stresses the point we noted earlier about the difference between children brought up in varying social environments. She says babies behave in a similar way until they are about eighteen months. But at this stage, when they start to talk and move from a purely physical to a more cultural environment, middle-class toddlers forge ahead. She explains:

The children of poverty, in their crowded and disorganized homes, learn that the best way to stay out of trouble is to keep quiet. Whether they are cared for by an older sister, by an indifferent neighbour, or by their own exhausted and harried parents, the law is the same: curiosity is generally rewarded by a whipping. *Coincidentally their IQs begin to drop.*

All parents and teachers have seen the effects of a bad home background on a child. It is essential for us to remember that, while we are stressing the benefits a loving, sensitive parent can give a child, we must also warn of the harm careless, ignorant parents can do.

Siegfried and Thérèse Engelmann, in *Give Your Child a Superior Mind*, describe a child who is not achieving his true level of attainment. They say:

> A trained observer can quickly spot a child who has been led to believe that he is stupid. The child will manage to give the wrong responses even if the task is relatively easy for him. When he is asked a question he tenses up because he *knows* what is going to happen. He knows the wrong answer will slip out, and he won't be able to hold it back. He pauses and his eyes dart. He fights down several words; then he says the wrong answer and he seems almost relieved. . . All healthy children are intelligent. . . The human animal is the only one on earth so intelligent that it can actually *learn* to be stupid.

But my task is to give you as much help as possible to avoid harming your child, and to provide as many concrete suggestions as I can to enable you to be your toddler's first 'teacher'. If you agree that you must help your child before he starts school, and must help him develop his abilities, your next question is: *how to do it?*

How to Teach the Pre-school Child

You can help your toddler in a vast number of ways. You can take great care in choosing toys. You can read to him as much as possible, and make sure the books he uses are suitable. When he starts school you can cooperate with the teacher by buying the supplementary books to the reading scheme used in his class, so that you are not presenting him with a vocabulary which is too easy or too advanced. You can make shopping trips a way of giving him an idea of mathematics, and you can turn even a chore such as washing-up into a science lesson. You can recognize that a rich vocabulary springs from a child's experience, and try to give him as many interesting experiences, such as visits to the zoo or the seaside, as possible. Above all you should realize how much children need *love*.

A mother is a child's most logical teacher. No one else has as much reason to love him and to want to make him feel secure and important. No one else has as much motive for being truly patient with his errors, his naughtiness or his stupidity. A mother begins her role as teacher in the first days of his life. By altering the tone and rhythm of her voice as she leans over the cradle she is teaching him that talking is not mere noise : it is a means of communication.

The first important 'Don't' is one which most modern mothers are aware of : 'Don't use baby-talk'. Every time you use a 'baby-word' instead of the correct word, you are making it more difficult for your child when he reaches infant school and when he takes his first steps in learning to read. Mothers-in-law, fathers-in-law and childless middle-aged friends still confuse toddlers in this way. You should try to persuade them to avoid not only words like 'bow-bow', 'tootsie-wootsie' and 'moo-cow', but also words such as 'nano' for 'piano' and any special names children make up for animals, objects or people. Once your infant has picked up a dozen or so words you should begin to be on your guard against these 'baby-words'.

I know it is amusing when a child says 'strangled egg' for 'scrambled egg', or 'Alice–andra' for 'Alexandra', but once you have noticed how quickly he drops incorrect words when he has heard you use the right one, you will realize how keen a toddler is to say the proper word. There is no need to correct a child by picking out the misused word and saying it loudly over and over again. This can inhibit him, and inhibition can grow into a handicapping lack of confidence. There is no cause to raise your voice, and certainly no reason to make it too obvious to him that he has made a mistake. Just work the correct word into your reply, and he will soon use it naturally in the right way, in the right place.

Mothers get frequent opportunities to enrich a child's vocabulary and to satisfy his curiosity about words. Every time you dress or play with him, you can name parts of his body and various objects around him. By the time he is two he should be able to locate – with very few lapses – all parts of his body. At a rough count this means at least thirty new words to add to his vocabulary. They are all useful words, and this lesson grows naturally out of the mother–child relationship. The most effective learning in the home usually arises out of some normal everyday situation, out of the proximity that a loving mother and dependent child experience, and need.

You should adapt his 'lessons' to his activities and surroundings. When he is eating, talk about the names of food, cutlery, and so on. There is the risk of wrecking a child's appetite by turning the meal into an interrogation or a quiz, but your own common-sense will tell you how far to go. Most mothers do chatter to their children when dressing or feeding them. It is a natural thing to do, but the wise mother makes sure these daily conversations are as fruitful as possible. You should try to speak whole sentences instead of phrases or brief commands. It is better to say, 'Give me your left arm' than, 'Now the other arm'. It helps a toddler more to give him a choice of three similar cereals, and to ask him, 'Which is your favourite today?' or 'Which do you like best?', than to place a bowl in front of him saying, 'There's your cornflakes.'

Sentences, expressing simple ideas and containing several common nouns, which spring spontaneously from the domestic situation, are the best stimulant to his mind. Consider how much a child's vocabulary is broadened by sequences like this : 'Do you want to wear your sandals or your plimsolls? Sandals are nice, aren't they. Where are your sandals? Under the bed. Now give me your right foot, and I'll put on your white sock. You are getting a big boy, aren't you? I'll just buckle your brown sandal. There you are. Just a minute, your shirt needs buttoning up.'

By the time a child is two and a quarter he should be able

to use words such as spoon, bib, cup, toothbrush, toothpaste, toaster, socks, etc, in simple sentences. When you use words like 'over', 'behind', 'underneath', 'next', 'in', and so on, you can often demonstrate the meaning visually. You can, for example, say: 'I'll put the egg *in* the eggcup, and place the eggcup *on* the saucer.'

Before taking him to the zoo you should buy a well-illustrated book of animals, preferably one with pictures of baby animals with their parents. Toddlers love to identify themselves with the young in animal families. The visit to the zoo will be a thousand times more enjoyable if he knows the names of his favourite animals *before* the trip. It may be twenty years since you went to the zoo, so it is wise to spend a few minutes planning the visit.

It is best to choose a cool September day when the zoo is not too crowded. I always take a small picnic lunch or tea because there is nothing more annoying for toddlers than to be expected to stand still in a queue for tea, or to wait for ages in a café, and then be told that some drink or favourite food is not available. You will know from his reaction to the picture book which animals he most wants to see. Try to memorize the map at the entrance to the zoo so that you can move swiftly from elephants to lions, or from seals to monkeys, and so on. There is so much to see on a first visit that it is best to allow an hour for the animals he wants to look at, and then to anticipate that he will be tired, or bored. My own little boy went to the Regent's Park Zoo chattering about yaks and elephants and I knew he would get over-tired and over-excited. I realized the yaks were a long way from the elephants, so by making a cunning short-cut past the bird-house, which I knew would bore him, I got him to the yaks while he was still in the first flush of excitement.

You may think this degree of care and planning is unnecessary, but many parents have told me their visit to the zoo was a disaster. Their children were bored, and more interested in ice-creams than in the animals. In many cases the children couldn't understand why their parents were so excited on their behalf about the zoo. 'What's a zoo?' the toddlers asked. They had not seen any animal pictures. The only animals they knew were dogs and cats. Suddenly they arrived in a crowded, smelly place, and they were confused. Their parents kept showing them strange beasts, and using unfamiliar words. They were tired, and their parents' puzzlement at the toddlers' ingratitude grew to bad temper and sometimes anger.

You may not have even a tiny zoo near you. You may not be able to afford to visit one. (Most fathers are shocked when they find how expensive a brief visit to a zoo can be. This is another reason for taking your own snack with you.) I have discussed a visit to the zoo as an example to emphasize why it is worthwhile ensuring that a child's early experiences are as rich as possible. But it applies to other similar visits – to the seaside or even a walk in the park – just as much. There's no need to make the trip as well organized as a military exercise. I am not suggesting the planning should cover every small detail, or that the family should be regimented into 'enjoying themselves'. I am pointing out how much a child can miss if you don't do a little thinking before you set out. Family outings will broaden a toddler's vocabulary and teach him what a wonderful, varied place the world is. He will be stimulated into expressing his new experiences in new sentences – and he will be puffed up by his success.

Children do not learn to talk systematically. However much you take my advice in this chapter, most of his 'learning' will arise spontaneously. But by the time a child reaches school he should have a vocabulary of several thousand words. Children will have learned their vocabulary from their parents, and from their play with other children. The key to literacy is usually turned one way or the other before they reach the classroom. A child with a placid, shy, monosyllabic mother and no playmates will be grievously handicapped before he reaches the classroom.

I know a mother who is intelligent, and who loves her young son. She comes from a rich family and her husband has a good job in a fine profession. But her four-year-old son hardly speaks at all. She just puts his food in front of him, and leaves him to play by himself. He has plenty of toys but he is often bored and bad-tempered. His mother makes no effort to direct his play. He sees a huge pile of jumbled, broken toys each morning, and he is quickly fed-up and frustrated. His father's habit of watching television for nine hours on a Saturday does nothing to improve the situation. When the child asks his father to play, or asks him a question, the father says: 'Go and play with your toys.'

Every experienced infant teacher can spot the difference between children who come from homes where the parents *talk with* their toddlers, and those who are deprived. The former have a confident command of language, and the latter are inhibited and frustrated. It is not only the poorest children who are deprived in this way. Dr William Wall, the former Director of the National Foundation for Educational Research, once told me:

> For seventeen years I studied highly intelligent children who failed examinations – in no case was the fault due to the school. The fault usually lay in the home. Some highly literate parents produced children who weren't talking at the age of six. I suppose the fathers were talking too much for them to get a word in edgeways!

You must realize when I say 'talk *with* your children' I am urging you to *listen* to, answer them and talk for their benefit as much as your own. It is also essential to recognize that children need to learn how to listen (how to interpret) as much as they need to have practice in talking. Parents and primary-school teachers train children to *listen* when they read to them, when they hear music quietly together, or when they appreciate the sounds of nature – birds singing, streams flowing, bees humming and so on. A modern primary school tries to arouse a child's interest with display corners, investigation or discovery tables. These are designed to start the children thinking and talking. Parents can make some effort to design a child's room, or parts of the home, for the same reasons. At a small cost each month you can buy the magazine* *Child Education* which contains at least one huge colour picture. These pictures are not beautiful but they show traffic, or shopping, or work scenes, which are full of detail. Children are at their most curious between the ages of two and seven, and each picture provides at least an hour's fascinating 'discovery' session. (By the age of three and a half you should be able to place the picture on the wall at his eye-level – without his tearing it down.)

You can also further your teaching activities by putting labels on vases, chairs, candles, tables, stairs and other household objects and furniture. These labels will just say boldly, and clearly, 'Vase' or 'Sam's chair', and so on. Of course most of you will say: 'If you think I'm going to cover the house with printed words you can think again. Other people live in my home and it would be most unsightly!' I understand this, but I am only suggesting it *could* be done in moderation – perhaps in the child's own room? A few words at a time would be a help when you come to begin the early stages described in Chapter Four.

Indeed a number of my suggestions in this section must be considered in relation to Chapter Four. This is understandable, as the most vital lesson in the pre-school period is learning to read. In the present chapter we are mostly concerned with giving your child an early life based on love and pleasant, exciting experiences which stimulate both thought and talk. In later chapters we will try to translate an enthusiasm for *words used for speaking* into an interest in *words used for reading*. Whatever they are used for, the words themselves spring from the fruitful experiences *you* provide.

One of the best ways to make life exciting and instructive for toddlers is for your family to 'go into the publishing business'. It costs little or nothing to be your own publisher, and books you produce will often be far more fascinating

---

* Any newsagent, bookshop or station stall should be able to get *Child Education* for you but in case of trouble write to Evans Bros, Montague House, Russell Square, London WC1.

and much more valuable, in real terms, than most expensively bound books bought in shops.

First you find some old pieces of cardboard and some elastic. Or you may have an old school exercise-book of your own, an unused scrapbook, or some volume with thick pages into which you can glue white sheets of paper – they will all serve your purpose. Next you can find a largish photograph of your toddler and paste it on the front of the book. A little coloured ribbon or decorative paper left over from Christmas will help lend the book an air of special distinction. This is not essential, but children of this age respond strongly to being pampered in this way. You can say: 'Look, Colin – this is *your very own special* book.'

It is wise to have done a little planning before you reach this stage. There are two things to remember. First, it is surprising how many children start school without knowing books have a front and a back, and without realizing you turn pages from right to left. If you have his photo on the front he will not make the first mistake, and, if you are careful when you browse through the book together, he will learn how to turn the pages quite naturally the right way. Second, you should have some idea about the subject-matter of the book.

If your toddler is about two, you may like to illustrate his favourite words. If you do this you should prepare the groundwork by cutting out four or five pictures of his favourite objects – animals, and so on – from newspapers and magazines. Then, when he has proudly examined his own photo and experimented a little with some tentative page-turning, you can say: 'Look at this; here's a cat, just like Martha or Tibby who live with Sarah! Here's a postman just like the nice man who brought the card for your birthday. Here's a racing car.'

My young son was going through the stage of being almost totally preoccupied with cars and trains when we went into the publishing business. I used an old ring-book from my schooldays, and collected colour photos of cars from the Sunday colour supplements. He had a favourite book at this time, the 'Ladybird' book of cars, and he had learned how to spot an amazing variety of vehicles from the Regal Reliant to quite unusual cars such as Simcas. The excitement of the search through every magazine and newspaper (the spread of colour advertising helps here) was quite tremendous. When the newspaper boy delivered in the morning, my son would have his 'own' paper to read while I studied mine. He would interrupt frequently as he discovered Vauxhall Vivas or Ford Escorts. I would pretend that I couldn't find any cars in my paper – so that I could catch up with the news in his. When we found a special car, or some particular favourite of the week (eg, a tractor), we would plan to cut it out.

There were obvious difficulties. My wife would complain about the paper always being cut to shreds, when she finally settled down to read it after getting the little boy off to sleep in the evening. I found it difficult to keep up my interest in cars when he interrupted my reading of a report of a World Cup match or the previous night's big fight. But the rewards of patience in this activity are immense.

You can scrap pictures when his enthusiasms alter, and you can re-live outings by collecting pictures of some animal or activity which excited him. I found a major problem here: after our first visit to the zoo, I had to go to enormous lengths to find a picture of a yak. This volume from the Kemble Press contained no fewer than seventeen crocodiles and nine giraffes.

You must try to leave a space under each picture so that you can print a caption (*not* in capitals). By writing the name of the animal, object or whatever, underneath, and slowly saying it aloud, you are teaching him one of his most important lessons. He is learning that the purpose of the printed word is to convey facts and ideas. Later you can cover the word with transparent greaseproof paper so he can try to move his pencil over the letters, and have great fun 'writing' the word himself.

Such home-made books are wonderfully flexible. If you leave each left-hand page free, he can pretend to copy the picture on the right-hand page. All toddlers love to scribble. If you like to increase his personal involvement with *his* book, you can include the less successful photographs taken on family trips.

Toddlers can learn the lesson that words on paper are 'talk' written down, or printed, in many other ways in the home. I do not favour a systematic use of flash-cards, recommended by Glenn Doman in his book *Teach Your Baby to Read*. However much he tries to disguise the fact, this method (as I shall show in Chapter Four) is artificial and contrary to my belief that home-learning should spring naturally from the mother–child situation and relationship.

But some basic domestic activities cry out to be translated into home lessons. Consider how much your child learns if you get him involved in a simple business such as writing a note for the milkman. You say: 'Shall *we* write a note for the milkman? Where's my pencil? Can I borrow your pencil? Where's the paper? Here it is. What do we want from the milkman? Oh, yes! Three pints of milk – that's one for Mummy, one for Daddy and one for Colin. We need some butter, and four yoghurts for Colin. Now we shall fold the paper, and put it in the milk bottle. Do you want to help me put it outside? We will leave it here on the doorstep, and when we hear the milkman coming, we know he'll read our note – then we will go and see what he has left.'

If you do this about twice a month, he picks up some useful vocabulary, and ways of asking questions. He learns how to use pronouns, and he grasps this crucial idea that marks on paper are a way of communicating with people. It is of course important in this milk-ordering process that you dwell on the amounts of milk, eggs, butter, yoghurt, and so on, as you write the note. Then when you come to open the front door to see what has been left, you should go through the list in the same order if possible and he will realize quite quickly the point that the words on the note are the same as the words you are saying.

This lesson does not take up much time and he will enjoy it because he will respond to the pretence that he is 'helping' you with your work. Another activity which conveys the same lesson is sorting out the letters when the postman calls. Around the age of two and a half he will be delighted to take on the task of walking up to the front door and collecting the letters. You should then place him on your knee (physical proximity in most activities involving reading is most important – cuddles are a vital part of learning in the home) and you should go through the post, running your finger across the name and address on each envelope. You will say something like this : 'Here is a letter for Daddy – we must tell him when he comes home. Here is a postcard for Mummy. What's this? It's a card for Martin from Sally inviting you to her birthday party! We must buy her a present today. Her party is on Saturday. I wonder if John and Sarah are going to the party?'

Above all you should recognize the supreme value of bedtime stories. They are not just an entertaining way of persuading your child to go to sleep, they have considerable educational value.

You should take great care about choosing books. Your public library should be a help here, but if you buy books they can be expensive and you can reduce the cost considerably by sharing them with one or two other families. The best single guide for buying books for children of all ages is the 'Books for Children' pamphlet published by the Advisory Centre for Education.

In recent years the attitude of authors and publishers has changed about books for children. Leila Berg, the editor of the series 'Nippers' (Macmillan), is a poineer in the field. She realized that many children's books were fundamentally unsuitable for children. She argued that, as most children come from working-class homes, it was not wise for authors to write stories exclusively with middle-class backgrounds and characters. She attacked the conventional story-book for being 'unemotional' and 'irrelevant' to the lives of the vast majority of children. Children need books which arouse their feelings and which are related to the world they know. Most children cannot identify with tales about people living in large, detached houses, with gardens full of roses and chrysanthemums – where the tables are beautifully laid out for breakfast and parents greet their young saying: 'Good morning, children!' and they reply: 'Good morning, Mother!'

Mrs Berg, who has two children of her own and a home full of her young friends aged two to twenty, has designed her series 'Nippers' to avoid these mistakes. Her books have titles such as *Fish and Chips for Supper*, *The Jumble Sale* and *Jimmy's Story*. Not all the characters are nice, and not all the homes are pleasant. In *Jimmy's Story* the home is a crumbling terraced house in a slum with a bulging dustbin outside the front door. Jimmy's mum wears a scarf round her curlers and his dad wears a shirt without a tie. There are cracks in the walls and there is no sign of a garden, or even a window-box. The range of the social classes in her series is vast. In *Finding a Key*, for example, the characters are lower middle class – their car is second-hand, and the house is a typical suburban house in a quieter area than Jimmy's home. One story has a rather shady wide-boy in it 'with a mouth like a shark', and the atmosphere throughout belongs much more to the world we live in.

Mrs Berg, and those who think like her, has made an extremely important point. If the majority of children are given books about a world they do not recognize, they will feel subconsciously that 'books are not for us'. They will sense that books and learning are for people who live in large houses and talk differently. They will come to believe that their thoughts and enjoyments are not quite 'proper'. If, at the age of seven, they see middle-class children dominating the 'A' stream while the poorer children are placed in the 'C' stream, these feelings will be confirmed.

Books are such a central part of learning that we must make sure children grasp as early as possible that they are a source of real enjoyment. Once your child begins pestering you to 'read me a story' you will know he has learned one of his first vital lessons. The stories you read him will present new ideas and they will stimulate him to ask questions. As you read to a toddler, dwell on the details in the pictures and point out the items which add to the tale. His vocabulary will grow not only from the words in the story, but also from the commentary you give as you are reading. You will say: 'How do we know these are Jimmy's toys? Why is his dad putting up his umbrella? Where is Sammy's mummy? Do you think John fell down because he left his shoe-lace undone?'

You can begin reading when your child is quite young. When he is about ten months old he won't understand most of the words but he will understand more than you realize, and get great pleasure out of the rhythm and sound of your voice. It is difficult to judge the best time to interrupt his crawling and exploring, but if you are free and if he does not seem to be too occupied, then lift him on your lap and open a large, brightly-coloured picture book.

As he gets older, you can combine the idea of your own home-made books with the library you build up by buying books. If your child gets a sudden enthusiasm about some activity, object or animal, and you haven't the time to 'publish' a book, you may find something suitable on the subject in a shop.

It is important to keep up the child's enthusiasm for books by arranging regular trips to the library. When he starts school your role as 'teacher' is not over. If you go once a month to the library and enlist his 'help' in choosing books for the rest of the family, he will learn that books are for adults as well as for children. He will also see you borrow gramophone records, and get a chance to choose a record of children's music. Most big libraries have a gramophone section and a wide variety of records. A child benefits enormously if there is plenty of music in the home. He learns to express himself through music, and he learns new vocabulary from the lyrics of nursery rhymes and songs. I intend to deal with toys in a separate section in this chapter, but there is one toy which is relevant to this question of music for the under-fives : the drum.

Most parents learn to dread the toy drum. It is nearly

always the 'wrong' time whenever the child wants to play with it. You soon suffer the agonies of a 6.30 AM. Sunday morning session on the drum, when your dinner guests didn't leave until 2.30 AM, or when you both have a hangover. But although relatives without children, and those with children who ought to know better, get cursed for giving drums as presents, something can be said in their defence. If the drum is just left around for some idle bashing, its value as a toy is not obvious.

But if it is kept out of sight and produced on suitable occasions, you will be pleasantly surprised at the enjoyment it can provide. If used to accompany nursery rhymes and songs on radio and television, the toddler gets extra fun out of the programme. The drum can also increase the amusement to be found in singing or reading your own rhymes in the home. First, Mum can recite the rhyme while Jimmy taps out a beat after each line; then you can both chant the words with a drumstick each. By interrupting the words with beats on the drum you encourage him to pay closer attention to the words used, so that he can be sure to get his beat in at the right time. All toddlers love marching to military tunes with their drums, and the fun to be had with a radio programme of this kind of music, and a toy drum, is considerable.

It is very important not to inhibit a child from singing. A grown-up who says 'Don't sing, dear, you spoil it for the others', is putting the first obstacle in the path of a toddler. Some very sensitive children (and all children are more or less sensitive, particularly where singing is concerned) decide never to sing again after such a setback. They pretend to sing from this time on, opening their mouths, but letting not the tiniest sound come out. Such children lose all chance of practising singing. They never hear themselves sing, and so may lose the opportunity of discovering through their own experiments that one note is higher than another. They may even feel that as music is part of singing, and as they cannot sing, they cannot move rhythmically to music either, and they can't dance.

An experienced music mistress once told me:

This widespread effect of the inability to sing is not uncommon, and the attempt to break through it in later years is agonizingly difficult, causing weeping sometimes, while perspiration pours down through the effort and the difficulty of trying. We can help children to avoid this kind of situation, and we can break through it best, if it has arisen already, by encouraging them to sing their own made-up tunes. The child can see that these come into quite a different category from the singing of specific tunes.

If mothers and infant-school teachers take as many opportunities as possible, in the classroom and in the home, even if they cannot sing in tune themselves, to try singing these made-up songs, the inhibited child will gain confidence.

All mothers will have noticed how toddlers sing naturally as they play. The tiny boy pretends to be an engine, his body becomes the engine as he moves rhythmically, and he makes sounds which are an essential part of his game. He may sing words, or make sounds in rising or falling tones; your task is to encourage this instinct to sing, and to help it to be an accepted part of his life and play.

So far we have concentrated on arousing a child's interest in a great variety of experiences in order to stimulate his thoughts and enrich his vocabulary. We have seen how books, music and singing can help this important process. There is another aspect of his pre-school education which is often forgotten or ignored by mothers.

A child needs training in basic essential skills. This training can be done just as casually and naturally as your efforts at making books in the home, or your attempts to stimulate his interest in words by writing notes to each other, or to the milkman. Children must have practice in using their senses of hearing, smelling, seeing, tasting and feeling. It has been estimated that between five and fifteen per cent of six-year-olds have difficulty in 'understanding what they see'. These children may not be able to tell the difference between the background and the foreground of a picture, recognize right from left, or to focus their eyes on words on a page. Sometimes such difficulties have serious causes. Occasionally a child behaves strangely because a physical defect has not been diagnosed.

Miss Lesley Webb, an experienced teacher of children with special needs and unusual handicaps, gave some vivid examples in her study of 500 infants (one in six of whom had problems ranging from delinquency to reading backwardness). She described some of these children in her book *Children with Special Needs* (Colin Smythe).

Branwell was one of her problem pupils. He started school breathless with excitement, yelling: 'I'm at school! I'm at school!' He was deeply anxious to please, and frequently asked whether he had done something 'right' or was being a 'good boy'. But he was clearly unaware his behaviour was often unusual. He would take himself off for a walk to buy an ice-cream, without telling his teacher. After two terms his teacher realized he did not understand her reproofs. They puzzled him. He kept telling her he was really 'a good boy'. But a few minutes later he would be standing in the rain, sitting on the coke dump, or good-naturedly dismantling the work of another child. At the age of eight it was discovered that his conduct was caused by slight brain damage, and he was transferred to a special school.

This kind of handicap must be diagnosed as soon as possible, but often the 'clumsy' or 'stubborn' child is physically sound. His 'handicaps' are the result of emotional factors; he may just be inhibited. Teachers and doctors now realize that these children require special training to help them coordinate their movements, or to understand what they experience through their senses.

All children benefit from games and activities which sharpen their senses and their ability to comprehend what they sense. You can devise games to help your child in this way. You can organize a 'sorting' game, for example. You can place in front of him a bowl containing four different kinds of unshelled nuts. Then let him try to sort them into four separate dishes. When he can do this, let him try it blindfold. With younger children you should make sure they have a set of bricks as early as possible – about the age of eighteen months. When my boy was two I found a 63-piece set of wooden blocks, all the same colour but varying in shape. They were splendid for building anything – houses, roads or garages for his beloved cars. Such toys give you a chance to make simple shapes, and then to see if your toddler can copy them.

All games which involve feeling, judging distance, arranging different-shaped objects, selecting items from a pile or building, will heighten your child's skills. If he seems unduly clumsy at the age of five you should mention this to his teacher and she will see that the school doctor makes a point of testing his reactions. Jigsaws are probably the finest single way of sharpening a child's perceptions and coordination.

All parents have problems about buying toys. Any owner of a toy shop will tell you hair-raising stories of fathers buying toys for a three-year-old which are meant for an eight-year-old, or he will speak with resignation about how mothers buy over-expensive toys which won't stay in one piece long enough to be used at home. Here are a few hints about this important aspect of play and the education in the home of the under-fives.

Toys – Where, What and When to Buy

The first thing to realize about your crawling child is the immense powers of curiosity he possesses. His curiosity can be infuriating. He wants to investigate your teacup, to study his father's book, to probe your sewing-basket and to explore your bedside lamp. As a result he upsets your tea, tears the book, scatters your needles and pins and knocks over the lamp. It may seem like naughtiness but it is all a part of learning. It would be quite wrong to think a toddler in such a mood cannot pay attention to anything. He is of course paying attention to *everything*. We react to his attempts to learn about the world around him by feeling we have to give him toys he cannot break or by enclosing him in a play-pen.

Glenn Doman, in *Teach Your Baby to Read*, has a useful passage on this point. He says:

> We are doing our best to stop his learning process because it is far too expensive... We parents have devised several methods of coping with the curiosity of the very young and, unfortunately, almost all of them are at the expense of the child's learning. The first general method is the give-him-something-to-play-with-that-he-can't-break school of thought. This usually means a nice pink rattle. It may even be a more complicated toy than a rattle but it's still a toy. Presented with such an object the child promptly looks at it (which is why toys have bright colours), bangs it to find out if it makes a noise (which is why rattles rattle), feels it (which is why toys don't have sharp edges), tastes it (which is why the paint is non-poisonous) and even smells it... *This process takes about ninety seconds.* [My italics.] Now that he knows all he wants to know about the toy for the present, the child promptly abandons it, and turns his attention to the box in which it came. The child finds the box just as interesting as the toy – which is why we should always buy toys that come in boxes – and learns all about the box. *This also takes about ninety seconds.* [My italics.] In fact, the child will frequently pay more attention to the box than to the toy itself.
>
> Because he is allowed to break the box, he may be able to learn how it is made. This is an advantage he does not have with the toy itself, since we make the toys unbreakable, which of course reduces his ability to learn... *One wonders what our conclusions would be if the two-year-old sat in the corner and quietly played with the rattle for five hours. Probably the parents of such a child would be even more upset – and with good reason.* [My italics.]

Mr Doman also has some provocative thoughts about play-pens. He speaks of a cartoon which shows a mother sitting reading in a play-pen while her children play outside, unable to get at her. He comments on the serious truth behind this comic scene. He says the mother, who already knows about the world, can afford to be isolated, while the children outside, who need to learn, can get on with their exploring. He adds:

> We parents have persuaded ourselves that we are buying the play-pen to protect the child from hurting himself by chewing on an electric cord, or falling down the stairs. Actually we are penning him up so that *we* do not have to make sure he is safe... In terms of our time we are being penny-wise and pound-foolish. How much more sensible it would be, if we must have a play-pen, to use one which is 12 feet long and 24 inches wide so that the baby may crawl, creep and learn during these vital years of life. With such a play-pen the child can move 12 feet... in a straight line before he finds himself against the bars at the opposite end. Such a pen is infinitely more convenient to the parents also, since it only takes up space along one wall rather than filling up the room.

Doman vividly conveys his message by telling a tale of two five-year-olds standing in a school playground when a plane flashes overhead. One says the plane is supersonic. The other disagrees, pointing out the wings are not swept back far enough. The school-bell interrupts their debate, and the first child says: 'We've got to stop now and go back to stringing those damn beads.'

His comments on rattles and play-pens and his example of this playground debate show us how careful we *must* be not to underestimate our children. Choosing toys *is* fun for both parent and child, but it is also a very serious business, and when we have chosen correctly, we must remember how easy it is to spoil a toddler's enjoyment of them, or to reduce the amount he can learn through his play.

Leila Berg once told me of an example of how adults can wreck a child's learning. A doctor was visiting her with his small son. The boy went upstairs and made a terrific row with two small friends. Leila, with her instinctive understanding of children, introduced them to a simple construction game. The doctor watched them as they sat absorbed, but making many initial mistakes. He kept shouting angrily: 'Michael do this! Don't do that! Oh you are stupid!' Finally the children and the other adults present went silent, and he was left ranting hysterically on his own. He knew how silly he was being, but he found it impossible to watch the children stumbling through and learning by trial and error. In the end he had to force himself to stand away from their game, and to calm down by the door, embarrassed and humiliated.

This is an extreme instance of adult interference, but we are all guilty at some time or another of this mistake. As I mentioned earlier, I bought my son a set of hardwood blocks for his second birthday. It was an excellent bargain. These blocks provide hours of fun for all children between the ages of two and eight. But I must admit that my two-year-old got less out of his birthday present, for the first few months, than he might have. Whenever he came to me saying: 'Daddy build me a garage for my lorries and cars', I used to build an elaborate structure, without realizing just how much harm I was doing. When he first saw the bricks in the garden, he threw them around, and we managed not to disapprove, we just ducked and smiled. Then about ten children from houses nearby heard about the bricks and pleaded to come into the garden and help him play. They were children of all ages and I thought 'So far, so good. He'll see them building interesting things and he'll soon get the idea.' But for six months he rarely built anything himself. He wanted older children or adults to build things for him. Eventually I started building things on his bedroom floor when he was out playing, and he learned the potential of the bricks when he returned. By the time he was three he would play for hours with the blocks and needed no encouragement to play on his own. If I hadn't helped him so much at the start, he would not have been so reluctant to play on his own, or to try for himself when other children were about. *Parents must try not to short-cut the learning process.*

But in this, as in all aspects of pre-school learning, we must remember to use common-sense in our handling of children. It would be wrong to think that children's play must *never* be directed. The kindly woman in charge of an excellent nursery school near my home told me once of a boy who *had* to be directed. His father was a lecturer in a teacher-training college, and his mother was a secondary-school teacher. They had read every book on the pre-school child. They treated him as an adult. They never offered any discipline, never imposed their wishes. They allowed him to open the milk on the doorstep, and to put his muddy fingers in the bottles; he went to bed when he felt like it. By the time he arrived at nursery school, he was socially impossible. He was unable to play with other children. He couldn't direct his thoughts in any rational way because he had never been guided to complete any task. His behaviour was very muddled, although he was not wild. He drifted around the hall and didn't settle anywhere. Most children settle down for a few minutes at some activity whatever their level of intelligence. This boy was intelligent, but he had absolutely no concentration. The nursery-school supervisor told me how they got him to play with a purpose. She said: 'We simply directed him as though he were in an old-fashioned dame school. We set him up with basic skills, and gave him a standard to work at, and made him do things again, if we thought he could do better. He loved it, and thrived.' I must admit I found the idea of 'old-fashioned dame school' strictness a bit hard to accept, but with toddlers with this sort of problem, I realize a good deal of firm direction is needed.

Dr Spock wrote in the 1965 version of his famous guide to mothers *Baby and Child Care* (which had first appeared in 1946):

When I was writing the first edition, the attitude of a majority towards infant feeding, toilet training, and general child management was still fairly strict and inflexible. Since then a great change has occurred and nowadays there seems to be more chance of conscientious parents getting into trouble with *permissiveness* than with *strictness*. So I have tried to give a more balanced view.

Parents today realize it is often necessary to insist on something with firmness, when it must be done – whether the child likes it or not. They also know how to forbid something because it is dangerous or unwise. Home has its rules about meals and hygiene; school has its rules about behaviour and learning, and parents should not be afraid to bring a little order into the anarchic world of play. I am not urging you to regiment your children in having fun, but it is clear that toddlers benefit more from their play if they have some guidance. The key word in Dr Spock's remarks above is 'balanced', and I apply his general remarks about upbringing to the specific question of play. 'Guidance' becomes *interference* in the example of the bullying father with his son who visited Mrs Berg's home. 'Guidance' is justified *intervention* in the case of the muddled child in the nursery school who did not know how to play.

Parents are right to intervene and guide their children in certain general ways. For example, how many mothers think carefully about how a child's toys are stored? If you leave it to the child, the toys are left in the place where he finished playing with them. Even the least houseproud mother will clear these away when it comes to bedtime. *How* she clears them away is an important consideration. By the time a child is three he will have a large number of toys. If you pile them in the corner of his room, or put them in a toy-box, you are making two mistakes. First, you run the risk of breaking toys at the bottom of the pile. However stoutly the toys are made, wheels will come off cars, eyes will get squeezed off dolls, and cracks, dents and damage will spoil other beloved playthings. Secondly, you are making play difficult for your toddler when he approaches the toys next day. The toys he sees first, those on top of the pile, are those he played with yesterday. The toys at the bottom will not only deteriorate in condition, they will also get neglected and forgotten.

To avoid these mistakes I suggest you use the sort of

approach I mentioned in connexion with day-trips and outings. A little cunning is required. First, it is a mistake to give a toddler *all* his birthday or Christmas presents at once. A very young child is overwhelmed by the variety: he is 'spoiled for choice' as we used to say at school. Any mother who has visited a large toy shop with a child will know how alarming it can be. The child races around from section to section changing his mind, getting excited and flustered. The same sort of confusion occurs when he is confronted with all his presents at once. If he has been looking forward to one special present, say a bicycle or some bricks, you can give it to him along with the smaller items that make birthdays and Christmas so wonderful for a child. But if he is lucky enough to have four or five other toys, these can be saved for later. You will be glad you kept these toys back in the months after Christmas when foul weather or sickness make it impossible for him to play outside.

A new toy presented on its own will get more attention and give more enjoyment. As Glenn Doman says above, some toys provided only ninety seconds' fun – with their box or wrapping paper giving a further ninety seconds. If a child was given such a toy along with many others, it would get even less attention.

In order to preserve toys, and to make it easier for the child to start his play each day, I suggest you spend perhaps ten minutes each week checking and rearranging the toys. You will soon realize that an old favourite he has not seen for some time lies buried at the bottom of the box: it should be brought out and left in a prominent position for the next morning. Any toys he has grown out of can be removed during the rearrangement and these can be stored, in the loft or in a cupboard, for other children.

Really fragile toys should ideally be kept away from heavy items such as drums or large cars. I use an old second-hand bookcase for breakable items. The bookcase is far too large for my son's few books, but the shelves are ideal for jigsaws, tiny cars and brittle items such as his toy watch. A cheap bookcase (easily tarted up with a coat of white paint) has another obvious advantage over toy-boxes in that the toys are easily visible at the child's eye-level. Small boys love making lines of miniature cars and inching them forward one by one, and this game can be played on the second shelf.

I have spent some time on the subject of storing toys because little thought is given by the designers of modern houses to this question. In wealthy homes in the last century, children had their 'nursery' and an adult to watch over them. Today many children live in flats or in 'open-plan' homes where space is restricted. Toddlers love to play around their mothers, and toys have to be brought downstairs to the kitchen or dining-room each day. Ideally a child should have his own 'riot' room for messy activities and the use of another room for quiet play. But the vast majority of homes cannot offer such desirable facilities, and we have to make the best use of what little space we have. Parents wishing to solve unusual or tricky problems of play-space should study *Your Child's Room* by Lena Larsson. This paperback gives hints for parents who fancy themselves as do-it-yourself interior decorators or designers.

Another important point to remember about storing toys is that cupboards have their limitations. Everything you cram into a large cupboard has a tendency to fall out when you open the doors. If you get an extra-large chest of drawers when children are very young, and keep an eye open for cheap eye-level shelves, you can use vacant drawers and shelves for toys so that they are not all piled up in one place. You may also find it useful to keep one or two small tins about your child's room for the parts of toys (small men from vehicles, tyres, keys for mechanical toys, dolls' socks, and so on) which get lost most easily. Having separate tins or boxes for special toys or parts of playthings can incidentally help your toddler's learning. If all the boxes look alike and have lids, he will have to look at the labels (printed boldly in lower-case letters) if he wants to avoid opening every box each time he is searching for something.

Having considered the child's view of play, the adult's role at playtime and how to make the best of toys, we come to the vital question : 'How do we choose toys?'

The three main reasons for selecting toys wisely are, in order of priority, concerned with entertainment, education and finance. Although this chapter is devoted to learning in the home, we must never forget that toys are meant to be enjoyed. We choose toys because the child will get the maximum amount of fun and the maximum amount of learning from them.

One of my central points has been that toys give the most interest and amusement when the child's curiosity is aroused. If his mind is active, and he is developing his visual or manipulative skills while he plays, you will have chosen wisely. The third reason, money, must be mentioned. Many toys are far too expensive for the average parents, and it has been estimated that one child in six comes from a home where money is desperately short. I shall therefore give you as much help as possible to choose toys which are good value for less than 25p. I shall also describe some ways you can make your own toys.

Parents with no money worries also need reminding that the best toys are not necessarily the most expensive. Even the most affluent father will want to avoid spending £5 on a toy which is damaged or useless by Boxing Day or by the evening of his child's birthday.

The first thing to realize is that grandparents, childless friends and other relatives frequently choose toys in the wrong spirit and for the wrong reasons. They go for large and expensive toys because of a subconscious wish to out-do everyone else. They want *their* toy to evoke the biggest squeal of delight on Christmas morning. With tact you can point out that simple, cheap toys such as a ball or a small teddy-bear are among his dearest favourites. You can say : 'That rabbit you bought when he was born is still the best buy of all.' From this you can get across the message that it is much better to give toys with lasting interest. It is sad to see relatives looking around the playroom for the gigantic panda or the monster truck they thought would give months of fun.

In most cases the panda received a cuddle or two, and was then forgotten. Children like to sleep with a cuddly toy, but once they have chosen a favourite in this line, other similar animals rarely get much attention. As for the giant truck, it may get some use as a place for storing smaller toys, or it may get the odd push across the floor, but its possibilities are limited (you cannot sit in it or drive it) and it is not good value.

Here is a list of suggested toys for children in each age group. But please bear in mind that if your child does not enjoy the toys I suggest for his age group, it does not mean he is necessarily backward or unusual, *it probably means he doesn't like them*.

Toys for Infants up to Eighteen Months

Your baby needs strong colours. White, wishy-washy pinks and blues and palest yellows don't make any impression on babies. But bright, primary colours do. His toys should be lightweight and of varied texture, and preferably washable. They should be too big to swallow, and certainly have no rough edges or corners. Be careful about rattles. Some split after a few vigorous bangs. It is best to go for a stout wooden one. He will like to see 'mobiles' – lightweight shapes, attached to a wire frame, which move in a draught. Wooden, unpainted dolls which can be chewed or banged together are also suitable for this age.

His first really educational toy can be something like a solid board with holes for pegs. Somewhere around the age of ten months he will enjoy removing the pegs, rolling them about, crawling after them, and eventually he will be able to put them back in their holes. An essential for toddlers of about fourteen months is a nest of brightly-coloured boxes, or failing this, yoghurt pots will do for a start. He can play with you at this game : you build, he knocks down, you fit them, he separates them, and then he builds and fits by himself.

At about eighteen months it is a good idea to stick a long

blackboard just above floor level so that he can chalk away when he likes. If you cannot find a really long, oblong blackboard, you can make do with any piece of stout board if you can stick paper on it. Old rolls of white wallpaper left over from decorating can be fastened on to such a board. Most toys that can be fitted together and pulled apart are good value at this stage, and will sharpen his coordination. As I have said earlier, do not forget to buy large picture books with animals and children in them.

Further ideas for this age group include : bath toys, tinkle-blocks, rocking toys, 'Baby Bouncer', 'Baby Walker', giant beads (wooden and undetachable or he'll swallow them), bells, tambourine, abacus, and coloured wooden rings on a rod.

Toys for Toddlers from Eighteen Months to $2\frac{1}{2}$ Years

This is the stage when children enjoy the simplest jigsaws and should be able to play with a picture tray (where pictures are painted on plywood and the objects in the picture can be removed and replaced). Push, pull and pedal toys are ideal for active play. Cars are usually a top interest for boys by this time. Girls like dolls' prams and tiny garden brooms to imitate adult behaviour.

Additional suggestions : a sandbox, screw toys, digging equipment, music box, posting box, building blocks, rag doll, plastic and metal dishes, 'washing and ironing' equipment, water-play toys, wooden car to ride, sand pit with bucket and spade, rocking horse, toy telephone, clay, Noah's Ark and nuts and bolts (large enough not to be swallowed).

Toys for $2\frac{1}{2}$ to Four Years

By this stage he should be quite inventive with his wooden bricks and blocks (which will fascinate him until he is eight). Paints with large brushes will also delight him. A toddler-size table and chair will come in useful for his more complicated jigsaws and for when he wants to scribble.

A difficult and worrying problem at this time is when to buy a tricycle, and how big should it be? It is quite likely that your child in this age range will have friends who own a tricycle or a go-kart or even a bicycle (with little extra wheels to keep it upright). When one child is given anything of this sort, it causes jealousy among the children whose parents are not able to afford such an expensive toy. If you buy a tricycle after his enthusiasm has switched to a go-kart, or if you wait to get a go-kart until you can afford it, by which time his friends have bicycles, you may find you have bought an expensive toy which gets little or no use. Nine out of ten parents will not be able to afford the full range of vehicles for the age group. It is difficult to say exactly at which ages he will ask for each. Some children have tricycles at about the time of their second birthday, about six months later they see friends with pedal-cars and go-karts, and, when they are three, they are old enough for a bicycle (which can cost about £16). It will be difficult for some parents to afford the £3 or so for a tricycle, but this is probably the one toy in the range that will be wanted the most. There is no simple answer to these questions, but it is worth remembering that such toys give hours of pleasure and, compared with many other expensive toys, they are good value.

Further suggestions for the under-fours include : bubble-blowing equipment (soap, not detergent), simple puzzles, bean bags, corrugated cartons and boxes, blunt scissors, fire engines, farm layouts and garages, larger jig saws, and dolls.

Toys for Four to Six Years

If you are lucky enough to have a garden, you should think seriously at this stage about a climbing frame. Children want to climb; it makes them feel bigger and more important. Such a frame helps them to develop physically and become more agile, and they can see more. Sets to help imaginative play (dressing up as nurses or policemen) are well received at this time. Equipment which helps them play 'post offices' or 'shops' is also a good idea. Five-year-old girls will want a doll's house and furniture (be sure to look carefully at toys of this kind, as they are liable to break easily unless they are soundly constructed). The doorway to the house and its interior must be large enough to make it easy for the child to arrange the furniture inside.

Further suggestions: garden tools, larger jigsaws, scales, pots and pans, glove puppets, wooden letters, sewing kit, sculpting materials, scrap book, humming top, table games with dice, skipping rope, hoops, stilts and a very simple carpentry set.

Now you have some idea of what and when to buy toys, the next question is where to buy them. Here is a list of shops which have high standards and which welcome *postal* inquiries. Some of the larger shops do half of their Christmas trade by post. You need not worry, therefore, if none of these is in your own district.

Larger specialist shops: Paul and Marjorie Abbatt, 94 Wimpole Street, London W1.

James Galt, 30 Great Marlborough Street, London W1, and at Brookfield Road, Cheadle, Manchester. At Christmastime Galt toys are also sold at Harvey Nichols (London), Hopewell's (Nottingham, Derby, Leicester); Lee Longland's (Birmingham); Maskrey's (Cardiff, Newport, Cwmbran); Maples (Bristol); Shepherd & Hedger (Southampton) and at Dunns (Bromley).

Hamley Bros Ltd, 200 Regent Street, London W1.

I advise you not to telephone these shops between October and December, as they are then so busy that you will probably not get through to anyone who can spare enough time to deal with your inquiry. All publish catalogues which are free. If you write in August or September for a catalogue, you will have a better chance of getting what you want.

Smaller specialist shops: John Dobbie, 79 High Street, Wimbledon, London SW19; The Owl and the Pussycat, 11 Flask Walk, Hampstead Village, London NW3; The Boy and Girl Shop, Emson Close, Saffron Walden; James France, 7 Gun Street, Reading; John for Toys, 20 Sun

Street, Canterbury; Tridias, 8 Saville Row, Bath; Play and Learn, 144 High Street, Maidenhead; Keith and Maggie Barnes, 13 York Villas, Brighton 1; Judith and Douglas Cook, Ding Dong Cottage, Newmill, Penzance, Cornwall; Tim and Rosalind Green, Crowdy's Wood Products Ltd, The Old Bakery, Clanfield, Oxon; John Gould, 154 Main Road, Sidcup, Kent; Susan Wynter, 31 Onslow Gardens, London N12.

Toy departments of large stores: Heal & Son Ltd, 196 Tottenham Court Road, London W1; Harrods Ltd, Knightsbridge, London SW1; A. W. Gamage Ltd, Holborn, London EC1. Your local store is likely to give advice, catalogues and send toys by post. Clements of Watford, for example, have many regular customers as far away as Plymouth and Bournemouth.

Educational suppliers: The Educational Supply Association Ltd, Pinnacles, Harlow, Essex; Adventure Playthings, Queensway, Glenrothes, Fife; Tube Plastics, Severnside Works, Stourport-on-Severn, Worcs. These are all increasing their direct contact with the public, although none began with the idea of supplying toys. The ESA now produces an excellent booklet for parents called *Playwork*.

Mail-order firms: Graves, Sheffield; Marshall Ward, Bridgewater Place, Manchester 4; Oxendales, Granby House, Manchester 1; J. D. Williams, Dale Street Warehouses, Manchester 1; Ambrose Wilson, Vauxhall Bridge Road, London SW1; Davis, Denmark Hill, London SE5. You should check in your local shop in case the toy you pick from a catalogue is available there. The price for a postal sale is often ten to fifteen per cent higher than it would be in a shop. But one advantage of buying through the post is that you get free credit for up to thirty-two weeks and you can try out toys on approval for up to a fortnight.

Many parents may still feel worried about the expense of the toys mentioned above, and those of you who do not live near any of the shops named may find the extra cost of getting toys by post puts them out of your price range. Although I have included shops as far apart as Penzance, Fife,

Bournemouth and Harlow, it is certain that some readers will still have difficulty getting toys. Here, for the benefit of such parents, is a list of about forty toys, all of which cost little more than a packet of cigarettes, and I shall end this section by describing how you can make your own toys at home.

Bargain Toys

Aston Martin DBF construction kit (Airfix); Bar Magnet (ESA); Beads, oval wooden (Galt, James France); Chubbie Stumps; Coffee set in plastic (Galt); Compass (James France); Craft outfit, junior gummed-paper outfit (Butterfly); Crayons (Feart, Galt, James France); Dolls' cutlery (James France); Felt and stuffing kits, choice of elephant, penguin, duck (ESA); Football rattle, wood (J. Dobbie); Ford Taunus Supercar (Lone Star Products); Gummed paper and scissors (James France); Handcuffs and key (Master Model); Horseshoe magnet (Galt); Interceptor jet-strike aircraft (Airfix); I-Spy Books; Jigsaws (Abbatt, Galt, ESA, etc); Laces, multi-coloured with tag ends for threading large beads (Galt); Lego (British Lego Ltd); 'Let Me Sew Too' (Abbatt); Letters – a set of 114 printed, glazed capitals and small letters (ESA); Lotto (Spear); Magnetic ladybirds, mice and spiders (John Dobbie); Modelling board (ESA); Money (James France); Mosaic wooden tiles (Galt); Mustard-and-cress farm (James France, John Dobbie); Nature viewer (magnifying glass in which an insect or flower can be enclosed); Origami papers (John Dobbie); Padlock-and-chain construction set (ESA); Paint brushes (Abbatt); Plastic painting palates (Galt, ESA); Untippable painting pot (Galt); Two-tier pencil box (Galt); Pop guns, wooden and cork (Galt); Metal puzzles (Galt); Raffia (ESA); The-Same-Not-The-Same recognition game (ESA); Sewing cards (Abbatt, Galt); Modelling shape cutters (ESA); Skipping ropes (ESA); Snakes & Ladders (Berwick); Tiddly Winks (Merit); Pull-apart bulldozer or steam-roller (Galt); Whips and tops (James France); Wooden-wheel rabbit (Abbatt).

At the time of writing none of these playthings costs more than 30p. The list is not meant to be exhaustive, and you may be stimulated to think of other similar toys while reading through it.

Toys You Can Make

It is worth remembering that John Lewis and branches have fine trimmings and haberdashery departments, and Woolworths are cheaper than most other shops for stuffing, tools, nails, castors, etc.

1. *Wooden bricks or blocks* can be cut to any size from a length of wood.
2. *Leather holsters and gun belts* can be made from old handbags from jumble sales or junk shops.
3. *A pull-along toy.* Cut an animal shape with a fretsaw from thick plywood, screw it to a wooden base, attach four wheels (sold by bicycle shops), sandpaper and paint it in bright colours with lead-free paint.
4. *Crocodile.* From an old plank or plywood cut two crocodile heads and twelve pieces for the body, ending with a tail shape. Screw these on either side of a length of Pirelli webbing, and screw on six cotton reels to make it run along. Paint it with lead-free paint.
5. *Jigsaws.* Paint a simple picture onto a square of thin plywood. Now cut it into large pieces with a fretsaw – you must adjust the number of pieces to fit the age and skill of the child. Jigsaws with up to fifteen pieces are suitable for children under three and a half.
6. *Baby's swing.* Use nylon rope with a breaking strain of 1,000 lb. The seat is a piece of one-inch-thick plank, 11 ins × 14 ins, drilled at each corner. Make the bars from one-inch plastic garden hose, two pieces front and back, one piece at each side, supported by five-inch pieces threaded on the nylon rope. Plastic hose can be easily drilled as long as it is firmly held. The seat, to prevent accidents, could be covered with samples of carpeting begged from a local shop. Permanent loops on the tree, of nylon cord, out of reach, can be

easily connected to the ropes on the swing by something similar to (but less lethal than) meat hooks. This means the swing can be taken in out of the rain, an important point if the seat is carpeting. Cost is under £1.

7. *Scrapbooks.* Successful with two- or three-year-olds for looking at (and occasionally recognizing words), and with babies under a year for chewing, picking at and just looking. You need sheets of brown paper or sugar paper, folded into pages 18 ins × 12 ins or thereabouts. It must be large because scraps tend to be bigger than one might think. Cover each edge of each sheet with drafting tape so that the pages themselves cannot be torn, and staple down the spine very closely. Get the scraps from magazines, newspaper colour supplements, architect's and seed catalogues. Stick them in with ordinary paste. A lot of pictures can be simply captioned, eg, car, pig, boat, etc.

8. *Paper doll with clothes.* On stiff cardboard draw and cut out a human figure of any size, shape or sex, standing on a rectangular base. Make a support for it to fit onto by cutting a strip of cardboard one inch wide and four inches long (larger, of course, if the doll is a big one). Bend it in the middle to form a 'V', and make two half-inch slits near each end of the upper side. Make two similar slits in the doll's base, which will slot onto the stand when you want to keep it upright. A child can now paint or draw a face and underclothes on the doll and it is ready to be dressed. Using the doll itself as the matrix, carefully draw round it (leaving out the head, hands and feet). You can use either coloured wrapping paper or plain white paper on which you colour an elaborate design afterwards. Make tabs at shoulders, wrists, waist and ankles which bend back to keep the clothes in place once they are put on the doll.

9. *Working model of television set.* Take any small cardboard box or packet (the 'variety pack' cereal box does very well), remove the back and cut a piece out from the front to form a screen. Stand it on end and push two pencils or round sticks through the sides, above and below the screen. These are the rollers on which to fit the programme scroll. Now

cut a long strip of white paper a little smaller than the width of the box, and mark it off into frames the same size as the screen. Inside these frames draw your story, starting at the bottom of the scroll. Through the back of the box fix the top edge of the scroll round the upper pencil, and the bottom end round the lower pencil. In each case the paper should roll round the side nearest the screen. Now wind the lower pencil slowly round so that the pictures pass across the screen. You can decorate the box with paint or coloured paper.

10. *Jack-in-the-Box.* The basis of this is a cardboard roll of any size. Make a puppet small enough to fit inside the roll, with a little stuffing in the head and hands. Now fix a stick about 8 ins longer than the roll into the head and tie it firmly round the neck. Push the puppet up inside the roll so that it pops out at the top, and glue the lower outside part of the puppet's skirt on to the inside top of the roll. The puppet can now be drawn in and out like a jack-in-the-box. Use a strong glue such as Copydex.

11. *Matchbox chest of drawers.* Just glue three pairs of matchboxes on top of each other to form a chest of drawers. Cover the top and sides with coloured paper or Fablon. Handles can be made from picture hangers.

Science in the Home

Apart from making toys in the home, you should also realize how many household objects are playthings which can give a child his first steps in science. Right from the cradle you can use quite commonplace objects to develop a child's skills and powers of observation. In this matter I was interested to read a comment from Dr Mary Sheridan, a research fellow and consultant in child development at Guy's Hospital. She said:

> We do a test with babies, from about six months old, to see that they can hold an object in each hand without dropping either. Most people use cubes, but I use wooden spoons. Spoons have a meaning in the child's life, in the

home. The mother cooks with them, children are fed with them. There's no better toy than a hard wooden spoon in the first year – you can suck it, bite it, bang it, stir with it...

Your home is full of science lessons and scientific equipment. The pans from the cupboard stand easily on their flat bottoms, and not so readily on their sides. They make noises when you bang them. So does a tin full of marbles, and yet the same marbles in a different tin or box make different sounds. The pan is shiny and makes your face look wide and funny. So does a tablespoon – until you turn it over and look into the hollow side.

Children do not think in 'scientific' terms. They simply take the materials and they examine them. Their questions are not posed as questions: they are expressed in terms of their actions. The child does not say: 'I wonder what note this milk bottle will sound if I tap it with this spoon?' He just taps it, and notices what happens.

Mothers often give science lessons without thinking how important they are to their child's mental development. But if they slightly increased the amount of activities of this kind, they would be helping their child enormously. Think for example of the amount of learning a child can take in at the kitchen sink. The water wets your skin but not always everywhere, for sometimes it stands in globules on the greasy surface. It offers resistance as you push your hand through it, especially when you push with the flat of the hand rather than the edge, and you can feel the smooth flow over the surface of the skin. A panful of water is heavy, and feels even heavier if you hold the handle near the end. It makes fascinating sounds when you pour it into cans and bottles. Some things will float on it. A table-tennis ball bobs up to the surface when you let it go. A tobacco tin floats only if you don't fill it with water. A flat piece of wood sinks further and further if you put more weights on to it. A block of foam plastic soaks up water and looks a different colour when it is wet.

Playing with water may not seem to be *science*, but these experiences are your child's first approach to scientific ideas about density, viscosity, flotation, the refraction of light and Archimedes' principle.

Once again (as in the role of the parent in a child's play) it is important to know how much to *intervene* and when not to *interfere*. A child will repeat his activities many times for all sorts of reasons: maybe he gets pleasure from the sounds of water gurgling out of a bottle, or maybe he is still not sure that he cannot stand a fork upright on its prongs. All the time he is learning. He won't need you to tell him when he has had enough play with the sieve that lets water through. Outside in the garden and on the paths he discovers soil can be dug, squeezed, smelled and crumbled. Every stone is concealing a mysterious world underneath. Leaves make interesting sounds when you scuff your feet through them.

Pets are also a great source of learning. Children see how vital it is to feed them regularly, and to treat them with care and respect. They spot the soft warmth of the cat's fur, the sensitivity of the rabbit's whiskers. As they hold a hamster they feel his heart beat, the rapidity of his breathing. They notice his teeth are large and not the same as ours. Sometimes a rabbit gets pregnant, and they remember she has been with a buck. They watch her grow and perhaps feel the unborn young moving under her abdomen.

Parents would be more tolerant about their children's destruction and damage to toys if they viewed *some* of it as the spirit of curious, scientific inquiry. It is essential to take some things apart if we are to learn what is inside them. This is why children poke their fingers into sponge-rubber balls or tear the cardboard from the outside of a torch battery.

Ronald Wastnedge, a former lecturer at Kesteven College and a pioneer of primary-school science teaching, sums up the business of science in the home in this way:

The young child does not really need a chemistry set or any special scientific apparatus. The home is full of equipment. The kitchen scales give experience in weighing, as do the bathroom scales and a spring balance. *The experience is better if the variety is wider.* Remember the boy who thought that a magnet was a metal bar, painted red in the middle and with an N at one end – his experience was severely limited. So the greater variety of scales the better.

We have seen so far in this chapter how you can have home lessons in a number of differing ways. We have noticed the role of books, toys, trips and, above all, the dominating importance of *talking* and listening to children. We have examined the learning and pleasure that music, dancing and singing can give. We have seen how children develop their physical coordination and powers of perception by simple games. You can of course teach your children many other lessons and skills in your home. You can teach them to knit, sew, cook, carpenter, swim, row, skate and fish. They can learn how to identify birds, trees, plants, flowers, stars and the sounds of musical instruments.

As they grow older you can teach them to build a fire and to use matches safely; to read a map and a thermometer; to replace a fuse; to change a baby's nappy; to use a telephone, typewriter, sewing machine, bus timetable, compass, catalogue, dictionary; to make a bow and arrow, a catapult, a go-kart, a paper boat and a periscope; to draw up a family tree and to identify family relationships ('She's my second cousin once removed'); to tell the time, days of the week and so on.

No teacher will be annoyed if you teach these kinds of skills and activities. They may be upset if they find your child thinks he already knows how to do long division when they start to teach it. This is the kind of 'parental interference' they are afraid of. The teaching of formal academic skills should be left to the school. Parents as teachers of their own children (in the classroom sense) are like husbands teaching their wives to drive : they are not detached enough, and the situation quickly becomes impossibly emotional. But if your contact with your child's teacher is close enough, and if you feel up to it, there *are* some more formal lessons which you can give. If your small son is, for example, crazy about cricket, and pesters you to tell him how batting averages are worked out, you should tell him (if you can). You don't need to tell him to wait until this subject crops up at school. This case is clearly one of the child *leading you*; it would only be wrong to teach such knowledge if you were dragging him along behind you.

Once you know a skill has been taught at school there are endless possibilities for practical activity in the home. This requires imagination and patience while he works things out for himself. Mothers can let a child follow a recipe and measure out the ingredients, and they can let him read the scales to see how much baby weighs. Fathers can allow him to calculate the number of screws or the amount of wood needed for a carpentry project. Fathers can also enlist his 'help' when it comes to working out routes, mileage and petrol for a family touring holiday. Home problems such as 'How much sand do we need to fill the sandpit?', 'How many turves are required to re-lay the lawn?', 'How much wallpaper or paint do we need?' and 'How much material should we buy for the curtains?' are all chances of improving his skills and knowledge.

A great deal of school-learning is still artificially created, and the problems in many arithmetic books are still abstract. But the problems in the home are real and meaningful. Send your child to the door to pay tradesmen you know and trust. Take him with you when you go to vote. Let him sit with you when you fill in forms or look up telephone numbers. A simple lesson about objects expanding and contracting with heat and cold can be learned from putting an obstinate screw-cap under the hot tap.

Sometimes his hobbies and pastimes will seem a little arid, but you can adapt them for his benefit without undue interference. If he wants to stand by the gate all day writing down numbers of passing cars, you might suggest he could borrow your watch and record the time-lag between them. If he enjoys this, he might find it interesting to write and draw a chart of the traffic-flow, with a list of which cars occurred most frequently.

At this stage a lot of parents may be saying: 'You suggest so many things, and I'm sure this is all very well, but I've got four other children and a house to take care of – I have no time to "teach" as well.' I accept that these added responsibilities may appear daunting, but I am sure that there are many occasions when both of you would be happier if you did teach him something. For example, think of a mother waiting with a small child in a shop, at a railway station or doctor's surgery. The child behaves badly because he is restless and confined. He runs about, he may do damage, and it can all end with a good hiding. But the mother could have anticipated that he would be troublesome if there was a wait – and there usually is. They could have played some kind of reading game or guessing game. In a shop, they could have explored together and she could have shown him pictures on boxes or interesting items on the shelves. He is badly behaved because he is bored. Anything which gains his interest will be good for both parent and child. You have to spend this time together anyway, so why not spend it reading, talking or playing?

But however much you do in the home, however well you buy toys, give lessons and arrange your toddler's play, he still needs the company of a wide variety of other children, and greater opportunities for play than you can provide. In a sense *nearly all children are deprived*. They cannot get enough space at home to play and make a mess in. They cannot meet as many children as they should if they are to learn how to play alongside them. Playing with other children is a vital means of working off their frustrations and sorting out their emotional difficulties.

SUGGESTED READING

Bruner, Jerome, *The Process of Education*. Harvard University Press: Cambridge, Mass, 1960.
Doman, Glenn, *Teach Your Baby to Read*. Cape: London, 1965.

Engelmann, Siegfried and Thérèse, *Give Your Child a Superior Mind*. Frewin: London, 1968.

Hollamby, Lilian, *Younger Children Living and Learning*. Longmans: London, 1962.

Kent, Jill and Pendarall, *Nursery Schools for All*. Ward Lock Educational: London, 1970.

Pines, Maya, *Revolution in Learning*. Harper & Rowe: USA, 1967. Allen Lane, The Penguin Press: London, 1969.

Reich, Ilse O., *William Reich*. St Martin's Press: USA, 1969.

Spock, Benjamin, *Baby and Child Care*. New English Library: London, 1967.

Thompson, James, J., *Educating Your Baby*. Oldbourne: London, 1967.

Webb, Lesley, *Children With Special Needs*. Colin Smythe: London, 1967.

CHAPTER THREE

Nursery Schools and Play-Groups

Toddlers need relationships with adults other than their parents, neighbours and relatives. The relationship they have with the women at nursery schools and play-groups is different and valuable for them. Many older mothers still do not realize how much a child gains from spending a few hours a week at school or a play-group. If you live in a large detached house in Surrey, a back street in some industrial slum, or in a flat, the arguments for finding somewhere for him to play and learn away from the home are very strong. The child in affluent Weybridge is likely to be isolated from other children – and toddlers need their company at this stage of development. The slum child may have a large number of brothers and sisters, and many relatives living near, and even a safe street to play in, but his home may be overcrowded and impoverished both culturally and materially. The toddler in a flat, whether it is council-owned or a luxury penthouse, may be getting the worst of both worlds : limitation of space and isolation from playmates.

Parents as well as children need nursery schools. Some mothers are far happier if they can go out to work, and they do need some relief from running noses, chores, and frequent requests for admiration and attention. The nation also benefits if they are enabled to return to part-time teaching or other vital jobs where skilled woman-power is scarce. Mothers who are lucky enough to find a play-group or nursery school usually become *better* mothers because of the welcome relief from worry and responsibility. I recall a mother saying on television:

> When my child was able to go to a play-group for a couple of hours on two mornings a week, I used to stroll around the shops quite light-headed at having the freedom to walk without having to watch her in case she darted into the road, and without having to reply to 'Mum can I have an ice-cream?' all the time.

Husbands often get irritated because their wives don't read the papers or have anything but children's activities and mishaps to talk about. It is nearly impossible for them to understand what it is like to be up all night tending a sick toddler, to be woken up at 6 AM, and then to be unable to finish a sentence or a conversation with a neighbour without having her skirts tugged, or her attention distracted in some way. It is no wonder she finds herself reading Monday's morning paper on a Friday!

Many mothers (my own for example) who managed without the relief a nursery school brings will say: 'When you have children you must expect this. They are young for only a brief while anyway.' But when the child returns from his nursery school or play-group, his mother is better able to devote attention to reading to him or playing with him, because she has been able to get on with the chores undisturbed. These fortunate mothers not only get relief while he is at school, they also get a rest when he returns. Instead of the confined child being bored (and therefore naughty) you now have a child who has tired himself out by two hours of exciting play, and he will probably have a nap after lunch. He may also come home with new ideas for play which he wants to pursue.

Children who live in remote parts of the country are in special need of this early schooling. They often have to travel quite long journeys, in all kinds of weather, and in darkness, when they begin primary school. The break from home is more of a shock because they suddenly start attending at the age of five from 9 AM to 4 PM and the contrast with the life they have led is too great. If a child gets a slow start in his emotional, physical, social, moral or intellectual development, and lives in such an isolated rural area, there is a strong possibility that he will not recover from his deprivation.

Of course, the children who need nursery schools and play-groups most are, at present, the ones least likely to be able to attend them. These are also the children who, when they finally reach school, are most likely to be in over-large classes.

Although educationists have been warning since 1825 that proper provision *must* be made for children under five, only a tiny proportion can go to nursery schools or play-groups at present. Although Section 8 of the 1944 Education Act stated that 'Local authorities should have regard to the need for securing provision for pupils who have not attained the age of five years by the provision of nursery schools ... or nursery classes in other schools', by 1960 a Government circular admitted: 'It has not at any time since the Act came into operation been possible to undertake any expansion in nursery schools.'

The Labour Government set about this problem after being elected in 1964, and it was made easier for new nursery classes to be set up to enable married women to return to teaching. In 1969, nursery education received its biggest boost for 30 years when nearly £1½ million was divided among 23 areas so that they could give 5,250 toddlers a chance of nursery schooling. But nine out of ten children were still unable to go to such schools. In some areas one child in four gets a place, but in others there are *no* schools or classes available. At the last count* only 150,749 went to nursery schools or classes. Over 87,000 of these (that is 5·9 per cent of the age group) went to State schools or classes, and about 63,000 (4·1 per cent of the age group) went to independent schools.

* I am indebted to Dr Tessa Blackstone of the London School of Economics for these figures. Her book, *A Fair Start* (Allen Lane, 1970), is the best survey of provision for the under-fives.

Since only 28,442 of the places provided by the State were at nursery schools, the remaining 58,784 being in classes attached to other schools, we can see how small the chances are of your child getting a place.

But to be fair to the politicians, we should remember that children in Britain start school one, or two, years earlier than most other countries, and that in 1969 there were 220,000 children aged under five in primary schools, so the State is not doing *quite* as badly as it may seem.

You can help improve the nursery facilities in your area by pointing out two facts to your MP and to your local teachers and councillors. There is evidence that some local authorities are inefficient and extravagant in this matter. Some claim it costs as much as £6,000 to alter a classroom in an infant school and to convert it into a nursery class. This job should cost no more than £4,500 at 1970 prices. Hundreds more places could be available if your local authority is made aware of the need for this vital provision, and if you keep up pressure to make them cost-conscious.

The second fact that needs great publicity is the Ministry of Education's belief that nearly all the most underprivileged children can be spotted by teachers and welfare workers. They say there is sufficient close contact between the schools and the local authority for these children to be known and helped. Most experts outside the Ministry doubt this. The Ministry says that if a primary-school child from a large family is seen to be poor or deprived, efforts are made to get his younger brothers and sisters into nursery schools. I find this hard to believe. There are good grounds for believing one child in six suffers from a degree of poverty, yet we know that only one child in ten gets a nursery place. The parents of deprived children are the least likely to join parent–teacher groups. They are the mothers and fathers whom teachers see least often. If you bring up this matter at your parent–teacher group, you will not only benefit children in most need of help, you will also be aiding your own child. The earlier we help the deprived under-fives the better-equipped they will be to learn and enjoy when they start primary school. If you support the nation-wide campaign for more nursery places in your area, you will be improving the standards in the classes your child attends. Your child's teacher will be less harassed and more able to devote time to each pupil.

One headmistress with twenty-six years' experience described to me how handicapped some deprived children are when they start school. Some of her pupils from tall blocks of flats were unable to communicate with their schoolmates at the age of five. She said:

> They have difficulty talking to their teachers, and they find the playground a vast, unknown wilderness. They are frightened of other children. Teachers find they have a social problem to deal with before they can start to educate them. They don't run, jump or skip easily. To them any mild gymnastics is frightening.

Her evidence would be supported by nearly all those teaching in infant schools. In 1964 six headmistresses, writing in an official publication on primary education and mental health, said that children who had been to nursery school were better able to learn and better able to make human relationships than pupils who had not been so fortunate. They then urged that seven special categories of children should get places. These were (a) children in towns, living in confined housing conditions, and therefore denied the open spaces of the countryside; (b) only children, who are often to become the cosseted or withdrawn that need social life to enable them to participate fully in school later on; (c) children from inadequate, delinquent or culturally deprived backgrounds; (d) handicapped or backward children; (e) children from recently-arrived immigrant families; (f) children whose mothers are urgently needed by the community, eg, teachers, doctors and nurses; (g) children whose mothers already go out to work.

They also quoted evidence from psychiatrists working in London child-guidance clinics in 1954 who said that more than 80 per cent of the mental disorders detected in their new cases *had started in the pre-school years.*

These arguments in favour of providing nursery schools for *all* children under five so impressed the Education Minister, Edward Short, that he said: 'If I had to state my priority for educational advance, I believe I would put first an advance in nursery education.' The case is certainly persuasive. It is no wonder that the National Campaign for Nursery Education claimed in 1969 that it had the backing of 'practically every MP in the House'.

Play-groups

In spite of all this powerful support, however, mothers have realized that it will take another generation at least before we get every toddler a nursery-school place. They have therefore taken the law into their own hands and set up independent play-groups. By 1968 this movement had 3,000 play-groups serving 83,000 children.

About 2,400 of these groups are in proper halls, and about 600 in houses. In most of the halls about twenty to thirty children play under the supervision of three or four adults. Six out of ten of these hall groups are run by qualified people. Nearly all (87 per cent) are financially independent and get money from fees and fund-raising activities. Fees are normally about 25p a session, and each session lasts about three hours. Seven out of ten experts in the field estimated in a 1969 survey that a group could be started on a capital of £50. The Pre-school Playgroup Association (87a Borough High Street, London SE1, and 304 Maryhill Road, Glasgow NW) is campaigning to persuade local education authorities to provide grants to suitable people to start groups in their areas. Mothers are performing miracles all over the country in an effort to get groups started. The PPA, for example, estimated that about 1,000 play-groups had been set up in the previous six months – which means six new groups every day.

If you would like to learn about the best way to set up a play-group, or if you want to know the nearest one to your home, you should write to the PPA (at either of the above addresses, depending on whether you live in England or Scotland). The Association publishes an informative magazine which would give you a fuller idea of its work. It will tell you how to contact professional play-group advisers, PPA area organizers, or helpful teachers from nearby nursery and reception classes.

I know it sounds rather daunting, but anyone wishing to start such a group needs to consult the Children's Act, 1948, Section 46(2), the National Health Service Act, 1964, Sections 22(1) and 22(5), and the Physical Training and Recreation Act, 1931. The PPA, your local library or your local education authority will help you find these documents.

I also advise any mothers who decide to launch a group to club together to buy *The Playgroup Book*, published by Souvenir Press. It is an American book, but it has been adapted for British readers, and it contains a great amount of practical information about organizing play for the under-fives. If you have any special query, I suggest you contact the Advisory Centre for Education in Cambridge, which is, as we have noted earlier, helpful in giving tips on toys and equipment. Mothers who cannot find or launch a group should consider joining the 'Nursery 3–4–5' postal service at 92a Old Street, London EC1 (telephone 01–253 3550). It offers tips on educational toys, and for a few shillings you can receive a monthly booklet with ideas for play in the home.

Nursery Schools – State and Private

I know some parents are reluctant to approach their local authority office, but many questions about the nursery schools in your area can be answered *only* by such a visit. You should start investigating when your child is about one year old, certainly no later than eighteen months. In certain areas, especially in the South-East of England, you may well get a place. Your local education authority's offices can be traced in the *Education Committees Year Book* in your local library. This book gives the address and telephone number of all departments, and names the members of the education committee together with their special interests. Don't be afraid to ask them about private nursery schools in your area if they cannot find your child a place in one of their classes.

When mothers start looking for a nursery school, they might be confused by the existence of both 'nursery schools' and 'nurseries'. The difference lies in the word 'school'. A day nursery meets a social need, it looks after toddlers while their parents are at work. A nursery school, on the other hand, is an educational institution, and it looks after a child's early learning and development. Nursery schools operate during normal school hours and observe school holidays. Day nurseries are normally open for longer and remain open for most of the year.

There is another important difference in that State nursery schools are (at the time of writing) free, whereas you are charged according to your income for day nurseries. I say 'at the time of writing' because David Howell, MP, is trying to empower local authorities to make charges for nursery schools in certain areas. This idea was supported by Lady Plowden and by seven other members of her committee which investigated and reported on primary schools, in 1967. They were outvoted by the majority of the committee, but her suggestion that parents ought to be charged 25p per half-day attracted a lot of support. It is likely that the Conservative Government will introduce such a scheme. While not insisting on the fee being 25p, the Conservatives have pointed out that any charge made would help local councils to provide more of these desperately needed schools.

The Advisory Centre for Education and the Nursery School Association (89 Stamford Street, London SE1) will give you additional advice on any special problem. If you are one of the tiny few who do have a *choice* of nursery schools in your area they will help you make up your mind.

Private nurseries, of course, charge fees ranging from a normal 25p a morning or £1 a week up to £50 a term.

Nursery schools run by the local education authorities and those independent schools recognized as efficient are staffed by certificated teachers with special training in this kind of work. They are helped by assistants holding the certificate of the National Nursery Examination Board, and often by students in training. A nursery class in a primary school should have one teacher and one full-time assistant to thirty children. In a separate nursery school the regulations say there must be one teacher and one full-time assistant for every twenty full-time children. In nursery schools, unlike other schools, the limitation on the size of classes is *strictly enforced*.

The question: 'What do I look for in a good nursery school?' is hard to answer because it depends partly on the needs of your own child. But if you can visit the school to watch, as unobtrusively as possible (so you see it functioning naturally), there are certain criteria to watch out for. See if the staff have a sensitive understanding of the requirements of children of this age. Have they made some attempt, for example, to ensure that the smaller the child the bigger the pencil, the bigger the brush or brick and so on? Any school which hangs pictures at adult-height, and fails to make as much as possible child-sized and child-centred, is just not doing its job.

Try to discover if the following range of activities is catered for: percussion, dressing-up, painting, sand-and-water play, sawdust, clay, dough or possibly mud, examining nature (plants, animals, leaves, twigs, and growing things like carrot and parsnip tops), playing 'houses' with pots, pans, washing line, etc, playing 'shops' with money bags and items to buy, and looking at books and pictures.

A good indication of the quality of a school is the use it makes of space. It is not much good having a wide variety of books if there is nowhere for the child to sit quietly with them. Some schools are wonderfully equipped and you should look to see if the toddlers get the maximum use out of things by being unobtrusively led by the staff when, for example, they spot a child doing something interesting. But the best schools know it is not only the most elaborate equipment which is the most effective. A bit of junk, a toilet roll with a face and hair on it, a cardboard box: any of these can be the basis of a stimulating game.

One crucial question about under-fives is how best to *ease* them into school with the minimum of tears and heartbreak. You must consider how your toddler feels on his first day at school. Remember how *different* this experience is from anything else he has encountered. The nearest experience he has met is going to a party, but that would normally take place in a house (where the rooms are smaller), and he would probably know most of the children and adults there. For many children, going to school is their first experience of being separated from their mothers for any length of time. The first few mornings will seem like an eternity.

These new arrivals tell the teachers and assistants it is time to go home after about an hour! The hall is huge to them, and they feel lost. The noise seems overwhelming and often rather frightening. The other children will be rushing about. The helpers are strangers, the equipment is unfamiliar, and on top of all this their beloved Mummy has left them to cope with everything, on their own.

There is absolutely no rule that certain children will get on better than others in coping on their first mornings. Teachers ask the mother, before her child comes to school, how she thinks he will react. But mothers often make poor predictions. Sometimes an only child, who has been expected to make a fuss, will walk in and find something to do as though he has been there before. It turns out, when you discuss this with his mother, that he has been minded a lot by friends, or he has gone out a lot to tea with other children. Occasionally a child from a big family, who has been expected to settle in easily, will be very nervous. The family is so self-sufficient it has not been necessary to take him out. His mother has always been busy, and his brothers and sisters have had each other to play with.

The worst time for a child to start nursery school is when there has just been an upset in the family: father has gone away from home on a job, or mother is in hospital. School will only add to his troubles. The teachers have many methods of making new arrivals feel at their ease. They can suggest that mothers bring them for a brief visit before they start at the school. On this occasion they can meet the helpers and the other children, and find out where the toilet is. (Nursery schools expect a three-year-old to be toilet-trained, but if the child is not very good at asking for the pot, some schools will make an exception.)

If the child decides he would like to paint a picture to take home to Daddy (my son brought me a brown splodge which he insisted was a yak) on this preliminary visit, he will be encouraged to do so and get some idea of the fun to be had at school.

Other children will prefer to be left alone. Some will like Mother to stay on the first full morning. Some will sob for a few minutes, but stop if every adult in the room has the sense to ignore them. Others will have a long look round, sum up the situation, decide no one is going to eat them, and then find something to do. Some will like to be taken to the paints or constructive toys to play quietly on their own, until they get used to things. But of course there is always the child who charges in like a hurricane and joins in some violent game with a whoop of glee.

The vast majority of three-year-olds will settle in and surprise their mothers by making little or no fuss after the first week. But some children are not really ready to start school. If they have nightmares, cry all the time, and do not settle down after a few weeks, the teacher has to tell their mothers to keep them at home a little longer. Of course this creates a problem when they restart school, for they remember how unhappy they were on the previous occasion. The parents of such a child should be encouraged in the meantime to take him to visit other children as often as possible, to make fleeting visits with him to the nursery, and to talk about how lovely it will be when he is big enough to go to school.

The *worst* thing you can say on the way to school for his

first morning is : 'You won't cry when you go in there will you?' This suggests to the child there might be something to cry about, and it makes him suspicious. Unfortunately a mother may be so attached to her child that if he *does not* cry she feels he is not showing how much he misses her, and she has lost face. If the *mother* can take the whole thing in her stride, the child will as well in most cases.

Mrs Iris Grender, an experienced teacher who has a nursery school in Kent, and who runs the 'Nursery 3-4-5' service, has been coping with these problems for years. She made me realize how hard it is to take your own advice. She told me that she had to choke back tears when her first child went to school : 'I took back all the terrible things I'd said about mothers who made a fuss.'

One other important aspect of a school to watch out for is its attitude to discipline. Of course no school recognized as efficient will be really harsh with toddlers, but there are differences of emphasis (often revealed in a prospectus) which are worth considering. If you are fortunate enough to have a choice of schools, I would think twice about one which put 'good behaviour' or 'good speech' at the top of its list of priorities. A nursery school is not a finishing school for toddlers. It is pleasant to hear a child saying 'please' and 'thank you' in melodious tones, but it is not a school's first aim to teach such things. The essence of good discipline is firmness tempered with tolerance, common-sense and love. Children should be allowed to be as uninhibited as possible, but they should not be so wild as to endanger their own or other's safety, and they should not be able to disrupt the life of the home or school. They have to learn 'social' lessons, how to adapt themselves to the needs of a group, as well as educational lessons.

Since the Second World War a great deal of interest has been shown in the work of A. S. Neill, the headmaster of Summerhill School, and his mentor, Dr Wilhelm Reich. Some people still have the idea that these men preached that the child is always right, that we must never use any 'discipline' in the home or school. Their theories are known as the philosophy of the 'self-regulated' child. They contend that there is far too much punishment, and they believe that children should be given as much freedom as possible. But it is nonsense to think they never say 'no' to children.

Dr Reich's wife reveals in her biography of her husband how he distinguished between freedom and licence. She tells how he allowed his son to paint on his play-room wall:

> Letting the child paint all over the house would have been licence. But showing Peter his freedom to paint was restricted by the *freedom* of others to have their part of the house clear of his paintings, gave the child a practical example of how freedom involves responsibility towards others ... I can remember only two occasions when Reich was really angry with him. Once when Peter was about four years old, he played with matches, and almost set the house on fire. The only other incident I remember was when Peter was accused of having taken candy from another child, and he denied it. But the candy was sticking out of his pocket, and Reich punished him severely, not for taking candy but for lying.

Parents looking for signs of a school's attitude to discipline could keep these examples in mind. There is hardly ever any need to punish a toddler. Ilse Reich can only remember *two* examples and we doubt whether there were more than two others. There is still far too much slapping and thrashing going on in homes and schools. (I know a woman who used to smack her boy when he was still in a shawl.) If the teachers at your nursery school seem to combine firmness with gentleness you can leave your child in their care with confidence.

Useful Organizations

1. Nursery School Association of Great Britain and Northern Ireland, 89 Stamford Street, London SE1 (telephone: 01-928 7454).
2. Pre-School Playgroup Association, 87a Borough High Street, London SE1, and 304 Maryhill Road, Glasgow NW.

3. Playgroups are also run by: (*a*) The Save The Children Fund, 29 Queen Anne's Gate, London SW1. (*b*) The Church of England Children's Society, Old Town Hall, Kennington Street, London SE11. (*c*) The Mothers' Union, Mary Sumner House, Tufton Street, London SW1.

4. Training for work in a play-group can be obtained at some adult-education institutes. If you wish to take such a course the Advisory Centre for Education (32 Trumpington Street, Cambridge) will help you find one near your home. The London colleges are (*a*) Morley College, 61 Westminster Bridge Road, London SE1. (*b*) Camden Adult Education Institute, 87 Holmes Road, London NW5. (*c*) Woolwich Institute, Burrage Grove, London SE18. Further information on these courses is available from: National Institute of Adult Education, 35 Queen Anne Street, London W1 (telephone: 01–580 3155); or Scottish Institute of Adult Education, Education Offices, Alloa (telephone: Alloa 2160, extensions 35 and 36).

5. National Campaign for Nursery Education. Secretary: Mrs V. Ross, Flat 9, 26 Highbury Grove, London N5.

6. If your child seems amazingly precocious (Mozart was composing at the age of eight) you may like to contact The National Association for Gifted Children, 27 John Adam Street, London WC2. They have centres in Birmingham, Essex, Gloucester, Leicester and Wolverhampton.

7. If your child is blind and you need help with some special problem you might contact: (*a*) The Royal National Institute For The Blind, 224 Great Portland Street, London W1. (*b*) Jewish Blind Society, 1 Craven Hill, London W2. (*c*) The Deaf-Blind and Rubella Children's Association, 61 Senneleys Park Road, Northfield, Birmingham 31. (*d*) The Scottish National Federation for the Welfare of the Blind, 4 Coates Crescent, Edinburgh 3.

8. If your child is deaf you may need: (*a*) The National Deaf Children's Society, 31 Gloucester Place, London W1. (*b*) Royal National Institute for the Deaf, 105 Gower Street, London WC1. (*c*) Scottish Association for the Deaf, 158 West Regent Street, Glasgow C2.

9. If your child is one of the 700,000 backward children in our schools, you can get help of all kinds from the Elfrida Rathbone Society, Toynbee Hall, 28 Commercial Road, London E1.

10. Parents of the mentally-handicapped may like to contact: (*a*) The National Society for Mentally Handicapped Children, 86 Newman Street, London W1. (*b*) National Association for Mental Health, Maurice Craig House, 39 Queen Anne Street, London W1. (*c*) Scottish Association for Mental Health, 57 Melville Street, Edinburgh 3. (*d*) Camphill Village Trust, Denrow House, Millfield Lane, Aldenham, Herts. (*e*) Cottage and Rural Enterprises Ltd, Blackerton House, East Anstey, Nr Tiverton, Devon.

11. If you suspect your child is *autistic* (unable to communicate, unable to understand speech, dislikes looking at people, hates being cuddled), and there are at least 5,000 such children, you should contact The National Association for Autistic Children, 1a Golders Green Road, London NW11.

12. A new organization has been set up to help children who have difficulty learning to speak. It is the Association for All Speech-Impaired Children, 63 Alicia Avenue, Kenton, Harrow, Middlesex.

13. Old toys are welcomed by: (*a*) The British Red Cross Society, 14 Grosvenor Crescent, London SW1, or your local branch. (*b*) Oxfam, Oxfam House, Banbury Road, Oxford. (*c*) The Spastics Society, 12 Park Crescent, London W1. (*d*) WRVS, 17 Old Park Lane, London W1, or your local branch. (*e*) National Children's Home and Orphanage, 85 Highbury Park, London N5. (*f*) National Society for the Prevention of Cruelty to Children, 1 Riding House Street, London W1. (*g*) National Society for Mentally Handicapped Children, 86 Newman Street, London W1.

SUGGESTED READING

Winn, Marie, and Porcher, Mary Ann, *The Playgroup Book*. Souvenir Press: London, 1968.

CHAPTER FOUR

The Most Important Lesson – Learning to Read

Half the pupils in our schools cannot read properly. They can get a little information from newspaper headlines, and they will, when they leave school, be able to check a football pools coupon, but they cannot comprehend and criticize the printed word.

This is alarming not only because it is a symptom of low teaching standards but also because the health of a democracy depends on the reading ability of voters. If electors cannot examine intelligently the written efforts to persuade them, if they cannot cope with the printed vocabulary of politics, they can be deluded by charlatans.

Learning to read is the most vital lesson taught in schools. From infant schools to industrial-training courses (how can you retrain a man who cannot read?), every step depends on a pupil's literacy. But for thirty years the evidence has mounted to show that large numbers of children over the age of eight never learn this crucial lesson.

In the 1960s experts stepped up their efforts to warn the nation of the dangers of complacency in this matter. While the Ministry of Education was content to point out, quite plausibly, that reading standards had risen since the Second World War, specialists revealed the scandalous facts about literacy. In 1961, for example, F. J. Schonell, in his book *Psychology and Teaching of Reading*, said: 'Too often schools believe that children will develop powers of concentration and study skills for themselves. While this is true of the top 34 per cent, *it is not true of the majority*.' In 1966

Dr Joyce Morris alerted the educationists with her book *Standards and Progress in Reading*. She claimed that about 10–14 per cent of fifteen-year-olds were poor readers. At that time there were about 650,000 school-leavers, so it is reasonable to estimate that about 70,000 of these could not read properly.

But in 1968 Keith Gardner, of the Nottingham University Institute of Education, angered the teachers' unions and the Ministry of Education by claiming that Dr Morris had *underestimated* the problem. He said there was no evidence that standards of literacy had risen since 1939 : 'It is likely that about half the school population *never* become literate in the sense that they can easily understand, criticize and evaluate the printed word.' He challenged the Ministry to *prove* that standards had risen. The seriousness of the situation had been masked, according to Gardner, by attempts to show standards were improving : 'National survey figures, however, give a misleading impression. They merely reveal that we have caught up on losses sustained during the Second World War.'

Warnings like these were backed up by the shocking evidence in Dr Morris' survey of 60 primary schools in Kent which had about 8,000 pupils aged between seven and eleven. She discovered that nearly *half* the children in their first year in junior school needed teaching which was normally given in infant schools. One child in five could not read at all, and one in four of the rest was unable to make progress without *skilled help*.

But skilled help was not always available. Dr Morris found that three out of four teachers of children needing to be treated as infant-school pupils were *untrained* in infant methods. She also found that one teacher in six was neither familiar with infant-school practice, *nor had any knowledge of how to teach reading*. Many teachers, she said, began their careers imagining that they would rarely have to cope with pupils who could not read – and were shocked when they found this was not the case.

In April 1968 Dr Morris pointed out that low reading

standards were a problem not only in primary schools, but also in our *universities*. She wrote in *The Teaching of Reading* (Ward Lock):

> Recent research indicates that a sizeable proportion of undergraduates have not sufficiently mastered the more complex reading skills to enable them to complete a degree course. Reading disability of one kind or another is therefore a matter of concern in Britain.

But by September 1969 the authorities were still ignoring these warnings. Education Minister Edward Short, an ex-headmaster, was still claiming that standards were higher than ever. In a speech at Blackburn he said:

> It is no exaggeration to say British primary schools are among the best in the world. It is rather a pity that their excellence is sometimes better understood abroad than it is in some quarters in this country. Standards of reading have risen steadily – whatever Bruce Kemble of the *Daily Express* may say.

But as usual he was quoting the old, disputed Ministry figures which Dr Morris and Keith Gardner had already exposed as unreliable. He was also ignoring the evidence of his own Ministry Inspector, Gilbert Peaker, who supervised the tests on which Mr Short based his case. Mr Peaker says that at the last count nine out of ten 11-year-olds could not read *The Times* editorial, and one out of ten was unable to read the simpler parts of the *Daily Mirror*. This means that about 70,000 school-leavers a year cannot read well enough to cope with the day-to-day demands of life. It also means that, by the highest standards, over three-quarters of teenagers cannot criticize a serious written argument such as an election speech or a social debate.

The whole of this controversy centres on the question of what we mean by 'reading properly'. It is obvious that Dr Morris is not claiming that undergraduates cannot read the

Daily Mirror when she says they cannot read well enough to get a degree. Most experts believe that the Ministry's definition of 'reading properly' is too low. The Ministry argues that it is unrealistic to define 'reading' as 'being able to understand, criticize, and evaluate the printed word', as Keith Gardner does.

But whatever the true state of literacy in Britain today, and whatever the rights and wrongs of the arguments between those in possession of the evidence and those who ignore it, parents need help so that they can make sure *their* children can read well enough to cope with life. Teachers, officials and parents should raise their sights and aim to improve the teaching of this vital subject so that *all* children can read a newspaper editorial, and understand it well enough to argue about it.

Parents usually ask four questions about this problem: (*a*) When should a child start learning to read? (*b*) Should mothers try to teach under-fives to read? (*c*) Which is the best method for teachers to use? (*d*) What should the Ministry of Education do to raise standards in our schools?

The short answers to these questions are: (*a*) As soon after the age of two as the child is ready. (*b*) You can help your child learn to read but it is unwise to use a teaching *method*. (*c*) There is no *one* perfect method for *all* children. (*d*) We should copy other civilized countries and have a National Reading Research Centre to find out the truth about literacy standards in Britain. It would examine the methods used in schools and settle arguments about their effectiveness. The Americans are willing to spend nearly £400,000 on *one* research project but our Government failed to find a mere £40,000 to keep a tiny research centre in London going. It has been forced to close, and its records are now gathering dust in a trunk in a Bloomsbury basement.

These are the brief answers to your commonest queries. But you will need much more help than this if you are to give your child a chance to enjoy our finest literature. I shall therefore deal with some of these questions at greater length.

When Should a Child Start Learning to Read?

It used to be thought that no child could learn to read before the age of six (some nineteenth-century educationists said ten). This myth has now been exploded and many children learn to read much earlier. About one child in four starting school this year will be able to read after a fashion.

Most normal children are *physically* capable of reading at the age of twelve *months*. There are many examples in history of precocious babies who made an exceptionally early start. Sir Francis Galton, the famous nineteenth-century pioneer in the study of hereditary genius, could identify all the capital letters when he was only one year old.

Many educationists believe that children should begin learning to read when they are two. They preach that the longer you delay after this age, the harder it becomes for the child to acquire reading skill. These teachers, who are mostly Americans, say that at the age of two or three a child has powers of curiosity and an ability to absorb information which will never be equalled later in his life.

But there are several dangers in telling parents that toddlers of two or three can start reading. A child could be put off books for a long time, perhaps for ever, by over-ambitious parents. You have to ask yourself : 'Does the child *want* to read, or does he appear to want to learn to read because he senses *you* want him to?' A mother who starts lessons prematurely, perhaps to show her child off to the neighbours, is likely to confuse and harm the toddler's development.

Dr John Downing, a leading expert on literacy, contends that unless early reading is taught well, it should not be attempted at all :

> To pressurize unwilling children into reading at an earlier age is a retrograde step. Educators need to beware of too great a swing of fashion at the present time. Some children still cannot learn before six.

It is clear that any idea of there being a fixed age, say six, when a child is 'ready' to read, is nonsense. A child may speak his first words at any time between ten months and three years; the onset of puberty has a range of five years; children are 'ready' to read at any age between two and eight.

In a sense, a child is reading from the instant he recognizes his mother's face as she bends over his cot. He goes on reading as he observes the world around him, sees pictures, recognizes his first letter or word, and finally reads a book. It is wrong, therefore, to divide this continuous process and speak of an age of 'readiness'.

But, although we cannot generalize about an optimum time to begin teaching reading, we can state certain conditions which must be present before formal teaching starts. The handbook for the 'Ladybird' reading scheme lists nineteen such conditions in question form. They are : (1) Can the child see and hear properly? (2) Is he free from speech defect? (3) Is his general health satisfactory? (4) Are there any other comments of significance on his medical record? (5) Does he appear to be seriously retarded in intelligence? (6) Does he ask questions, does he want to know about the objects and happenings in his environment? (7) Does he understand oral instructions and can he carry them out? (8) Does he listen satisfactorily to a story? (9) Can he re-tell a simple story in fairly logical sequence? (10) Can he see similarities and differences in simple drawings? (11) Does he play constructively with apparatus? (12) Does he draw in a representational form? (13) Has he grown out of babyish behaviour such as baby-talk, temper tantrums, excessive shyness and stubbornness? (14) Is there any evidence he is being subjected to undue stress and strain? (15) Is he generally self-reliant, eg, not continually asking for help, and able to work on his own for short periods? (16) Is his home background reasonably satisfactory? (17) Does he cooperate reasonably with others? (18) Can he match word with word? (19) Does he show signs of wanting to learn to read?

Some of these questions are a shade vague and unhelpful. I do not think it is necessary, for example, for a child to have *completely* grown out of 'tantrums, shyness and stubbornness' before he can start reading. Many *adults* behave in this 'babyish' way. Also I am not sure what is meant by a 'reasonable' home background. There is a great deal of strain and tension in some affluent homes, and there are many excellent parents living in slum conditions.

The final condition, as we have noted earlier, is ambiguous. Dr Spock makes interesting observations on this point. He says:

> Often the parents themselves are more ambitious than they perhaps realize. When he is playing childish games, or rough-housing, they pay only a normal amount of attention. But when he shows an interest in reading, their eyes light up, and they help him enthusiastically. The child senses their delight, and responds with greater interest. No harm essentially, but we may not be using the child's pure, spontaneous interest, so much as creating it – so we must not be too surprised if it soon flags.

Donald Moyle in his book *The Teaching of Reading* lists the following six conditions for reading 'readiness': (1) The perceptual maturity to recognize the shapes of letters and the varied patterns of the printed word. (2) The ability to recognize the sound units from which spoken words are formed. (3) A good speech vocabulary and an ability to use and understand spoken language. (4) A wide range of experiences. (5) An interest in books and the ability to treat them in a respectful manner. (6) Ability to concentrate.

Again, this list is not entirely helpful. Mr Moyle himself points out that it is not much use talking about a 'good' speech vocabulary unless we tell parents and teachers what is considered 'good' for each age.

But these lists of conditions teach us two lessons: they urge us to be cautious about starting toddlers reading before they are ready, and they remind us of the vital pre-reading process. We have seen in Chapter Two how it is desirable to broaden a child's vocabulary, to give him a 'wide range of experiences', to create an interest in books, and to talk and to listen to your children. I shall now extend this advice so that *your* child can begin reading earlier.

We can answer the question: 'When should a child start learning to read?' by saying that he can read before the age of six *if* he has the ability, *if* he has had the appropriate pre-school experiences, and *if* school conditions are suitable. We must hope that in your child's case the school conditions are 'suitable'. My task is to ensure that your child has had the 'appropriate' pre-school experiences.

How Can Parents Prepare Children for Reading?

The process of learning to read is a team effort involving the parents, the school and the child. Teachers provide the learning of skills, and many of a child's experiences. Parents give him a background of talk, interest, encouragement and the majority of his experiences. Any parents who suspect they are not patient enough to help their children in these ways should be on their guard before trying to carry out any of the suggestions in this chapter. A substantial cause of reading failure is the nagging of impatient mothers.

Many parents wonder whether their child's teacher will be angry if they help him before he gets to school. The truth is quite simply that teachers will be delighted if you provide the background and preparation suggested in this book, but they may be annoyed if you use some amateurish teaching 'method' (eg, sounding out words instead of merely telling the child the word); formal skills are best left to schools. One sound way to please teachers and to help your child is to ensure he attends school regularly, and to avoid moving homes if you possibly can when children are aged between five and eight. No two schools follow exactly the same syllabus, and if your child misses lessons he may never recover.

But there is no need to go to extremes in trying to please teachers. If parents listened to some teachers they would spend a lot of time trying to *stop* children having contact with words. It is impossible, and silly, to prevent children recognizing words in print. They see them on the cornflakes packet, on signs outside the garage, on television adverts, in books and newspapers and on the labels of birthday presents. But parents should not misconstrue the recognition of whole words as 'reading'. Children will spot whole words before they know anything about individual letters or the sounds of letters. If you make this mistake you may well think he is making quicker progress than he really is – and then get impatient when you discover the truth. Another common mistake is to believe that when a child recognizes a whole word correctly he is seeing it as clearly as you are. In most cases he has recognized part of the word, or seized on one letter, or even guessed the word because you read the rest of the sentence. A child may say, for example, 'That's my name – Charles', but you may well discover that he cannot really read the word when he sees 'Church' and repeats 'That's my name – Charles'. Some parents use flash cards at home with large words printed on them. They tell you with glee that 'Sally can read thirty words!' But often you find Sally can spot a word only because the card has a gravy-stain on it, or has a bent corner.

Hunter Diack, a senior tutor at Nottingham University and a veteran teacher of reading, defines the problem in this way:

> The real stage of learning to read occurs when the child is learning to translate the letters in a word into the correct sounds, in the correct order, and then associating the sound of the word with the meaning. Now this is a slow process, and the very slowness of it, contrasted with the *apparent* speed with which the child learnt whole words, may lead to a fair amount of upset in both parent and child. It is not unusual for a child, who has learned to recognize as many as 50 words by the age, of say, three and a half, to be unable to understand the significance of letters for another two to three years. Small wonder that many parents who are aglow with the early success of their young readers, get depressed about the slowness of the progress later on.

He also points out the difficulties, and dangers, of parents using their idea of 'teaching methods' at home. If a parent uses the old-fashioned 'drilling' method (spelling out simple words to a child using the alphabetic names of letters) the child finds the whole business very confusing. How can a child be expected to see the connexion between 'see-ay-tee' and the sound of the word 'cat'? If a parent tries a slightly more sophisticated approach and uses her idea of 'phonics' (teaching the child the sounds of letters), the child is again likely to find things puzzling. Children do not respond to being told 'ker-a-ter' is 'cat'. If you were thinking of trying your 'phonic' scheme on your child, ask yourself how you would describe 'bicycle'. Mr Diack says: 'I have heard children say "ber-er-ker-yer-ker-ler-er – bicycle", which just shows how incredibly accommodating children can be. But here we have a real difficulty, the fact that English is so irregularly spelt.'

The crucial difficulty of the learning-to-read stage is getting the child to blend the separate letter-sounds into words. This is why teachers use graded reading material beginning with regular spelt words such as 'man', 'bus', 'animal', 'caravan', and moving on to each stage of complex words. Once a child, and I am not speaking about very backward children, has got insight into the function of letters, he will usually make rapid progress, given suitable books to read. The 'Ladybird' series, or the 'Royal Road' readers (Chatto & Windus) are two popular and effective graded schemes.

People sometimes talk about there being two 'schools' of teachers of reading: the 'whole-word' approach and the 'phonic' approach. This is nonsense. No one ever taught a child to read by concentrating entirely on whole words or on parts of words. No one has ever been able to describe *how* a child learns to read. Some people, such as Dr Downing and Hunter Diack, have made some brave attempts, but it has proved impossible to convey the whole complex business in words. But we can say, however, that children learn to read once they have begun examining the structure of words and seeing them as a whole. If you do not encourage children to look closely at how a word is constructed, you find they will quite happily read 'agriculture' as 'aeroplane', or 'general' as 'George'.

Parents should leave the teaching of 'sounds' of letters and groups of letters to teachers; they should concentrate instead on hearing their child read, and telling him words he does not know. But you can sharpen your child's powers of observation and heighten his interest in the structure of words by pointing out some obvious aspects of words which may have a special fascination for him. When children start asking questions about words, and are getting near to the vital stage in 'reading readiness', they can be reminded of some of the shapes and sounds of letters. Every child knows the sound of his own name: John knows the sound of 'Jo' and 'n'. They will also be aware of the names of pets, relatives and special family objects. There is no harm in saying: 'Look at that "S", isn't it like a snake? How does a snake go?' You mention that a 'T' looks like a tree, an 'h' looks like a house, an 'e' like an egg in an egg-cup, an 'F' looks rather like a flag and an 'O' like an orange.

When a child begins writing you can encourage him to form letters correctly. No teacher will object to your trying to prevent him forming bad habits in his writing. Stanley Johnston, a teacher with twenty years' experience, has given some sound guidance on this question in his book *Achieving Reading Success* (Cambridge Aids to Learning Ltd). He says:

> Most printed letters should be formed from a long, upright stick, or a short, upright stick, a curve, a circle or a cross-piece. Broadly speaking the letters need forming from top to bottom, and from left to right, as far as is reasonable. That is to say that 'b', for instance, is formed by making the stick first from top to bottom, and then the circle. 'D' is formed by making the circle first and then the stick. Circles can be done clockwise or anti-clockwise. Cross-pieces, as in 't, f and e', should be from left to right. As in all aspects of reading do not labour these points too

much, but guide gently. It may be necessary to undo a lot of bad writing patterns.

Mr Johnston is here writing for teachers but, if parents observe these simple rules, it will not be necessary for teachers to have to unteach bad writing habits. By following these rules you will be able to combine his love of drawing (forming letters is only an extension of drawing) with a lesson in writing and some useful information about letters, and their sounds, as suggested above.

You will realize by now that there is no *one* best method of teaching reading. There is no approach which works for all children in all circumstances. Each child has his own best method of learning, and by knowing that each child is unique, and by approaching him as an individual, we can help him discover it. Children will further their progress by learning from different aspects of their environment. Much of their learning will be independent of, and in some cases in spite of, the 'method' used in school. You will want to learn more about the 'methods' used in schools, and I shall explain one more of them later in this chapter, but at this stage you will probably like some more suggestions for helping your child at home.

I have already urged you to build up your child's vocabulary, to talk and listen to him, to use home-made books to increase his interest in fascinating experiences, to use pictures in his room as a subject for conversation, to realize how notes for tradesmen and letters from friends can be steps towards reading, and above all to read to him. If you follow these suggestions your child will probably 'pick up' reading, just as he miraculously 'picked up' speaking. Once we realize the written word is a token for the spoken word, and that a child learns to speak because we have taken trouble to talk to him and to listen to his own efforts, it is logical to expect that he will learn to read when he is surrounded by the printed word as a natural and enjoyable part of his daily life.

Sadly, many homes do not have anything like enough

books in them. It is hard for some people to accept but, even in these days of free libraries, a recent survey showed that one child in three in junior schools had fewer than *five books* in their homes. These books were the possessions of the whole family – not just the children. Parents who want to give their youngsters a chance should recognize how hard it is for them to learn to read, and to keep up with their classmates, if they are not provided with enough books in the home.

Children are quick to copy adults, and if you do not use books and show enthusiasm for reading, your children will not recognize the value of literature. But it is also dangerous to go to the other extreme. Parents who love reading should realize how infuriating it is for their children to find them engrossed in a newspaper or buried in a novel when they need attention. You will not convey an enthusiasm for reading merely by being *seen* to read. You may even make a child resentful of an activity which stops him playing with you or getting your affection. The wise parent will discuss pictures in a newspaper with his child, or talk about the child's own books.

Of course the best way to give him some idea of your joy at reading is to arrange to read together. Sunday mornings can be more fun for children if, for example, they know *they* can look through the colour supplements, while *you* study the women's page or the football reports. In such ways pleasant experiences are *shared*. I remember once telling my own little boy of a story in the newspaper about a 28-stone gorilla which picked up a woman and hugged her so hard it broke both her legs. Of course *he* thought it was very funny. Then he wanted to see a picture of the gorilla, but the newspaper had printed only a head-and-shoulders. My son asked: 'Why don't they show us the gorilla properly? Where is the poor lady? How big was she?' When I told my wife about his questions he felt puffed up.

My point here, and it cannot be repeated too often, or stressed too strongly, is how the use of the printed word in the home should arise out of some natural, spontaneous experience. My three-year-old son was interested in gorillas.

He had been to a zoo. He liked the idea of being able to take part in a grown-up discussion about why there was not a large, full-length picture in the paper.

But if you use flash-cards with words on them, and hold them up for him to read, the lesson is not a spontaneous one. It is an attempt to create an artificial learning situation. The words on the card, as in the Glenn Doman method described in his book *Teach Your Baby To Read*, may be homely and they may be words he hears every day, such as 'Mummy' or 'foot', but it is difficult to see how a card-quizzing session can be started naturally.

When you consider the love and humanity involved in other pre-reading activities, I am sure you will agree the Doman approach seems too arid. For example, how many times does your toddler ask to have his nursery-rhyme book open at a favourite page, while he is eating his meal? You pretend to feed Old Mother Hubbard's children with the spoonful intended for him. His affection for his book, his pleasure at eating, and his knowledge of his mother's love, are all combined to make these moments a bond in your relationship. You cannot, in my opinion, enhance his learnings or deepen your relations to the same extent by holding up cards for him to read. He may appear to be delighted when you shout your approval if he guesses a word correctly, but he will not be learning anything important, and the experience will be rather superficial for *both* of you.

But books are not the only way we can make children aware of the use of the printed word. I have mentioned letters, tradesmen's notes, newspapers and catalogues. There are other activities which may not immediately occur to you.

Suppose your child has been playing in the garden and comes in to find you watching television. He may say: 'I want to see my programme.' If, instead of merely telling him it is not on, you suggest you find the newspaper or the *TV Times*, and you look it up together, he will have learned once more why adults are always reading.

When your child is about three or four he will begin to notice most of the hundreds of words all around us, everywhere we go. He sees the labels on food in the kitchen, the words on the side of the ice-cream van, signs in a field which say 'Danger' or 'Keep Out', and the names above shop-windows. Each word on display is a chance for you to make him realize how important, and how much fun, reading can be. If you go visiting one of his friends who happens to live in a street where all the houses are the same, he will learn about numbers, why we need them, and perhaps why we count in sequence. At the start of the road you might say : 'Janet lives at number 35 – let's look for the numbers on the front of the houses and see if we can find her house.' Of course this lesson is best learnt in a street where the houses are not numbered alternately.

Your child will also learn quite quickly that he is surrounded by individual letters as well as words. There is the 'L' plate on a neighbour's car, the 'H' and 'C' on the taps in the bathroom, the initials on handkerchiefs and the 'P' on parking signs.

Dorothy Glynn, in her book *Teach Your Child To Read*, is very encouraging about these simple lessons. She says :

> Thus it will be seen how in many interested homes young children can make acquaintance with words and letters in a visual form, and so come to accept the printed word as a necessary and proper part of their daily lives. It is in this way that those children who are ready for it acquire fluency in reading, almost as naturally as they acquired fluency in speech. *It is indeed possible for some children (though by no means all) to learn to read in this apparently effortless way, even before they are admitted to school.*

Because of the importance of this kind of home-learning, it is tempting to say that teachers only succeed with children who are going to read anyway. This is unfair on thousands of skilled teachers, with a touch of genius, who manage to help deprived children from bookless homes with inarticulate parents, but nevertheless the case can be argued. Consider the implication behind Mrs Glynn's statement. She is saying that many children start school at the age of $4\frac{1}{2}$ to $5\frac{1}{4}$ able to read, and according to the estimates of experienced teachers, these represent about one child in five. We know that only one child in five succeeds academically in our education system. These are the children who fill the 'A' streams, who surmount the hurdle of the eleven-plus exam, who leave school long after the official leaving-age, and who go to universities and technical colleges. While they are reading and acquiring new skills, the remaining 80 per cent of children are still learning to read.

Even if we admit that some children manage to succeed even though they could not read before starting school, it is quite clear how crucial the parental role is in teaching children their most important lesson. The parents who take the advice offered in this chapter are really giving their children a head-start in the academic race, and providing them with a happier childhood.

But you may ask: 'I agree with all you have said but your suggestions are mostly designed to create a favourable attitude to books; when do the children begin reading?'

Mrs Glynn answers this point. She says:

They *are* learning now, and they have been doing so from the beginning, even though your efforts to teach them cannot be described, or laid down in clear-cut stages. In all these early books, whether published or home-made, children are constantly meeting, in different contexts, printed words with which they are already familiar through their everyday conversation. You will read books to them, and with them, and you will enjoy them together. You will encourage them to make bold attempts to read for themselves. Many children because of a genuine interest soon appear to know the text of their favourite books by heart. They can make sense of the printed material because they have a good idea of what is there. Soon, however, they begin to associate individual words with their meanings, and then to pick out the key words and phrases in different books and in unfamiliar contexts.

Finally they begin to recognize the parts which make up the words; in this way many children learn to read as naturally as they learn to talk. Such 'natural readers' seem capable of becoming fluent without any teaching of phonetics or word-building, and appear to need very little help in the analysis of words.

I must stress the importance of encouraging your child to draw, paint and eventually write. I have already mentioned the idea of your writing captions under pictures in homemade books. I said you could put transparent paper over them and get him to copy the words. You can extend this idea and put captions under his own paintings and drawings. You can leave a small blackboard beside his bed and put a tiny drawing on it with a simple message. For example, you could leave an apple near the blackboard, and the message could just read : 'John's apple'. You could also fold a piece of paper (perhaps stuck on cardboard) into a concertina-like shape, and draw simple pictures of objects and animals on each section. On the outside you could put a letter, say 'B', and in this case you should make sure that all the animals and objects begin with 'B'. These concertina booklets could also contain pictures of items which contain the same sound – such as 'watch', 'church', 'satchel', 'chair' and 'torch'. The lesson he learns from these booklets can also be learned by playing 'I Spy' games which are sold in most bookshops.

Now it only remains for me to complete the answer to the third of the four questions I posed earlier : 'Which is the best method for teachers to use?' I have already covered most of this issue by pointing out there is not one 'best' method for all children. But many mothers will want to know more about a method which is rapidly gaining ground in our schools : this is the Initial Teaching Alphabet, usually called i.t.a.

What is i.t.a.? Is it Good for All Children?

The i.t.a. has 44 characters instead of the 26 letters of the traditional alphabet. It originated in 1837 and is taught to about one in six of primary schoolchildren. It has been enormously successful. Many experts believe that, because children learn earlier with i.t.a. than with the 26-letter alphabet, the case for introducing it into *all* schools is overwhelming. When children using i.t.a. for their first year were compared with pupils learning with the normal alphabet, the i.t.a. pupils were able, at the end of the year, to read twice as much as the others. Their writing vocabularies were nearly fifty per cent greater, and in creative writing they wrote fifty per cent more.

You will probably wonder what happens to the children who arrive at school well-advanced for their age in reading the normal alphabet. There is no need to worry. If your child can read the first two books of the 'Janet and John' series, which is used in seven out of ten primary schools, the headteacher will probably agree there is no point in putting him on to i.t.a. Dr Downing tells of a boy who read so well when he started at school that he was given his own library and read merrily away while the rest of the children began their first steps in i.t.a.

Parents often ask why anyone considers it necessary to teach pupils a strange 44-letter alphabet for two years and then to make them return to the 26-letter alphabet.

The case for i.t.a. is based on the difficulties caused by the vast number of inconsistencies in English spelling and pronunciation. The obvious example of this is the variety of sounds in the words 'tough', 'through', 'enough', 'bough' and 'though'. The i.t.a., as designed by Sir James Pitman, aims to cut out these inconsistencies so that any one sound is represented by a single symbol. For example, the letter 's' used in the word 'sad', is the same as in the 26-letter alphabet, but the 's' in the word 'houses' is represented differently in i.t.a. The word 'island' becomes 'ieland' in i.t.a., and the word 'light' becomes 'liet'.

Supporters of i.t.a. point out that the simplified spelling gives pupils a chance to read at the speed they want to read. This confidence, when added to the joy of reading what they want to read, gives them a boost so they are able to tackle the return to the 26-letter alphabet without great difficulty.

But although the case for this alphabet is very persuasive, and although 99 per cent of teachers who use it say they would never go back to teaching with the normal alphabet, the arguments about its use are still going on. In September 1969 two researchers at Manchester University, Prof Frank Warburton and Mrs Vera Southgate, did a great deal to hearten the advocates of i.t.a. They reported that:

> The experimental results so far obtained suggest very strongly that i.t.a. is a more efficient medium for teaching reading to beginners than traditional orthography (the 26-letter alphabet). The magnitude of the differences found in its favour in many different researches is unusually high . . . In the majority of schools, although not in all, infants using i.t.a. have learned to read earlier, more easily, and at a faster rate than similar children using traditional orthography.

But critics of the alphabet claim that the advantage children gain by reading earlier is often wiped out when they return to the normal alphabet. More research is needed into i.t.a., but I am impressed by arguments stressing its benefits in starting pupils to read earlier. In view of the urgent need to teach children as much as possible as early as possible, the benefits of i.t.a. are considerable. No one is really certain why it is so successful, but it is thought that its efficiency stems from the way the strange symbols direct a child's attention to the structure of words. As they learn the 44 letters they are made to examine language in the very way needed to teach them reading. I am sure Dr Downing and Dr Joyce Morris are right in urging Sir James Pitman to modify his alphabet to iron out certain anomalies, but the changes they suggest are not great enough to support those who think the spread of i.t.a. should be halted.

Other Problems – What to Do?

One important point about the controversy over methods emerged from some research published in November 1968. Mrs Vera Southgate, in the magazine *Educational Research*, wrote that:

> The most decisive factor influencing children's reading progress is the beliefs and attitudes of the staff about the *importance* of reading. In those schools in which the staff consider reading of prime importance, and favour an early beginning ... most children do learn to read, early and well, *almost regardless* of the media, methods, materials or procedures adopted. In those infant schools in which the staff are convinced of the value of delaying the beginning of reading tuition, little or no reading drive is in force, and children's reading progress in their first year or two at school is noticeably slower. There is an obvious difference in the reading standards of children in two such infant schools, even though they are in similar areas, and have children of equal ability.

The second most important factor affecting a child's progress, according to Mrs Southgate's investigation, appeared to be the skill, training and experience of the teacher.

These findings confirm for us the basic causes of low reading standards in our schools. Teachers do not receive the right training in the nation's 170-odd colleges. They are not made to realize the desperate need to teach children to read as early as possible, and they are not able to give sufficient individual attention to slow-learning pupils in overcrowded classes. Mrs Southgate's point about the attitude of teachers, and the importance of their believing in the decisive role of reading in a child's whole life and career, reminds us of our reasons for urging mothers and fathers to do what they can to make their children literate. Parents have a greater motive for wanting their children to read, than any teacher faced with a class of children belonging to others.

But you may well ask what should be done if your child is a backward reader or handicapped in some way. If teachers are far from perfect you will feel your child may need some extra help. Two of the commonest reasons for reading failure are poor physical conditions and severe emotional disturbance. (This is why the 'Ladybird' list of conditions for reading readiness lays such stress on a child's physical and psychological state.) If a child's speech development is poor for his age, a parent should arrange through the school for him to see a speech therapist. If the school cannot find a therapist for you, your local doctor will help. If your child is physically or psychologically handicapped, you should consult your local child-guidance clinic. You could also find out the name of your local educational psychologist by looking up the list of officials in the *Education Committees Year Book* in your library.

If your child seems perfectly normal, but still cannot read at the age of seven or eight, there are four things you can do. First, you can try a different approach to reading, in an effort, as Mrs Glynn says, to 'surprise' him into reading.

If your child shows little inclination to read books, you could try working words into another activity. A seven-year-old is quite capable of helping you with recipes or handling a simple scientific experiment. As you prepare the recipe, or perform the experiment, you will find you can quite naturally write down information on cards or record findings in a special book. In the excitement of the game he will forget his distaste for reading. If you get him concentrating on the fun of the activity you will often find he is looking at the words on your record, or in the recipe, without thinking. If you build up a special book of his science experiments, such a book would have more interest for him than reading the books he finds so difficult. His science book will be something he looks on with affection, and he may be 'surprised' into reading. Such ploys should only be used for older children, however, and you ought to consult his teacher about the vocabulary suitable for his age.

Another note of warning here. If you are one of those

mothers who are horrified by the idea of comics, you should remember that comics sometimes have some educational value. Your child is likely to have a stronger motive for reading his favourite comic than many of the rather boring books provided by schools.

My second piece of advice for the parents of slow-learning children is to have a chat with his teacher. Sometimes a child can have something wrong with his eyes and his disability may go unnoticed. Teachers are advised to watch out for children who display certain symptoms of poor eyesight, but they may not notice that *your* child needs attention. The symptoms are: blinking, frowning, watery or aching eyes, headaches, and omissions, repetitions, reversals and line-skipping in their reading. Children with these symptoms may need to change their seat in the class, or avoid close work for a while until they have seen the doctor.

Thirdly, you should consider either joining the Advisory Centre for Education, or contacting Educational Explorers Ltd (40 Silver Street, Reading). The ACE will advise you on how to handle a school if it does not respond to your worries about a child's slow progress. It will also help you with titles of books to suit your pocket, if you think a new book would help your child regain interest. The Educational Explorers have tiny resources, but I have always found them very successful with children considered as 'failures' by schools. If you live near enough to Reading to take your child there, they will examine him in a friendly way and suggest a new approach.

Fourthly, you should ask the teachers if they think your child may be suffering from 'word-blindness', known as dyslexia. There is a great deal of controversy over this disability. Many children who are thought to be 'word-blind' are suffering from some other handicap. But much more is known about this condition now, and your local educational psychologist may feel it is necessary to put you in touch with the Word-blind Centre (93 Guilford Street, London WC1. Telephone: 01-837 8914). Other organizations which may prove helpful are listed at the end of this chapter.

But above all I cannot urge you too strongly to start as early as possible with your 'teaching' in the home. If you love your child, and show him you love him, if you talk to him for at least half an hour a day, and let him share in your activities, such as shopping, you will be doing much to avoid problems in the future.

SUGGESTED READING

Books for Children. Advisory Centre for Education: Cambridge, 1969.

Glynn, Dorothy M., *Teach Your Child to Read*. Pearson: London, 1964. (Now available from Hamlyn.)

Johnston, Stanley. *Achieving Reading Success*. Cambridge Aids to Learning Ltd: Cambridge, 1969.

Morris, Joyce, *Standards and Progress in Reading*. National Foundation for Educational Research: London, 1966.

Moyle, Donald, *The Teaching of Reading*. Ward Lock Educational: London, 1968.

Schonell, F. J., *Backwardness in the Basic Subjects*. Oliver & Boyd: London, 1942.

Wood, Anne, *A Parents' Guide*. Transworld: London, 1971.

Anne Wood is the founder of the Federation of Children's Book Groups, 100 Church Lane East, Aldershot. Telephone 0252–23111.

There is an enormous number of books published each year for children beginning to read. From the classic series by Beatrix Potter (Warne) to the latest by Brian Wildsmith (OUP and other publishers) the choice is vast. It would be impossible for me to select a reasonable number to recommend here. The best plan is to go to your local public library and ask the advice of the children's librarian. Usually small children take great delight in choosing their own books, however, and this enthusiasm can be guided so that the most suitable choice is made. For the fullest available information you should see the *Books for Children* pamphlet published by ACE; there is also a leaflet, *Books for the Under-fives*, available from the National Book League, 7 Albemarle Street, London WIX 4BB (10p).

Among the popular series there is the very inexpensive Ladybird Key Words Reading Scheme, stocked by many newsagents as well as booksellers; there are the *Barbar* books by Laurent de Brunhoff (Methuen), Leila Berg's *Nippers* (Macmillan), *The Happy Lion* books by Roger Duvoisin and Louise Fatio (The Bodley Head), *The Little Red Engine* stories by Diana Ross (Faber). A popular series of factual books is *This is London* – and many other cities around the world – by Miroslav Sasek (W. H. Allen).

Here are some of the reading schemes used in schools. None of them is exciting and some of them *barely* functional. It is time these standard schemes were changed; at least one has remained unaltered since 1932. But you should certainly be familiar with the scheme used in your child's school.

Janet and John. Donnell, M. O. and Munro, R. (Nisbet).

Happy Venture. Schonell, F. J. and Serjeant, I. (Oliver and Boyd).

The Pilot Reading Scheme. Devenport, P. (Arnold).

Gay-Way. Boyce, E. (Macmillan).

Growing and Reading. Bakewell, R. and Fletcher, D. (Macmillan).

The Honey Family. Black, M. and Brearley, M. (Educational Supply Association).

John and Mary and *Mac and Tosh.* Ashley, E. (Schofield and Sims).

DYSLEXIA ASSOCIATIONS

Bath Association for the Study of Dyslexia, 18 The Circus, Bath, Somerset.

North London Dyslexia Association, Mrs M. L. Heath, 78 Whitehall Park, London N19.

Scottish Association for the Study of Dyslexia, 3 Coltbridge Avenue, Edinburgh EH12 6AF.

North Surrey Dyslexia Society, J. G. Meiklejohn Esq, 9 Moorhayes Drive, Laleham, Staines, Middlesex.

West Surrey Dyslexia Aid Association, Mrs P. A. Jones, 13 Springhaven Close, Crawley Road, Guildford, Surrey.

Northern Ireland Dyslexia Association, Bryson House, 28 Bedford Street, Belfast BT2 7SE.

Cambridge Dyslexia Association, Mrs J. F. Mitchell, 22 Sedley Taylor Road, Cambridge CB2 2PW.

Essex Dyslexia Society, Mrs J. C. Norton, Round Hills, Ramsden Heath, Billericay, Essex.

Publications on Dyslexia and Where to Get Them

Reading and the Dyslexic Child. Souvenir Press, 95 Mortimer Street, London W1 (£1.50).

Dyslexia or Very Severe Reading Difficulty. Reading Services, c/o 91 King Street, Cambridge (60p).

Dyslexia: A Guide for Parents and Teachers. Margaret Newton, Department of Applied Psychology, University of Aston, Birmingham (5p post-free).

Anne Allen's Sunday Mirror Book-List for Children

I have tried to judge the age that each book is suitable for but if your child is advanced or is having reading difficulties you might like to see the book before buying.

FICTION

Under Four

SHREWBETTINA'S BIRTHDAY by John S. Goodall, published by Macmillan at 75p.

Adorable story of a shrewmouse's birthday party, all in pictures. Small and easy to hold.

SHAPES by Janet Williams, published by Ernest Benn at 75p.

A very nice present for the smallest children. You could sit him on your knee and spend a happy time talking about different shapes and what they make. Very clear illustrations and words.

JOHNNY'S BAD DAY by Edward Ardizzone, published by The Bodley Head at 60p.

All pictures and Edward Ardizzone at that! What more could anyone want as the perfect present for (perhaps) a grandchild who likes sitting on knees with a book.

Under Six

BABAR AND THE OLD LADY by Jean de Brunhoff, published by Methuen at 30p.

Another sweet little story of Babar the elephant.

TIM'S FAMILY GOES DOWN THE HIGH STREET and TIM'S FAMILY GOES TO THE SEASIDE, by Pat Albeck, published by Nelson at 62½p each.

Both these are attractive and should give immense pleasure. Pictures in black and white and three colours. The titles give a good idea of what they are about.

FIND THE GOLDFISH, FIND THE YELLOW CHICKEN and I KNOW ABOUT CARS by Alain Gree, published by Methuen at 30p each.

These are in the 'Look Around Books' series and Alain Gree has written five others. They are nice simple little books with bold pictures.

THE EARLY BIRD by Richard Scarry, published by Collins at 50p.

Bold, clear pictures on every page illustrate a story about a bird – who goes out to find a worm to play with and gets a bit muddled before he is successful. A very nice present to read to a four-year-old and older.

Four to Seven

A BAD CHILD'S BOOK OF MORAL VERSE, by Charlotte Hough, published by Faber & Faber at £1.05p.

Plain, but nice, pictures illustrate some poems which I think far too old for the children this book is obviously intended for. But if you like reading highly moral rhymes, these are they.

THE RAIN MAN by Helga Aichinger, published by Dobson at 90p.

A story of a little girl and her two pets who went for a ride in the sky with the rain man. Each page is a picture with the words in bold, black print.

MR BEAR'S TRUMPET by Chizuko Kuratomi and Kozo Kakimoto, published by Macdonald at 95p.

The fourth Mr Bear book and likely to be just as loved. Simple pictures which leave room for your own imagination. This time Mr Bear gets in an awful muddle trying to learn the trumpet in a circus.

I CAN LICK 30 TIGERS TODAY by Dr Seuss, published by Collins at £1.00.

If you know Dr Seuss you will have a mental picture of his bold witty pictures. This book seems to me rather better than earlier ones.

TIBOR GERGELY'S GREAT BIG BOOK OF BEDTIME STORIES, published by Hamlyn at £1.05.

A very nice, good-value, present for children who like being read to and looking at pictures.

THE TRUCK ON THE TRACK by Janet Burroway, published by Jonathan Cape at £1.00.

Fantastically pretty pictures by John Vernon Lord. If the reading matter had been as good I would have picked it book of the year. But it has no 'start', which is muddling, and the words are a bit sophisticated for small children. Have a look though if you can. You may feel the fun of its gay rhythm suits a child you know.

THE LAUGHING DRAGON by Kenneth Mahood, published by Collins at £1.05.

A really lovely present for a child who loves looking at pictures at bedtime. £1.05 is a lot of money but the illustrations are gorgeous. The story is about a dragon in Japan whose hot laughter proves a fire hazard and then a comfort in a cold winter.

IF I WERE A GROWN-UP by Eva Janikovsky, published by Dobson at 50p.

A funny, delightful book with simple 'scribble' drawings illustrating a child's view of the joys of being grown up. One of the nicest books recently.

JASPER AND THE GIANT by Nicholas Brennan, published by Longman Young Books at 90p.

A smashing present for anyone who loves Red Indians and magic. The pictures are so good that I foresee the book becoming a treasured friend for hundreds of little boys.

THE BEARS WHO STAYED INDOORS by Susanna Gretz, published by Ernest Benn at 80p.

An adorable story of five bears (one blue, one brown, one red, one yellow and one black) who do various things to pass a wet day – with help from a Dalmatian called Fred.

THE VELVETEEN RABBIT by Margery Williams, published by Heinemann at £1.25.

(Preferably read aloud.) First published in 1922 and very 'vintage' feeling. Well worth a new edition, a charming story about a velveteen rabbit who knows that only toys who are really loved become 'real'. I can only say that I am thankful there is no longer a need to burn toys because of germs. (But it is all right – the velveteen rabbit has a happy ending.) A few pictures but mostly writing.

MR GRUMPY'S OUTING by John Burningham, published by Jonathan Cape at £1.05.

Every year hundreds of us must look forward to the new Burningham. This one is as good as ever and will be the basis of hours of bed-time cuddle. Mr Grumpy is a farmer who loves animals.

MOG THE FORGETFUL CAT, by Judith Kerr, published by Collins at 90p.

A nice story about an interesting cat who is always in trouble, until he catches a burglar. Pictures on every page and simple words. Might help a learner-reader.

TIMOTHY'S HORSE by Vladimir Mayakovsky and Flavio Costantini, published by Dobson at 90p.

Good clear pictures illustrate the building of a 'hobby horse' for a little boy.

BOLLERBAM by Janosch, published by Dobson at 90p.

An anti-war book about a bird who stops a silly king from enjoying his cannon. Super bright pictures.

Five to Eight

123456789 BENN by David McKee, published by Dobson at 90p.

A gorgeous book about Mr Benn (who last appeared in Mr Benn – Red Knight) in prison through a bit of a mix-up. And it really is surprising what a little enterprise can do to brighten up the place!

THE LITTLE RED COMPUTER by Ralph Steadman, published by Dobson at 90p.

A really lovely story about a little red computer who is in disgrace because he can't add 2 + 2 but ends up a hero because he knows that 'beyond the golden star there are cascades of falling stars'. All of which takes him into space.

PUNCH AND JONATHAN by Bill Binzen, published by Macmillan at £1.05.

This time the illustrations are colour photos. Very nice. The story is about a little boy who loves Punch and Judy – and eventually learns how to 'work' them.

MR TOAD PLAYS A TRICK ON MASTER FOX (£1.05), MR TOAD INVITES A FRIEND TO DINNER (80p), MR RAT GOES OUT TO DINNER (80p), MONSIEUR MAUGRET AND THE BURGLAR (80p), TOUTOU FINDS A HAT (50p), THE LONELY LITTLE BLACK CHICK (80p), AUNT MARIANNE'S GARDEN (50p), all by Robert and Gordon Davey and published by Chatto & Windus.

The pictures are adorable, the writing clear script and the stories racy. Try and see one of them.

THE BEGINNING OF THE ARMADILLOS by Rudyard Kipling, published by Macmillan at £1.05.

A Kipling story newly illustrated, very attractively, by Giulio Maestro, on every page.

TWO CATS IN AMERICA by Mischa Damjan, published by Longman Young Books at £1.10.

A super story about the first two cats in the USA illustrated with lovely bright coloured pictures. The whole thing crammed with Red Indians, sailing ships and early America.

THE RUTH AINSWORTH BOOK, published by Heinemann at £1.50.

Ruth Ainsworth has collected some old favourites amongst her stories and added some new ones and the whole thing is most attractively illustrated in black and white. A really nice present (perhaps for a family of children).

PILLYCOCK'S SHOP by Margaret Mahy and Carol Barker, published by Dobson at 90p.

If you have met Carol Barker's beautiful drawings before you will definitely want this too. It comes with a charming story about a little boy and a magic shop and a wicked man who gets defeated in the nick of time.

THE TALE OF DRIVER GROPE by Richard Ingrams and Ralph Steadman, published by Dobson at 90p.

A lovely, beautifully illustrated story of a nice engine-driver, a wicked man and a train that was needed after all. The pictures will be loved by boys who like cars, bridges, traffic signs and trains.

CHRISTMAS AT BULLERBY by Astrid Lindgren and Ilon Wikland, published by Methuen at 90p.

Anglicized version of a Swedish tale about how seven children who live on neighbouring farms spend Christmas. Well written with colourful, full-page illustrations.

DIMPLE, THE ADVENTURES OF A LITTLE DONKEY, published by Hamlyn at 52½p.

A reasonably priced and pretty story about a donkey from Ireland who goes through all sorts of adventures and sadness — but is happy in the end.

ALBERT'S CHRISTMAS by Alison Jezard, published by Gollancz at 80p.

The fourth book about lovable bear Albert, and this time he is working as a temporary Christmas postman in London, from which other adventures ensue.

WHERE THE WILD APPLES GROW by John Hawkinson, published by Muller at 80p.

A story about a girl and a white horse who live undisturbed in a quiet valley but have their peace shattered when a party of trippers arrive from the town. Illustrations in black and white and rather dull colours.

Six to Ten

THE GOOD TIGER by Elizabeth Bowen, published by Jonathan Cape at 80p.

If only the best stories were always with the best pictures! I didn't like the illustrations of this one bit but the story is lovely. About a tiger who likes cakes and escapes from his zoo to live happily in a wood.

STEVIE by John Steptoe, published by Longman Young Books at 80p.

A lovely story of a little Negro boy who is infuriated by a visiting toddler, but misses him when he goes back home. Soft pictures that leave a lot to your own imagination.

THE WONDERFUL POTION AND OTHER STORIES by Nicholas Brennan, published by Longman Young Books at 60p.

A small, easy-to-hold book overflowing with pen drawings. Its great advantage is that any grown-up doing the reading must enjoy it. It is about an absent-minded professor who makes a magic potion that lets him hop over roofs, etc.

WILLIAM TELL, adapted from the Rossini opera by Alan Blackwood and Tom Bailey, published by Bancroft at 75p.

If you liked this publisher's version of Peter and the Wolf *this will give you pleasure too. Plenty of pictures. Very difficult to age but I think six to nine or ten.*

ANN IN THE MOON by Frances D. Francis, published by Bancroft at £1.05

A highly topical story about a trip to the moon by a girl – a sort of little sister to Alice in Wonderland. *It deserves to sell well because it is full value at £1.05. I am not drawn to the pictures but others may go overboard for them.*

DINOSAURS DON'T DIE by Ann Coates, published by Longman Young Books at 90p.

A really nice story about a little boy who gets friendly with a dinosaur who has escaped from a museum, hoping to find if he is 'made right'. Mostly writing, but lots of pictures too.

PADDINGTON TAKES THE AIR by Michael Bond published by Collins at 75p.

A new Paddington for his fans. How I wish I had never met this lovely little bear so that I had the pleasure of reading them all for the first time ... However this one (about a dentist, show-jumping, dancing and pages and pages more) has been a treat to read.

ALLSORTS 3, edited by Ann Thwaite, published by Macmillan at 75p.

According to the publisher, Allsorts has 'all sorts of things in it for all sorts of children' and it has. Puzzle pictures, word-games, codes, quizzes and stories.

OLD MACDONALD HAD SOME FLATS by Judith and Ron Barrett, published by Longman Young Books at 90p.

A very funny book. Mr MacDonald is a caretaker who loves farming. After pages of pictures all the tenants of the flats have left and he has turned the block of flats he cares for into a four-storey farm.

THE CAT WHO COULD FLY by Alexy Pendle, published by Muller at 80p.

A lavishly illustrated story of a cat who not only learns to fly but gets as far as Africa, with its many animals. A really nice present.

THE HUNTING OF THE SNARK by Lewis Carroll, pictures by Helen Oxenbury, published by Heinemann at £1.10.

If you know Helen Oxenbury's illustrations already you will know this is a gem. If not do try and see it. It is a beautiful new look at Lewis Carroll's old ballad. But it does need a rather 'intellectual' child.

Seven to Ten

ARTHUR by Ernest Dudley, published by Muller at 90p.

Arthur the white cat who eats with his paw on television is the basis of this story – then well embroidered with adventures and royalty by Ernest Dudley (the BBC's Armchair Detective) and well illustrated by David Nockels. A must for cat-lovers.

ELIAS THE FISHERMAN by Papas, published by Oxford at £1.00.

Papas always does lovely pictures and this is possibly his best yet. Elias is a young fisherman who day-dreams himself into danger – and into a whole new future.

THE BIRTHDAY UNICORN by Janice Elliot, published by Gollancz at 90p.

I loved this story about a rich, rather lonely, boy whose (rather unusual) parents give him a unicorn and a dodo. I do hope that this is the first of many children's books from this author.

STARDOM FOR HIMSELF by Kenneth Bird, published by Macdonald at 90p.

Himself is a dog who can talk. He has appeared in two previous books. This is well up to standard with hectic hair-breadth escapes from the circus people and a do-or-die adventure to save a good dog-meat firm from nasty competitors.

CLEVER, CLEVER, CLEVER, FOLK TALES FROM MANY LANDS, selected by Jeanne B. Hardendorff, published by Macdonald at 90p.

A collection of folk stories from several countries. Nice to read aloud or give a little girl who loves good stories that can be read over and over. A few pictures in black and white.

THE WISHING POOL by Elinor Lyon, published by Brockhampton Press at 80p.

A nice book for the child leaving picture books and not quite ready for children's novels. A little boy who thinks that a statue standing in a pool in a deserted garden grants wishes and two girls who decide to help the magic along.

MARMADUKE GOES TO ITALY by Elizabeth Chapman, published by Brockhampton Press at 80p.

Marmaduke is a lorry who finds that Italy is a pretty exciting place.

Nine to Twelve

THE LAST MAN ALIVE by A. S. Neill, published by Gollancz at £1.20.

This book by the founder of Summerhill School was first published in 1938. Neill and some of his pupils are the only people left alive after a strange green cloud has turned everybody on earth to stone.

THE JENNINGS REPORT by Anthony Buckeridge, published by Collins at 65p.

A good addition for Jennings fans.

THE HUNTING OF WILBERFORCE PIKE by Molly Lefebure, published by Gollancz at £1.20.

A smashing children's novel for cat-lovers.

THURSDAY'S CHILD by Noel Streatfeild, published by Collins at £1.25.

A romantic little girl of ten or twelve would love this. It is a typically excellent story by one of England's best writers of books for children, about an orphan found with three sets of clothes 'embroidered with crowns' and some exciting friends and a horrible matron.

THE BLOW-AND-GROW YEAR by Margaret Potter, published by Dobson at 90p.

The second novel about the three Sinclair children. They have just moved back to the country and meet lots of new friends and new adventures.

A PENNY FOR THE GUY by Jill Chaney, published by Dobson at 75p.

Some children fear that 'Guy Fawkes' may be happening all over again.

FAIRY TALES FROM JAPAN by Miroslav Novak, published by Hamlyn at £1.05.

A super book for reading aloud but not, I feel, much fun to read to oneself. Very oriental illustrations.

Ten to Fourteen

CUSTER'S LAST BATTLE by Paul and Dorothy Goble, published by Macmillan at £1.05.

The story of the battle of the Little Bighorn told by Red Hawk, a Red Indian boy who was 15 at the time. Super illustrations and added historical notes.

THE DAYBREAKERS by Jane Curry, published by Longman Young Books at £1.10.

Set in America, this is a novel for 'real readers'. It is a mixture of ancient history and magic and two children trying to cope.

THE FIGHT FOR ARKENVALD by Thomas Johnston, published by Collins at £1.05.

A novel for boys – say 11 to 14 – who enjoy fantasy, ancient history and adventure. A good way to spend a book token.

OUT OF THE BANDBOX by Marjorie Gayler, published by Macdonald at £1.00.

Ideal story for a little girl who already has her eye on going out to work. It is about Judi working in a boutique and the people she meets there.

MYNA BIRD MYSTERY by Paul Berna, published by Bodley Head at 90p.

A racy and exciting children's novel set in France. Excellent value.

THE HOUSE AT WORLD'S END by Monica Dickens, published by Heinemann at £1.05 and Pan Books (in their Piccolo series at 25p).

A lovely, lovely novel for any child who loves a good read – and animals. The four Fielding children are managing on their own and they keep finding animals needing help. There are also problems at school, from a child-care officer and a ghost.

GIANNI AND THE OGRE, by Ruth Manning-Sanders, published by Methuen at £1.50.

A collection of Mediterranean folk stories, re-told by Ruth Manning-Sanders. I feel that £1.50 is a lot of money to pay for a book for a child, but it would make a lovely present for someone who loves books and enjoys reading folk stories.

NON-FICTION

Under Seven

COLD LANDS, AIR, SHIPS OF LONG AGO, UNDER THE SEA, MUSHROOMS AND TOADSTOOLS, 25p.

These are all in the Macdonald First Library range and cost 25p each. They are especially for pre-school and infant children and excellent, although I feel they must be for a child with an inquiring mind who loves to understand things.

MY FIRST COLOUR ENCYCLOPEDIA by Jane Werner Watson, published by Hamlyn at £1.25.

For very young children, colour illustrations.

PICTURE DICTIONARY, published by Young World Productions at £1.12½p.

Written in consultation with a psychologist this book is for children beginning to read. Each word explained clearly with text and pictures. Good value.

Seven to Thirteen

BEASTLY BOYS AND GHASTLY GIRLS, Poems selected by William Cole with drawings by Tomi Ungerer, published by Methuen at 90p.

A marvellous collection of 60 poems about naughty children. A lovely present for a grandparent to give – and read to – any child who likes to laugh and shiver at the horrors of boiling your sister.

THE FABER BOOK OF CHILDREN'S SONGS by Donald Mitchell and Roderick Biss, published by Faber and Faber at £2.50.

A really lovely present for the children in one of the rare families who still play a piano.

MY LEARN-TO-SEW BOOK by Janet Barber, published by the Hamlyn Group at 55p.

A pretty and exciting book with lots of ideas for sewing – simple clothes, toys and dolls' clothes.

MORE FUN TO MAKE by Colette Lamarque, published by the Hamlyn Group at 50p.

The ideal present for the child who makes things, clear with pretty illustrations.

KITTENS by Pat Taylor and PUPPIES by Wendy Boorer, published by Hamlyn at 65p each.

All about kittens and puppies with black-and-white and colour photos.

Eight to Fifteen

THE WORLD OF BALLET, edited by Anne Geraghty, published by Collins at £1.75.

A really handsome present for a child who is keen on ballet. Well written and illustrated with both photos and line drawings, it covers ballet history, autobiographies of the great dancers and personal experiences.

PURNELL'S CONCISE ENCYCLOPEDIA, price £1.50.

Very comprehensive and clearly set out with colour and black-and-white illustrations.

THE CHILDREN'S WONDERFUL WORLD ENCYCLOPEDIA, published by Hamlyn at £1.50.

Information on hundreds of subjects, nicely illustrated.

THEY MADE HISTORY by Plantagenet Somerset Fry, published by Hamlyn at £1.05.

Short biographies of 270 famous people from Britain's past. Colour illustrations. Good value for a child who likes history.

Twelve Plus

NELSON by Arthur Bryant, published by Collins at £1.50.

A lovely present for anyone who enjoys history (and this includes adults). Written as clearly as always with this marvellous author, and brilliantly illustrated.

THE BEST OF YOURSELF by Mary Young, published by The Brockhampton Press at £1.25.

A super book for a young teenage girl who is just beginning to experiment with make-up and think about clothes and worry about her figure.

PAPERBACKS

Puffins are always good value and here are a few of the most recent ones.

Picture Puffins for the Very Young – PUGWASH ALOFT by John Ryan, 17½p. ROSIE'S WALK by Pat Hutchins, 20p. THE PIRATE'S TALE by Janet Aitchison and Jill McDonald, 25p. OLD MOTHER HUBBARD AND HER DOG, 17½p. WHERE THE WILD THINGS ARE by Maurice Sendak, 25p. All have big colourful pictures and bold black print.

Two Young Puffins, for those just beginning to read – THE ADVENTURES OF GALLDORA by Modwena Sedgwick, 17½p, and FLAT STANLEY by Jeff Brown, 20p.

Novels for those a bit older

BEDKNOB AND BROOMSTICK by Mary Norton, 25p, for 8 and over.
ENGLISH FAIRY TALES by Joseph Jacobs, 20p, for 8 and over.
THE DOLPHIN CROSSING by Jill Paton Walsh, 20p, 10 and over, especially boys.
THOSE HAPPY GOLDEN YEARS by Laura Ingalls Wilder, 25p, 10 and over.
THE HOUSE OF THE NIGHTMARE AND OTHER EERIE TALES, 25p, 11 and over.
THE CHILDREN OF THE HOUSE by Brian Fairfax-Lucy and Philippa Pearce, 20p, 12 and over, especially girls.

Also look out for the boxed sets of four Puffins, for instance there is one of 'Popular Puffins for Boys of 8 to 10' and a set of the Borrowers books by Mary Norton.

Nine to Fourteen

TOM'S MIDNIGHT GARDEN by A. Philippa Pearce, published by Oxford at 30p.
One of the very nicest of modern children's novels reprinted in paperback.
THE EAGLE OF THE NINTH by Rosemary Sutcliff, published by Oxford at 30p.
First published in 1954 and now in paperback. Set in 117 AD with the Ninth Legion (Roman). An ideal present for a reading boy or girl who likes history.
SAFARI ADVENTURE by Willard Price, published by Knight Books at 20p.
First published in 1966, this is the story of two boys and a game-reserve in Africa.

CHAPTER FIVE

How to Choose a School

Your child is unique. You know things about him no teacher will ever know, although some teachers may get a more objective picture of his ability and personality. The problem of matching your child to his school requires most careful thought. It is one of the most important decisions you will ever have to make.

Bear in mind that you *do* have rights and a certain freedom of choice. Many parents believe their only choice is between a State school on the one hand and an independent school, which they cannot afford, on the other. Some think that at the age of five their child must go to the *nearest* primary school. Both ideas are mistaken. Confused by the eleven-plus, parents may think they have no choice in selecting a secondary school. This is also untrue. Though, for both age groups, accidents of geography may limit their choice.

The rights and duties of a parent are expressed in the 1944 Education Act – the basis of our education system. On the question of choice it reads :

> In the exercise and performance of all powers and duties conferred and imposed on them by this Act, the Minister and local education authorities shall have regard to the general principle that, so far as is compatible with the provision of efficient instruction and training, and the *avoidance of unreasonable public expenditure*, pupils are to be educated in accordance with the wishes of their parents.

The Act also states that :

It shall be the duty of the parent of every child of compulsory school age to cause him to receive efficient full-time instruction suitable to his age, ability and aptitude, either by regular attendance at school or otherwise. [The parent is also obliged to see children attend school regularly.]

The *limited* nature of parental rights is indicated by the use of the phrase 'have regard to'. Local authorities need not follow the principle, they need merely note it.

Geographically, ie, *where* you live, affects not only where your child goes to school but also *when*. The law says children should begin at an infant school in the term after their fifth birthday. But the national situation is varied. Some children begin the term after their fourth birthday. One child in Leeds had to wait for *nine months beyond his fifth birthday*. Most children in this country start at the beginning of the term *containing* their fifth birthday. A survey of 114 local education authorities, made by the ACE, showed that 60 of them consistently applied this principle for all children. A further 21 admitted *most* children at this time. Only five authorities admitted children at the beginning of the year in which the child was five. Twelve said they had some arrangement other than those listed above. These findings show your child may have seven, eight or nine months more or less than other pupils in the infants' school. Very few of the authorities said they made special provision for children unlucky enough to have birthdays in the summer – a factor which, as we noted earlier, can be crucial for a child's future.

Where you live is an important factor in choice of school. If you are unfortunate enough to live in one of the many areas where eleven-plus selection still operates, your child will, of course, be allocated to a school either on the basis of an examination or after investigation of teachers' reports, and your freedom of choice will be further restricted because of this system.

Fee Paying

Family income in most cases prevents parents from considering the fee-paying alternatives to the State system. In secondary schooling, particularly, fees average about £450 a year per child and they often rise as high as £600. These fees mean the total annual cost to a parent is usually about £1,000 once you add in the additional expenses such as travel, uniforms and pocket money. The high cost of private education is a matter of some concern even to the Headmasters' Conference, which represents 200 boys' public schools. They admit that :

> Only the better-off can afford to send their sons to us, and our parents, therefore, nearly all come from the upper-income brackets, and follow the occupations normal to those in those brackets.

But parents who cannot afford this alternative can take heart from the opinion of no less a body than the Public Schools Commission. Headed by the late Sir John Newsom, they revealed that giving a child an expensive education can be a *handicap*. For, as they pointed out, the most striking division between children of this country occurs at eight or nine years old, the age at which so many public-school children start to board at preparatory schools. Rarely do they get the chance of meeting their contemporaries in other social classes, as they would do if they went to a State school. This handicap is prolonged for the whole of their school life.

Clearly public schools reinforce, rather than diminish this division. For though a few schools attempt to increase their contact with the local community, they belong in a remarkable degree to a world of their own. This narrowness of atmosphere is worsened by the background of the masters who teach in them. Seven schoolmasters out of ten went to public schools themselves, and consequently have no experience, and little knowledge, of their State-school counterparts.

There are many other grave indictments of the whole independent boarding-school set-up made in the Commission's report. I am sometimes impressed with foreign comparisons which attempt to show how other countries educate their young more successfully than we do. I refuse to believe, for example, that teenagers in America, Norway or in England are *fundamentally* different. One particular foreign comparison, referred to by the Commission, makes the point rather well. Querying the claim that Britain cannot flourish without the leaders provided by public schools, and ignoring the counter-claim that we cannot flourish *with* them, the report questions whether it is any good for *anybody* that so many of these boys should be segregated at a small number of schools. 'Have other nations without such a system of education – the Israelis, the Japanese, the Swedes – no leaders? Have we no other sources of leaders?'

Another factor, again related to *where* you live, which restricts a parent's freedom of choice is the practice of 'zoning' primary schools. You cannot always choose a primary school for your child. You may have to live in the 'catchment' area of the school of your choice. This is particularly true when demand exceeds the number of places available at a certain school. A school may be popular because it is newly built, or has a lively headteacher, or good eleven-plus results. Pressure on one school may leave others half empty. The local education authority may then designate 'catchment' areas for all the schools in the district. In such a situation, there is always the suspicion that – whatever the authority says – the arrangement is one of administrative convenience.

How to Beat the Odds

In spite of all these limitations parents *can* make their individual wishes known, and get what they want for their children, within the State system. The Ministry of Education lists, in a manual of guidance to the 165 local authorities, a number of 'considerations' which are recognized as legitimate causes for parents to choose one school rather than another. These cover religion, language, convenience, medical reasons, 'special facilities', family associations, a preference for or a dislike of co-education, and academic provision.

You can ask for your child to go to a particular school which caters for children of your particular religious denomination. It helps if you can show you are a *practising* member of that denomination otherwise they may suspect that you have chosen the school for some other reason.

The commonest language consideration accepted by local authorities is given by Welsh, or immigrant, parents.

Two acceptable 'convenience' excuses are safety of travel (there may be traffic dangers involved or an absence of 'lollipop' men), and the obvious advantages involved in having a younger child join an older brother or sister at a school.

As to 'medical' matters, a sympathetic doctor or educational psychologist can work wonders with an official recommendation that your child would benefit from attending one school rather than another.

The Ministry also accepts the 'consideration' of school-meals provision (where both parents are working), and allows that a particular secondary school may do certain advanced work necessary for your child's chosen career. This last factor is usually applicable when a parent is faced with the choice between two secondary modern schools. Some, as we noted earlier, make little or no provision for pupils wishing to study after the official leaving age.

Bear in mind that you cannot expect the local authority to give way to your preference merely because you state one of the 'considerations' listed above. The Ministry is careful in its circular not to give parents the *automatic* right to select a school on the grounds given in their list. It states: 'These are considerations which may need to be balanced against each other before a decision is reached.'

But in practice the fact that so few parents are aware of their right to share in this vital decision has meant that a parent who takes a stand for these reasons has a good chance of success, provided that he uses tact and determination. There is little evidence that local authorities take positive steps to publicize the above 'consideration'. If more parents knew their rights and were aware of the Ministry list, local authorities would have to state more clearly why some children are accepted for a certain school, while others are turned away. At present it is too often a case of first come, first served. Mrs Margaret Thatcher, speaking to the North of England Conference in January 1971, said she was hoping to change the wording of the law concerning parents' rights. It is clear however that her officials are mostly concerned with making the process of deciding appeals from parents *quicker*. They are not anxious to give more power to parents.

The plain fact is there are not enough good schools to go round. A major reason for this is that many of the most powerful people in our society have opted out of the State system and sent children to private schools. Had the State system been fully comprehensive twenty years ago, these influential parents would perhaps have opted *into* it, and made sure the quality of schools was improved. They would surely not have tolerated the over-large classes, inadequate facilities and antiquated buildings that most working-class children have to endure. As we noted earlier, the parents who opt out are often not getting their money's worth. Only about 40 of the 200 public schools recognized by the Headmasters' Conference, only about 100 of the 500 schools recognized by the Preparatory Schools Association, and only about 50 of the 178 direct-grant grammar schools, are as good as the supporters of segregated education claim.

But even though these parents are opting out, it is up to others to apply what pressure they can. Only by thriving parent–teacher groups, parents' pressure organizations, effective spokesmen for parents and teachers among school governors and managers, and on education committees, can we end the anomalies, inconsistencies and injustices of our schooling system.

Meantime, parents must do their best for their child in the present situation. Although there are exceptions, it should be stressed that it is unusual for a local authority to change its mind once a child is allocated to a school, and it is difficult to make your voice effective unless you contact the authority well before your child is due to start at a primary or a secondary school. To be fair to the local authorities, it is very difficult for them to consider even the most valid reasons if the school in question is already full.

If you do fail to get your wishes accepted you can fight the authority's decision. You begin by appealing to your local Councillor, and through him to the Education Committee. If this does not work, you can appeal to the Minister (her full title is 'Secretary of State for Education and Science'). Appeals to the Minister can be passed on by your local MP. But if these approaches fail you can only carry on a kind of war of attrition, and, without an organization like CASE or ACE behind you, your chances throughout would be worse than slender.

How to Choose

How do you choose a school, early enough and fully aware of your rights, assuming that there is no 'catchment' area operating? Certainly not just on its new buildings, well-behaved children, or polite headteacher. Choosing a school is not like choosing a motorcar or a television set. It depends first on objective standards, and secondly (and this is equally important) on your own complex, personal values and needs.

At primary-school level there are several things you can do to help in making your choice. First, obtain a list of primary schools from your local authority office (its address is in the telephone directory). The office will not tell you anything more than the size of the school, name of the head, etc. For almost all the important information you will have to rely on your own enterprise and initiative.

Now look closely at say three possible schools, and watch for the material signs that may give you an indication of their character. Are the buildings new? Is there ample play space, imaginatively equipped? Watch particularly for notices of the 'Thou Shalt Not' kind : a sign saying 'Parents not admitted' can tell you something vital about a headteacher. Do the children wear school uniforms? You should also talk to the parents at the school gates, and to as many of your neighbours with children of primary-school age as possible.

The next stage is to make an appointment *in writing* to see the headteacher. Follow this up by a phone call to ensure your letter has been received and to show your resolve. On your visit remember (*a*) to look about you inside the school, and (*b*) to ask the head *any* question about the school or its organization : the more you show your interest, the more interest will be shown in you. Now you should repeat this process with two more schools.

There are many factors to be watched both when choosing a school and while your child is there. Bear in mind that headteachers often move on, and their replacements may have quite different ideas. Signs saying 'No Parents beyond this point' should ring alarm bells with every well-briefed, watchful mother. Such a sign ought to be taken as a warning that the headteacher is at best a traditionalist and at worst may be unaware of modern educational thinking which has made our primary schools the finest in the world.

One of the most difficult moments during your investigation is the meeting with the headteacher. It is crucial for parents to prepare themselves to cope with bland evasion and attempts to conceal important information. Headteachers are often highly skilled in meeting queries in such a way that parents do not manage to find out what the school is *really* like. Headteachers have, of course, years of experience in dealing with these interviews. You need to have your wits about you.

Brian Jackson, director of the ACE, described an interview which went like this :

Parent : 'My boy's quite bright, will he stand a chance of getting to a grammar school from here?'
Head : 'Oh, we don't believe in distressing children

over the eleven-plus, but we do very well, and everyone who deserves a grammar school place gets one.'

Mr Jackson's advice is to avoid seeking information in such a general way. If part of your interest *is* in the eleven-plus results, then you should phrase your questions so that you get precise answers. The specific query in this case would be: 'What percentage of children passed the eleven-plus from this school last year, and what was the percentage for the authority as a whole?'

Mr Jackson also advises that if you are troubled about your child being trapped for ever in the 'B' stream, don't ask: 'Can he get out?' Even the most rigid head will say: 'If he progresses well enough, he certainly can.' Ask: 'How many children moved from B to A streams in the school last year?' If possible get numerical answers, and use some *specific formula*, such as the 'last year' in the above example.

Ask if there is a parent–teacher group. If not, why not? Doesn't the school need one? Doesn't the head want one? If there is one, may you attend the next meeting? Will there be an Open Day soon that you can come to? (Though you should never forget that Open Days are usually as much 'advertisement' as informative.)

Other questions to press home: how many teachers left last year? Is the school *using* the advantage of its size? If it is large, does it have a specialist teacher for, say, music or remedial work? If it is small, does the headteacher know all the children? (His attitude to individual cases and his tone when talking about children will often show whether his answer to this last query is honest.)

These and many other questions should be followed through *politely and persistently*. Your first meeting with the headteacher may be your last chance to learn the detailed pattern of the running of the school. If you are a member of the ACE or CASE and you find a headteacher who refuses to give information, you will, of course, be able to report the incident to them. They often publish accounts of poor parent–teacher relations to off-set the reports from the

Ministry and the National Union of Teachers which try to claim that there is a full and frank cooperation between parents and teachers in all our schools. Any case of rudeness or outright hostility should certainly be passed on so that these groups can maintain a register of schools where there is room for great improvement.

The question of discipline is one of individual taste. Whether you believe in corporal punishment or not, you should be watchful for signs of how order is kept in the school. It is not only the presence or the absence of caning which is important. The whole atmosphere of the school can be revealed in many different ways. Perhaps you observe the children have a particular deference to the head. The boys might tip their caps when passing the headmaster's study window. This would delight some parents, and horrify others. Similarly a class might stand up if an adult came into the room, or go on as before, except that one child might go straight to the adult to show him his latest piece of work.

You must make of such observations what you will. Each parent will have a different personality and a different set of values. The reaction of children in many schools to classroom visitors may strike some parents as strange. They will say: 'In our day we always leapt to our feet whenever someone came into the room – it was just common courtesy.' Other parents will say: 'Lots of things have changed for the better since we were at school – and I would rather see a class, deep in fascinated concentration, which ignored me, than a well-drilled group of obedient conformists.'

Brian Jackson also mentions a point worth watching out for in connexion with a school's total atmosphere. He says we should watch pupils as they come out of school at the end of the day:

If they are uninterested or repressed, then they may burst out of school like a bomb exploding – sudden, noisy, disordered, disrespectful of each other. If the school *captures* their interest, and meets their growing needs, then they will still have steam to let off . . . but their exit will be quieter, slower, not such a kick-and-rush, and here and there will be children lingering over an unfinished essay, or experiment, just a little reluctant to leave the absorbing atmosphere of a first-class primary school. And there are few schools in the country better than our finest primary schools.

New Methods

Parents often have some difficulty in understanding modern teaching methods. Some still visit a modern, imaginative, creative infant class, and comment angrily: 'All they ever do is play.' Some are puzzled when children come home and say: 'I know how to make 5 plus 5 equal 13.' You are understandably shaken if you have not heard that it is possible to add up in *sevens* and units, as well as tens and units. If you are using sevens and units, then 5 and 5 do make 13. Parents wishing to grasp the 'New Maths' should buy a copy of *The New Mathematics Made Simple* (W. H. Allen), or the volume in the 'Teach Yourself' series.

But the important aspect of modern teaching methods which concerns us in this chapter is the new thinking about how a primary school should be organized. It will help you understand how the new ideas work in practice if I describe two different schools using different methods. Both schools are staffed by efficient and interested teachers, but the attitudes behind the teaching, and the atmosphere of the school, are based on different principles.

In the first school the hall is full of children. The teachers are clearly greedy for space, and they use every bit to its best advantage. You hear busy children calling out 'Move that barrow', 'Can we build this line right around?' 'Can I have some of your red paint?' and 'Why don't you put a propeller on your aeroplane?' There are children building, hammering, sliding, washing. The teacher may be scarcely visible among her class of forty or more. She will be helping Sammy with his building and keeping in touch with other pupils by calling out encouragement and advice. Children may be walking, dawdling, running, skipping (according to temperament), but they will all be quite clear *where* they are going and *why*. In the corridors you may meet a class going out to play with brightly-coloured balls, ropes, hoops and so on.

If you look through the windows and open doors you will see children standing before easels, or sitting on the floor, painting on large papers with fat brushes, putting dolls to bed, scrubbing tables, polishing handles, moulding clay, making sand-pies, measuring water, serving in shops, sewing clothes, doing sums, and reading to themselves or to each other or to a teacher. A child may be writing very carefully, and not very tidily, the word 'buttercup', which she will then put before a jar so that all may know and recognize the contents. Another may be scrawling the word 'daisy', while a beautifully written note 'Dear Alan, our rabbit has had some babies, what shall we feed them on?' goes into a pocket and is never seen again. There is a recognized right to move about freely. Tables and chairs are moved without fuss or inhibition. Pictures are hung so that pupils three feet high can look at, and touch, them. The school is *a child-sized world for children to move in and learn in.* Your total impression is one of *purpose*. You will be pleasantly surprised at the confidence and poise of the young child who escorts you to see the headmistress. She will entertain you with friendly conversation and information in a way which reveals that her relations with adults are easy and serene.

The second school is distinguished by its quiet. There is no talking, no laughing, no shouting, and the silence is broken only by the sound of a chant when a whole class recites a poem, or a table. You will wonder : 'Where are the children?' There may be none in the hall, because the teachers here are not so anxious to use space to its fullest advantage. When you come across children they will be in a group, all doing the same thing, and the teacher will be in front of them, striving by word, action and suggestion to influence the forty children in the direction she thinks is backward readers. A musically-gifted but unqualified teacher takes music throughout the school, thus getting to know all the children, And what a pleasure to meet a headmistress who admits that "*the parents must know their own children better than we do*".'

These comments make us realize what a really good school is like. Is your school anything like those described above? Could you imagine improving your child's school by encouraging both parents and teachers to work towards such high standards of cooperation? What would happen if parents 'questioned a teacher relentlessly' because they had a desperate worry or some burning interest?

Starting at School

A major factor to be considered when choosing a primary school is the difficulty many children have in making the transition from home to school at the age of five (if they are among the unlucky ninety per cent who have not been found a place at a nursery school). We can all recall our first day in the infants. I remember vividly the name of the boy, Paul Harmon, who said to the teacher, Miss Derrick, 'Bruce is crying.'

Here are three examples, reported by parents to the ACE, of the kind of crisis which occurs when children cannot cope with school.

When my first son was due to start school he began to dread it, and worry about it. I did not understand these things, but now I know he must have suffered agony. My sister brought him home on her bicycle at midday – but he was ill with the most dreadful, violent vomiting and diarrhoea. Life was a struggle, enhanced by his going off to school that day like a new penny.

My daughter was very tired on arrival home, ready for tea, and needing to be put in bed by 5.30 PM, whereas before she was never tired before 6.30 PM. This fatigue lasted throughout the term, and only now this term does she seem to be getting used to it.

After the first day he said he wasn't going there any more. He now begs each morning not to go and at lunchtime, and at last thing at night. He has nightmares almost every night (he's always had them occasionally) ... He has had two bouts of illness and has now been away for ten days. Each night he says: 'I'm still poorly, aren't I? I can't go to school?' I think I must send him back for mornings only – I'm quite prepared to argue with the attendance officer.

Until all children are given a place at nursery school when they are three years old, the kind of traumas described by these mothers will continue to occur. Five-year-olds without any previous schooling are very variable creatures. Many of them are simply not ready for the exacting demands of day-long attendance at school. Local authorities should examine more ways of making the transition from home to school more flexible and humane. It depresses everyone concerned with the well-being of young children how unimaginative many education authorities are in this matter. Other countries have a much more sensitive attitude towards children starting school, and they have shown that with staggered entry, or half-day attendance in the first year, much misery can be avoided.

It would be foolish to make part-time attendance *compulsory*. Such a move would only widen the gap between the small number of mostly middle-class children who have been to play-groups and nursery schools, and the deprived pupils described in my first chapter. But if there was proper contact between mothers and teachers, the children likely to suffer could have a special arrangement made for them. Local authorities could make it possible for problem children (or, rather, potentially problem children) to be able to attend part-time for up to two terms before full-time entry. Some children could be permitted to attend part-time until the age of six. Mothers should be encouraged to bring their children along to classes in the school, before they have to start at school. In this way they could get the feel of school by watching the infants or nursery section. Schools should recognize the benefits of allowing mothers to stay with children during the first days at school.

Parents can gain an important and significant insight into the ethos of a primary school by the simple method of discovering how other parents are treated on the day new pupils are admitted. In fact, if all the children are admitted on a single day it could well be a bad sign in itself. A sensible, flexible, humane school often spreads the whole business over a week. They admit a few children at a time, and they may invite mothers in for a chat a couple of days before the day of enrolment. Bear in mind that by the time *you* reach this stage with your child it is almost certainly too late to change your mind about your choice of school. Ask the headteacher how he handles this problem, and if it is all right for you to drop in for a few minutes on an enrolment day.

The bad school is often a distressing sight on the day of admission. Tearful children, anxious, overwrought mothers, and unsympathetic staff combine to convince the tiny child that education is a nasty business like castor-oil, eye-drops and visits to the dentist. I have heard of schools where large numbers of mothers sit in gloomy, Victorian-built halls waiting for a grim-faced teacher to come and put a label round their sobbing child's neck.

Every pressure should be brought by parents on education committees, parents in PTAs, parents who belong to CASE and to the ACE, to see that these scenes become part of our history.

Secondary-School Admissions

When meeting your primary-school headteacher you should also ask him about how his school copes with the problem of transfer to secondary school. One research survey showed that six parents out of ten had not been consulted by the headteacher six months before their children were due to leave their primary school. The best type of school will cope with this question by arranging a consultation evening some three weeks after the start of the school year. The headteacher and his deputy then let it be known they are available for further consultation and advice when the 'preference' forms are issued by the education authority. These senior members of staff, and, of course, the child's own form-master, are willing to discuss a child's strong and weak points, and interests and ambitions. They can also advise if parents can do anything at home to help strengthen any really weak aspects of the child's academic performance, and they may well suggest some activity, or outing, which could increase his interest in a certain subject. If there is sufficient mutual trust and respect between staff and parents (this can only be built up if parents are welcome, and frequent, visitors to the school) the teachers may even point out some aspect of a child's home life which is harming his life at school.

The bad school usually gives parents interviews of not more than ten minutes in the first instance. They are asked to state the school of their choice. If the head agrees, the form is signed at once. If parents 'aim too high', the head suggests his idea of a suitable school. He does not view the problem of matching the school to the child as being a complex issue, which could make or mar a child's whole life. He adopts a policy of first come first served. When parents state their preference he sometimes says: 'Lucky you did not choose XYZ, I already have my quota there.'

Parental Preferences

Parents taking part in a survey were asked to list in order of importance eleven factors affecting their choice of school. They were: (1) School's academic record. (2) Access to higher education. (3) Training and qualifications of staff. (4) Facilities such as laboratories, workshops and subject rooms. (5) Head's personality. (6) Accessibility from home. (7) School's attitude to discipline. (8) Size of classes. (9 Social-class composition. (10) Single-sexed or mixed. (11) Denominational or not.

The parents voted them in the order of preference given above. On the specific issue of co-education, 83 per cent were in favour and said mixed schooling was emotionally healthier, it made children more tolerant of the opposite sex, it produced a wider outlook, more mature judgement, and ultimately made pupils happier when they were married. They pointed out that segregated schooling is an inadequate training for life in a society which contains both sexes, and many social classes.

This overwhelming approval of co-education among parents is matched in the figures we have for the opinion of teachers on this issue. Reginald Dale, in his book *Mixed or Single-Sex School?* (Routledge & Kegan Paul), revealed that nine teachers out of ten believe mixed schooling is better than segregated schools:

> It is established beyond any doubt that most of the opposition to co-education stems from ignorance. The core of the opposition comes from those teachers in girls' schools who have never taught in a co-educational school, and probably from public-school men who will usually have had no contact with them.

Dale interviewed over 1,000 teachers and 750 school-leavers and said there was no evidence at all for the idea that co-education lowers academic standards. Boys do better in mixed than in segregated schools, and girls do as well, if not better. He also found overwhelming evidence that co-educational schools are much happier places than single-sex institutions.

The above list of eleven preferences will not only interest you as a way of comparing your views with those of other parents, it will also give you a basis for judging the secondary schools in your area if you have a choice.

Summer-born Pupils

If your child was born in the summer, you should make sure the teachers at his school are aware how he or she may suffer from this. You should also approach your local authority when your child is four years old to see if he can begin school earlier than is normally allowed. As we noted earlier, a few authorities do make special provision for these children. But you can make out a good case with most authorities if you base your arguments on any of the following points: (*a*) Mother has had a long illness. (*b*) The child comes from a large family, which makes home-life difficult. (*c*) Your doctor agrees the child should begin school earlier because of psychological or physical difficulties.

As education is mostly concerned with the training of the mind, you may find doctors and authorities willing to translate the word 'psychological' as meaning 'educational'. They will then be able to urge special treatment for your child.

Private-School Pitfalls

If, after investigating local State schools, you are *certain* that they are not academically sound, and *if* you are one of the lucky few who can afford it, you may wish to find a private school. Before settling on a particular preparatory school it is worth consulting the Incorporated Association of Preparatory Schools, whose headquarters are at 138 Kensington Church Street, London W8. The IAPS has detailed information about the 500-odd schools it accepts as worthy institutions. The full list of public and preparatory schools can be found in the *Public and Preparatory Schools Year Book*, which should be available in your local library. Information about girls' preparatory schools can be obtained from the Association of Headmistresses of Preparatory Schools; girls' public schools are listed in the *Girls School Year Book*, which you will also find in the library.

If you are not advised by an organization such as the ACE or the IAPS, you are in danger of making a dreadful mistake.

Parents have for years been swindled by schools who proudly proclaim they are '*registered*' with the Ministry of Education. Many unsuspecting parents have believed this meant the school was 'recognized' as efficient by the Ministry. There is an important difference between the words 'registered', and 'recognized'. Schools get 'recognized' as efficient by the Ministry *only* after a fairly tough, invited inspection. When a school says it is 'registered', it is merely telling you what you know – it is saying it exists. Every school in the country *has* to be registered.

In November 1967, the then Education Minister, Patrick Gordon Walker, gave 314 independent boarding schools (with over 26,000 pupils) five years to improve their standards and to submit to an inspection. But it was clear that he and his colleagues intended to warn a further 1,343 unrecognized day schools to become sound educational institutions or risk being closed down. By 1971, this purge had slowed down but in four years it had caused many schools to 'shut up shop'. Many of these closed down before the inspectors arrived. Not all these schools were really bad but it seems clear that a school which closes rather than undergo a routine inspection cannot inspire confidence. When the Tories won the election in 1970, the campaign against bad private schools was called off. Education Minister Mrs Margaret Thatcher said she planned to make the registration of schools a more meaningful business, but the drive to force unrecognized schools to improve soon lost its impetus.

Parents should realize how many of these schools are far from suitable for anybody's children. If a school refuses to be inspected, it would seem a clear indication that it is frightened of the consequences. If they do not believe in themselves, why should you entrust your child to them?

One way to expose a fraudulent school is to examine the letters after the headmaster's name. The Ministry defines a teacher as someone who is either a university graduate or a product of a teacher-training college (nowadays called a 'College of Education'). If a headmaster has some unusual letters after his name, it *may* mean his academic standing is negligible. As Peter Preston, the features editor of the *Guardian* newspaper, said in an article on this subject: 'You wouldn't pick a doctor because he played international rugger, commanded a motor boat, or painted a third-rate landscape. Nor would you pick a headmaster on such grounds.'

But the qualifications some heads are proud of, and think relevant to the problem of attracting parents, are bizarre to say the least. For example a head in Surrey tells us he is a DA. This could mean he has a diploma either in agriculture, architecture, or possibly anaesthetics! Another head has the letters FCIS, and FACCA, after his name. He is therefore a Fellow of the Chartered Institute of Secretaries, and a Fellow of the Association of Certified and Corporate Accountants. He may be a dab hand at the accounts, but what does he know about education? Many of the hundred-odd qualifications claimed by these heads *are not to be found* in any official list of academic or even military titles.

Parents trying to get a child into a public school need to know the facts about the Common Entrance. Just as public schools are not *public*, this entrance exam is not *common* to all schools. Girls take a different exam to boys, and only 146 of the 200 boys' schools recognized by the Headmasters' Conference require it. The exam is not the only way of getting into a public school. They nearly all offer scholarships, which are awarded on the basis of a separate exam.

At the last count, 1970, 9,000 boys sat the Common Entrance, which can be taken at three times during the year: mid-February, early June and early November. The normal age for sitting this exam is 13. The pass marks vary widely between one school and another. The exam consists of six compulsory subjects: English, Maths, French, History, Scripture and Geography. There are also four optional papers in Latin, Science, Greek and a further Maths exam. From June 1971 the schools plan to make science compulsory. If your child goes to a school which belongs to the IAPS he will have a very good chance of finding a place at a public school. Eight out of ten pupils from IAPS schools succeeded at the last count in entering a public school belonging to the Headmasters' Conference. A further 10 per cent went to other independent schools.

The Common Entrance is therefore nothing like so competitive, or so demanding, as the eleven-plus (which 75 per cent of candidates 'fail') or the GCE 'O' level (which is failed by 41 per cent of candidates). Indeed the most famous supporter of preparatory schools, Philip Masters, the author of *Preparatory Schools Today*, has admitted that one in three prep-school boys would have to go to secondary moderns if they were asked to sit the really competitive eleven-plus!

The girls' Common Entrance is used in nearly 100 schools, and it is held twice a year: in February and in November. About 3,000 girls take this exam each year. The subjects are similar to those set for the boys. If you would like your daughter to sit this exam you should contact Miss Helen Garnett, Secretary of the Common Entrance Exam for Girls Schools Ltd, 2 Bankfield, Kendal, Westmorland.

Educationally Subnormal Children

If your child has an IQ of 85 (100 is considered 'normal', and 120 is the level of most bright children) the local authority may suggest that he attends a school for the educationally subnormal. His IQ may be lower than 85, and it may vary above and below this figure slightly, but they can say he needs special schooling. At the last count it was estimated one child in ten needed such a school, but only two pupils in 100 were found places in them. You have the right of appeal against the authority's decision. But if the Minister rules that the decision is based on sound evidence, you will be compelled to comply with the law. Most authorities try to avoid using the law to force parents to obey, and they attempt to persuade them of the superior facilities for children of this kind in special schools.

Other Sources of Information

If you are a Quaker or a Catholic and you want information on schools for children with these beliefs, you should contact the two organizations which cater for your needs. Quakers should write to the Secretary of the Friends' Educational Council, Friends' House, Euston Road, London NW1. Catholics can obtain a handbook called *Catholic Education* from the Catholic Educational Council for England and Wales, 41 Cromwell Road, London SW7.

SUGGESTED READING

Ayerst, David, *Understanding Schools*. Penguin Books: London, 1967.
Burgess, Tyrrell, *A Guide to English Schools*. Penguin: London, 1964.
Dale, Reginald, *Mixed or Single-Sex School?* Routledge & Kegan Paul: London, 1969.
Douglas, J. W. B., and Ross, Jean, *All Our Future*. Peter Davies: London, 1968.
Douglas, J. W. B., *The Home and the School*. MacGibbon & Kee: London, 1964.
Ford, Julienne, *Social Class and Comprehensive School*. Routledge & Kegan Paul: London, 1969.
Gardner, D. E. M., *Experiment & Tradition in Primary Schools*. Methuen: London, 1966.
Holt, John, *How Children Learn*. Pitman: London, 1967.
Holt, John, *How Children Fail*. Pitman: London, 1969.
Masters, Philip, *Preparatory Schools Today*. A. & C. Black: London 1966.
Neill, A. S., *Summerhill*. Gollancz: London, 1962.
Murphy, Patrick, *The New Mathematics Made Simple*. W. H. Allen: London, 1969.

CHAPTER SIX

Educating Girls

I hope this chapter may do something to diminish the widespread prejudice against providing greater educational opportunities for women. Those who say that taxpayers' money is wasted on girl students are extremely shortsighted, for even if girls do not decide later in life to use their degrees to enter some profession, they will still be better mothers and happier wives. As Gandhi said: 'Educate a man and you educate an individual, educate a woman and you educate a *family*.'

Too often parents and teachers do not believe, or pay only lip-service to, the idea that the hand that rocks the cradle rules the world. But today's schoolgirls *are* tomorrow's mothers, and the quality of their mothering will affect the educational future of their children, and of the country. If parents are to play their full role in education, it must be admitted that mothers have the greater influence on children, in those crucial years from birth to five, than fathers. If mothers can be persuaded to do the right things and convinced of the need to *talk* to their children, the task of teachers will be easier, and the remedial classes for backward children will have fewer pupils. An educated mother is more *likely* to rear a child well-equipped for entry to school.

As to the intellectual differences between boys and girls, we know they mature at different rates, and in different phases. Up to puberty girls are, in the main, intellectually in advance of their brothers. During puberty they grow in '*emotional* stature', become more interested in people than in things and ideas, and are again more mature emotionally than a boy of the same age. Even so these points are often ignored in discussions of the academic achievements and progress of boys and girls respectively. Girls do somewhat better than boys academically during primary school. Indeed, were the places available, substantially more girls than boys would be offered selective places at grammar schools.

The following figures show how our education system is prejudiced against girls. In January 1967 there were 40,000 eleven-year-old girls in the grammar schools of England and Wales, and 38,000 boys. At this time female children outnumbered males. At sixth-form level, however, the position was reversed. Over 40 per cent of the boys had stayed on, compared with only 25 per cent of the girls. The few girls who do get to university (only three out of ten undergraduates are girls) still achieve remarkably good results: 82 per cent of girls get their degrees, compared with 76 per cent of male students. What happens in secondary schools to make girls drop out of the academic race?

A closer look at the situation reveals that girls are triply handicapped. There are, in any case, fewer places for women than men in the older universities. Also they are disadvantaged not only by having fewer 'A' levels per head, but also by having them in the wrong subjects – in arts rather than in science. Remember it is easier to get a university place in the sciences. Of course no university education is of such value in itself to be worth twisting a pupil's natural aptitudes to come up with the 'right' 'A' levels, so she has a better chance of a vacant place. But the reason why so few *girls* take physics and chemistry at 'O' and 'A' level is not that they inherently lack natural ability, but that *they do not get the same chances*. The exam pass rates are the same – the discrepancy lies in the entry. *Five times* as many boys take 'O' level physics, and *three times* as many boys take 'O' level chemistry.

If girls take science subjects, their chances of passing are as good as those of boys, and the hope of going on to university much *higher* than for arts subjects. A question which the Dainton report on science education considered in 1967 was why so few girls stay on to do science in the sixth form. As parents you should also be concerned, although you cannot bring about the immediate provision of laboratories and supply of science teachers. If science facilities at the girls' schools are inadequate, what *can* a parent do about it?'

The first thing is to discover what sort of science teaching is available in neighbouring schools. It is often possible for a girl to transfer to the sixth-form of a school (perhaps a boys' school) that is more favourably placed for science teaching. The damage, however, to your daughter's future may already have been done. If there is no adequate provision for teaching science to the senior girls, it is likely that there is insufficient enthusiasm for these subjects among the staff lower down the school. A school can unconsciously discourage a girl from considering these subjects, because of the lack of good teachers and facilities. As a nation we compare badly with other civilized, industrialized countries in the science education we give our girls. Although one undergraduate in three is a girl, only one in ten of science students is a female. In Russia half the student scientists are girls. The figures for Sweden, Norway and Germany also reveal a wider use of women's talents.

If you are still unconvinced that studying science is a 'proper' occupation for a young girl, look at today's science and engineering female students. They are as pretty and attractive as their arts counterparts, and as likely to make similar use of their attributes in their work.

It is not just a matter of facilities – very often it is one of attitudes and aspirations of the individual teacher. While the exam system persists as it is, teachers are naturally anxious that their own schools should acquire a substantial number of 'A' level passes. At the same time, for the sake of their own reputation, they do not want to enter candidates who do not show a very good chance of getting through the exam. It could be that women teachers are more cautious in this respect than men, preferring to put all their energies into coaching a few 'certain' pupils instead of a greater number of 'possibles'. As girls are, on the whole, more suggestible than boys, those not actively *encouraged* to embark on an 'A' level course may well feel they are not up to that standard. If your daughter says she is not taking an 'A' level, you must establish that the exam is genuinely unsuited to her needs, and that *she has not been discouraged for other reasons.*

Apart from the attitudes of the teachers, there may be other factors that put the girl off. Perhaps she has been swayed by her friends opting to leave school before the sixth-form. She may dread the risk of failure, and baulk at the long series of exams ahead of her. Or she may even be thinking of getting married. If the girl is at all afraid of exams, whatever her excuse, only the combined efforts and reassurance of *both* parents and teachers will rid her of the fear. The very degree of imagination shown by teenage girls exposes them to exam neurosis. Remind her that, like dentists and aeroplanes, exams are best tolerated, and usually found unpleasant by the old as well as by the young.

Advising parents on the best way to handle such talks (whether with boys or with girls) is always difficult. My own younger sister left school against her mother's wishes, and has since regretted it. Seven years later she decided to train to be a teacher and had to take her 'A' level course at night school. Clearly there is no *one* argument or method of persuasion which parents can use to prevent teenagers determined to leave from doing so. If a child is not *too* set on leaving, you *may* influence her by pointing out that four out of ten early-leavers wish afterwards they had stayed on. But leaving school is often an emotional decision ('I don't like being treated as a child', 'I want to earn a living', 'I cannot wear school uniform any longer') and it is not possible to alter emotions by quoting statistics.

On the other hand, if you give up the battle and say wearily 'It's your life – do what you want', later on your daughter or son may accuse you of not helping them when they needed guidance with one of the most vital decisions of their lives.

Until recently it was impossible to say how many fifteen-year-olds could have been persuaded to stay on at school. Most secondary modern schools could not offer them anything after this age. However, now there are more comprehensive schools and many children are being given greater opportunities. But children accept too easily that it was their fault they 'failed' at school, when often it was partly the fault of the *teachers* who could not capture their enthusiasm. Parents, careers teachers and class teachers should make a major effort to persuade a child with untapped ability – and a chance of benefiting from extra schooling – to stay on. You could attempt to describe as vividly as possible what it is like for a youngster to start, say in a factory, without qualifications. It can be miserable – especially as few employers have the right kind of personnel service to help these children. But, as a parent, you cannot do *everything*. Eight out of ten children are rejected by our education system. You cannot be expected to arouse their interest in something which failed them, and may have failed you.

The Role of Women

When parents think seriously of their daughters having a career, and a chance to take 'A' levels, women will start to make their presence felt in the professions. At present there are many key professions where, for no apparent reason, men outnumber women by twenty to one. Sue Keable, the assistant editor of *Where* magazine, put the issue this way:

> A hundred years after the pioneering days of Elizabeth Blackwell (the first woman doctor in 1859) women doctors form little under a fifth of the profession. There are more women in the Church than there are journalists and writers. There are nearly twice as many women teaching in universities as those working as architects or surveyors. There are more women on the stage than there are pharmacists. Indeed 'Do put your daughter on the stage Mrs Worthington', at least put her there if you want her to be a member of one of the few professions with a third or

more of women to make up its ranks. Don't, on the other hand, tell her to be a judge or a biologist or a chemist – unless of course she can put up with being outnumbered by one to twenty or more. But what seems really important is that the professions in which women predominate are the socially vital ones. If you ask someone to make out a list of all the professions, with the ones that the country could do least without at the top, then it is a fair bet that nursing, teaching and social work would all come pretty high up.

It is of considerable significance that 57 per cent of teachers are women. It is of greater significance that the proportion in primary schools is even higher. To take an earlier point, a child's first 'teacher' is his mother; it is very probable that his first schoolteacher will be a woman as well. We can therefore see the full, damaging circle.

Girls *are* treated as though they are not capable of studying, say, maths and physics. They attend schools which too often have inadequate facilities for such subjects. They become mothers, possibly primary-school teachers, and influence the next generation of girls through their apathy to these subjects.

The major factor in their professional inequality is male prejudice. Only in 1919 did the Sex Disqualification (Removal) Act win the right for women to practise as barristers or solicitors. Fathers must search in their hearts, when deciding on educational issues affecting their daughters, and try to make sure they are seeing the problem objectively.

Co-education

Prejudice and emotionalism also confuse the issue of co-education. The research by Reginald Dale already referred to has given those favouring mixed schools a sound factual basis for their preference. We have no evidence that single-sex schools are educationally unsound, but we do know that co-education makes pupils happier. Another recent study (of over 2,500 married people) showed that in marriage both men and women were happier if they had been to mixed schools. People who had enjoyed a happy home life as youngsters, who had come from church-going families, tended to be happier. Of all the groups questioned the ones least likely to be happily married came from *boarding* schools. The results of this and other surveys suggest that on the whole co-education helps people to mature emotionally. Among the many pertinent questions which arise from such research, one of the most important is whether the happiest school is the best. We cannot give a definite answer. It would seem likely that a happy school would be, in the best sense of the word, a good one. Certainly we can say, even without any direct research evidence, that an unhappy school is a bad school.

One could expect the single-sex schools, with their often higher 'status' and their rather better-qualified teachers, to have compared favourably with the unsung, 'unknown' mixed schools. Results suggest the pupils in mixed schools seem to have a *positive* enjoyment of school life which is not so keen in their rivals. In their book *All Our Future*, Dr J. W. B. Douglas and Miss Jean Ross established that middle-class *boys* tend to stay longer and get a higher percentage of passes at 'O' level in segregated schools, but middle-class *girls* stay on longer and get more 'O' levels at mixed schools. With working-class pupils there are no significant differences in the achievements of boys and girls at single-sex grammar schools. The girls stay on longer than the boys, but the boys get more good 'O' levels. Similar proportions of the boys and girls at segregated schools intend to continue with full-time study after leaving. It is still not proved that middle-class children do better at segregated schools.

I must stress again, in the light of the known evidence, that the ideal secondary-school system would be not only unstreamed (as far as possible), non-selective (no eleven-plus), non-boarding, and run by the local education authorities, it should also be *co-educational*. A truly comprehensive system – based on the principle of giving *all* social classes, and *both* sexes, an 'equal chance to be unequal' – would help to remove the present shortage of opportunities for girls.

Choice of School

A way to ensure that your daughter is well catered for is to take note of the different needs of the sexes when choosing the best available school in your neighbourhood. Though the attitude 'Girls are different from boys – they are inferior at academic studies' is demonstrably false, it is necessary to examine the *real* differences between the sexes when choosing a school. Remember, even at primary level, that you must see your daughter not merely as another five-year-old about to go through the educational machine, but as a little girl on the way to being a woman. What kind of woman will depend largely on what kind of schooling she gets, at the primary as well as the secondary level. For it is at the primary level that roles may be allotted : 'a boy does this', 'a girl is like that', and attitudes formed that may last for ever.

A good school recognizes that young boys and girls have different characteristics in their approach to learning or play. How should these differences be emphasized? Where does the 'girlness of a girl' and the 'boyness of a boy' shade into rigidifying the differences, and fixing limits on what girls do, and boys do? The answers will vary for each parent, according to how they think the sexes should have *distinct* roles. But it is worth looking at your daughter's school carefully to see how far the way it is run agrees with your view about what kind of separate treatment, if any, boys and girls should be given.

Look at the question : 'If there is choice between an infant/junior and a separate infant school, which is better for a girl?' It is important that, even if the juniors and infants are in the same building, they are regarded as separate departments. Not all little girls (or boys for that matter) can withstand the rough and tumble and general pace of a big age-range. A separate infant school may have a quieter atmosphere, which small girls often prefer. Since they mature more quickly than boys, being the 'big girl' at a small school may suit them more than being the 'little girl' at a large one. Should there be separate playgrounds for boys and girls? Watch for this when you look first at the school. Do boys and girls play together? If so, do the boys interrupt the girls' games and tease them? Depending on what you want, it is a crucial matter.

Look also at the balance of the subjects studied, and the overall emphasis of the time-table. Does your daughter's school have too feminine an approach to the curriculum? In some schools the approach may be completely women-centred – all dressing-up, shopping, dolls and keeping house – bad for girls and even worse for boys. If there are no men on the staff, opportunities must be given for the girls to get some insight into masculine life, either by fathers coming to talk about their jobs, or visits (say to the local fire station).

Menstruation

Even in the junior school girls should be given sex instruction and told about menstruation. Why should teachers be shocked if you mention sex instruction in the primary school? Many parents would welcome it. What do *you* think? Many eleven-year-olds have their *first* sex instruction at secondary school. A significant number of girls are by then already menstruating, and too often a first period (possibly occurring at primary school) is an unexplained and frightening experience.

For girls there is a need for sex instruction to be a part of the curriculum as soon as they are ready for it. This is one difference (between boys and girls) that many parents, especially those with daughters who are early-developers, would like to see recognized, so that girls are told about menstruation. Sadly, this is seldom done. It is up to you, as parents, to raise such questions, either at your PTA or, if there is no such group, with the teachers. At secondary all-girl schools it should be borne in mind that this one, all-significant, matter is too often swept under the carpet, or just not mentioned.

Reading

Parents should remember that girls are *not* inferior to boys at school work. In fact they tend to make *better* progress than boys in learning to read. One survey in America showed girls were ahead at each age for tests of reading speed, vocabulary, and understanding of the printed word. Boys tended to outnumber girls in the lowest three scores in all three tests, in a ratio of two to one. In Britain, too, girls learn to read sooner, have fewer reading problems, benefit from more formal reading instruction, and make better progress.

Before congratulating yourselves, consider the possible causes. Social pressures and expectations are different for boys and girls, From infancy we teach children to behave in certain ways considered by our society to be appropriate for their sex. As early as two, little boys may show more interest in bricks and vehicles, while little girls prefer dolls and prams. Generally speaking, girls have a closer identification with their mothers at an earlier age than boys with their fathers. Girls copy the tasks their mothers perform in the household.

Whether or not these sex-linked qualities are inherited or learned, there is evidence to suggest that from an early age boys and girls differ in certain language skills, and means of communicating. Certainly girls tend to articulate more clearly, make fewer incomprehensive utterances, pronounce consonants with greater clarity, and mispronounce fewer words. The first vital skill a child learns is the ability to speak, and the speed at which the child picks up this skill affects his (or her) efforts at learning to read. As we have seen, the timing of a child's learning to read, or the fact of not being able to read at all, or being an inadequate reader, affects the whole of a child's future.

Girls, with their mimicry of their mother's behaviour, probably have more experience of hearing both their mother's speech and their own. They obtain more 'feed back' regarding correction of phrasing and pronunciation. Their speech is not only clearer and easier to understand, there is also more of it. Evidence shows that girls use longer statements, more words, and make fewer grammatical errors than boys. There is also evidence that boys tend to have less favourable attitudes to school and learning. Girls are more willing to please adults and, if bored, less likely to show their boredom actively. It may be that teachers treat girls in a similar fashion, irrespective of their background, but boys are taught in relation to their attitudes to learning, and their willingness to be cooperative pupils.

Parents might become anxious about the comparatively slower language development of boys, and worry in case they continue to make slow progress at school. They should not try to rate their girl's ability just on her infant verbal fluency. You *can* help your daughter by talking about words and phrases she uses, and by providing a wide range of materials and constructional toys. This will enable her to gain the experience necessary for the development of abstract thinking, so that competency will be attained at school, not only in reading, but also in understanding the printed word.

Comparing the abilities of girls and boys in the primary school brings home to us the impressive academic potential of the so-called *weaker* sex. But, as we have seen, this potential is usually wasted because parents and teachers have so far neglected girls when they most need *positive* help: in their teens.

Further, we should question why girls should not study metalwork, if they want to, and why boys should not be taught housecraft. The vast majority of teenage and women's magazines encourage early marriage, and tend to be anti-education. The stories in them may urge girls to become fiancées and wives (excellent objectives provided they are not mere appendages), but they do not emphasize often enough the need for girls and women, wives and mothers, to become real people, and moulders of society. Parents can help their daughters make a wise choice if *they* have been allowed a richness of educational experience during their own youth. As yet the main difficulty is not to get a girl through an education, but to get her to embark on *any* course at all.

SUGGESTED READING

Educating Girls. Advisory Centre for Education: Cambridge, 1968.

Greer, Germaine, *The Female Eunuch.* MacGibbon & Kee: London, 1970.

CHAPTER SEVEN

Sex Education: Why, When, Where, Who, and How?

Every parent must be worried by the rise in the number of schoolgirl mothers, cases of pupils with venereal disease and teenage abortions. By July 1971 a leading Family Planning Association doctor, Helena Wright, said the number of British girls becoming child mothers, or getting abortions, was growing so rapidly that an *emergency* situation existed. Dr Wright pointed out that the number of babies born to girls under sixteen had risen from 483 in 1959 to 1,486 in 1969. She commented: 'Whatever is now being done is disastrously inadequate.'

Dr Wright, a founder member of the FPA, called for a crash programme by the Association's 1,200 women doctors in clinics throughout the country to take over the sex education of schoolchildren. She suggested mothers seeking birth-control advice and devices at the clinics could bring teenage children with them. She also said a complete guide to sexual intercourse, contraception, pregnancy and conception was an 'inescapable necessity' in schools.

These recommendations seem sensible to anyone who knows the facts about eleven-year-old mothers and girls who come to teachers saying 'I'm bleeding' and not knowing the reason why. But I have discovered that large numbers of parents ought to have pointed out to them the need for sex education. Many react to the news that illegitimate births are increasing among under-sixteens by saying: 'It is all *because* of this sex education in schools.' I am determined in this chapter to show such people that sex education is the only cure for, and not the cause of, the alarming situation in our schools. It is necessary therefore to repeat the essential facts to explain why experts such as Dr Wright are right to be so anxious. Many influential politicians, educationists and teachers are childless, and it is understandable that they do not feel as passionately about the need for some action in this field as parents – especially those parents with daughters. It is essential to spell out the consequences of ignorance. Unfortunately, many adults seem to think problems of unwanted babies, venereal disease and teenage abortions will disappear if we take no notice of them. Such people must be persuaded of the urgent need for sex education in schools.

Sex in the Seventies: the Facts

In April 1971 Dr John Slome, a Harley Street doctor, told a London medical congress: 'The kiss of the 1940s and 50s has now become the sexual intercourse of the 60s and 70s'. He reached this conclusion after studying 150 unmarried women who had sought abortions. Of these sixty-two pregnancies resulted from 'casual friendships'. He said: 'This group of patients illustrates the changed pattern of social behaviour during the past twenty years.' Dr Slome told the Third International Congress of Psychosomatic Medicine in Obstetrics and Gynaecology: 'I had the impression patients over the age of twenty-eight purposely became pregnant – to encourage their "consorts" to marry them. But the result was invariably the opposite. The men left them suffering from acute anxiety and depression.'

These sad stories are part of a national picture which clearly forces us to realize the need for useful and intelligent sex education for children *from the age of seven upwards*. Soon after Dr Slome's speech, I wrote a three-part series for the *Daily Express* about these problems, and suggested some solutions. During my investigations I spoke to teenagers, parents and teachers all over the country. I also examined the statistics for illegitimacies and abortions. Dr Ernest Miller, Medical Officer of Health in Birmingham, quite rightly insisted the figures for schoolgirl mothers should be seen in their social context. He linked 'sex stimulation, advertising, films and strip clubs' to the spiral in illegitimate births in his city. More than 10 per cent of babies born in Birmingham are illegitimate – this is far higher than the national average; but the national statistics were equally disturbing.

In March 1970 a report showed that the 'number of girls who become pregnant at school has shown a staggering rise'. The total of girls under 15 in 1967 who had illegitimate babies was four times as high as the figure for 1957, and six times as high as the number in 1947. The increase in the population in this period does not explain these statistics, but it is as well not to be too alarmist. There are about 2,400,000 girls aged 11 to 16 in our schools and there were, at the last count, 4,294 with babies. This is under one per cent of the age group. We start to have our complacency shaken, however, when we examine the breakdown of Dr Wright's figures for mothers aged under 16. Three were aged 11, eleven were aged 12, thirty-two were aged 13, 204 were 14, and the remaining 1,236 were 15.

If anyone is still indifferent to the case for more sex education to be given to more children at an earlier age, I suggest they visit a London Church Army school where the youngest mother is 11. This school cared for her throughout the last months of her pregnancy, and helped her readjust during a depressing post-natal period. Her schoolmates, aged between 13 and 15, all have babies. They spend their days at this residential school knitting toddlers' clothes, chatting about baby care, cuddling the babies – and occasionally doing some homework.

The other stark facts are equally disturbing. Around 4,000 of all the 11,000 babies born to girls between 15 and 19 in 1968 were illegitimate. By 1969 the number of girls under 15 who had legal abortions was 1,232. This is not, of course, any indication of the total number of young girls who had *illegal* abortions. It has been estimated that the total number of women, of all ages, risking illegal abortions, could be more than 110,000 a year.

Two points arise from these figures. Do schoolgirl mothers get adequate education? Does the school have to know when a girl has an abortion?

The girls in the London Church Army school are (in one sense) the lucky few. Most of the 4,000 mothers aged 16 and under (this total increases by at least 200 every year despite abortions, sex education and the availability of contraceptives) cannot continue their schooling. The National Union of Teachers admit: 'Local authorities are legally bound to provide education for everyone under 15, but few of them do.' A Ministry of Education survey showed that out of 206 schoolgirl mothers aged between 12 and 18 – only 65 had any education during their nine months of pregnancy. When this question was raised with Education Minister Mrs Margaret Thatcher, she said she knew of no authorities 'not doing their duties by adolescents'. Mrs Margaret Bramall, Chairman of the National Council for the Unmarried Mother and her Child, believes voluntary societies like her own will continue to bear the brunt of caring for schoolgirl mothers. She says: 'Britain is terrified of facing up to the problem. Some teachers think it is an infectious disease; if something happens to one of their girls, she has to be got rid of quickly. Some parents also object to their children mixing with pregnant schoolfriends. Everyone hopes the whole thing will be kept as quiet as possible.'

The boyfriends are a thorny problem. Legally they are guilty of carnal knowledge of minors and are liable to be prosecuted. But the law is inconsistently applied – social workers often reserve the right of keeping the name of the 'father' quiet during inquiries.

The question about a school's knowledge of an abortion performed on one of its pupils is difficult to answer with certainty. My inquiries show that in most cases, the school does *not* know. An article by Tim Devlin in *The Times Educational Supplement* in March 1970 supported this finding: he wrote: 'I spoke to one girl and heard about 26 other case-histories. Their abortions had been arranged by the Birmingham Pregnancy Advisory Service. In most of the cases the abortions had been arranged without the schools knowing anything about them.'

Two of the girls seen by Mr Devlin provided the kind of human information which we should bear in mind when trying to convince parents of the need for sex-education films and lectures. At least nine of the girls came from grammar schools. One called Jane disclosed to the general studies teacher that she was pregnant. She said: 'It was absolutely marvellous to be able to talk to someone. For a long time I could not bring myself to tell my mother. As for telling my headmistress – she is so bloody-minded and old-fashioned about sex that I would have been slung out.' The one woman teacher was the only member of staff to know of the abortion. For weeks before the operation Jane found it impossible to concentrate on homework or lessons. She broke down when she had to speak in class, and she found making excuses for not doing PE or games very difficult. Once the operation was over she had no regrets about having become pregnant. Before, she had planned to take her 'O' levels, and go into nursing. Now she turned against the idea of school and left to earn money 'for my family'.

Another girl seen in this investigation, a West Indian, knew about contraceptives but both she and her boyfriend 'disliked' the idea of using them. She became pregnant when she was 15, and had a baby in October 1969. It died within a month. None of her friends knew anything about her baby. By June 1970 she was pregnant again.

The story of Jane reminds us of the waste of human potential, and the personal tragedy, in these cases. The attitude of the West Indian girl and her boyfriend serves as a warning to those of us who talk (and write) as though it is only ignorant girls who get pregnant. Sound sex education seeks to inculcate a responsible attitude towards sexual relations. It is not just enough to provide information about contraceptives.

The raising of the school-leaving age to 16 is likely to

aggravate the problems caused by having schoolgirl mothers. Mrs Margaret Bramall says: 'One hopes the social climate will be such that all pregnant schoolgirls do not almost automatically have to leave school. Perhaps the position will be helped because in time more *married* girls are likely to be attending school. It is terribly important for them not to lose their educational opportunities. If they part from the child, they will be in great need to help them overcome their grief.'

In America (where pregnancy is the main cause of girls 'dropping-out' of secondary school) about 200,000 girls under 18 have babies each year. Nearly two-thirds of them are married at the time of birth. Those who marry between 15 and 19 are three to four times as likely to get divorced as older couples. As in this country, the provision of education for these young mothers is uneven. Out of a survey of 17,000 schools only 5,450 provided education for them. The traditional approach in those cases was to send a teacher to the home rather than to allow the girl to attend school.

Despite all this evidence that promiscuity and pregnancies are on the increase, some people still argue that there is little new in the present situation. They point to comments in history which show how many mothers under 16 there were. A Child Employment Commission in 1867, for example, reported: 'At the infirmary many girls of 14 years of age, and even girls of 13, up to 17 years of age, have been brought in pregnant to be confined here. The girls have acknowledged that their ruin has taken place . . . in going or returning from their agricultural work.' Such evidence does deter us from being over-alarmist, but it should not encourage complacency or inaction. There are plenty of experts who believe that the situation has got *worse* in recent years.

The last reliable figures on under-16 sex were published in 1965 and based on information collected a year earlier. These showed that by the age of 16 one girl in 20 and one boy in seven had had intercourse. There seems little doubt that the figures would be *higher* if they were recorded today. Dr Nicolas Malleson, physician to the University of London Health Service, says: 'Girls are discovering sex earlier and a growing number are already on the Pill when they come here.' As we have seen, the facts support his impression. The number of mothers under 16 more than doubled between 1963 and 1969. The number of under-16 abortions rose by 45 per cent between 1969 and 1970.

As I write I am reminded of two recent events which highlight two aspects of the problem. The first was a case in June 1971 when a 20-year-old girl trainee teacher was asked to face a college 'morals court', accused of sleeping with a married man. Her parents took the view that she was old enough to run her own life. The girl's union, the National Union of Students, attacked this 'outrageous' investigation of her private life, and promised legal help. The NUS aroused such opposition to the college authorities that the girl was not 'punished'. The fact that her private life was considered a matter of concern indicates one attitude to sexual activity among unmarried girls. It is of course significant that she was a student teacher. It is possible that we are approaching a time when secondary-school children will resent being taught by male and female virgins. We must decide whether in this case her action in loving a married man can be said to affect her teaching. I think it probable that the people who agree with the college's attitude would find it difficult to defend their view. Would they object to a student teacher (who might teach liberal studies one day) belonging to the National Front Party or an Anarchist group? Would they resent a student being a vegetarian? Would they be angry if their child was taught by a Jehovah's Witness?

The second recent event was a court case involving a 12-year-old girl who went missing from home for twelve days, and got 'involved' with nine youths. All the youths pleaded guilty to indecent assault. The Court heard she told the defendants she was 16 or 17, and indeed she did look much older than 12. With some of the men she instigated what happened, and in many cases 'actually seduced' these youths. The youths were all given an absolute discharge.

I mention these two events because it seems that the case

of the student teacher reveals one kind of *unreal* approach to life in our society in the 1970s, and the court case exposes the sort of unpleasant fact which too many people try to ignore. Twelve-year-old seducers need mature adults to give them care and attention. Eleven-year-old girls need to know how to avoid becoming mothers. We cannot help them with vague talk about gooseberry bushes, or 'morality'. They need help – based on love and facts.

Why Can't They Learn about Sex in the Playground Like Us?

Parents, teachers and teenagers are often unaware of their own ignorance about sex, and of the general level of knowledge among pupils and adults. Dr Robert Kind, Medical Officer of Health for Oadby, Leicestershire, says many adults only discover how little they know when they are shown books and pamphlets *intended for 10- and 11-year-olds*.

We have noted how the facts about illegitimacies, venereal disease and abortion indicate the need for sex education. We must now study the present provision of sex education in schools. It is hard to be specific about the national picture, but it is clear that too many children are getting far too little useful information. Parents have mostly opted out and left the teaching of sex to teachers. Some parents are worried even by the best available sex-education films. The whole subject is fraught with misinformation, prejudice and mythology.

David Barnard, a biology teacher, exposed the extent of ignorance in an article in *New Society* in April 1968. He said: 'How to get pregnant, and how not to, are equally misunderstood. Conception is believed to follow a number of activities such as being kissed, missing periods, and receiving "flying" sperms. Those teenagers who realize that conception requires entry of sperms in the female tract, may still believe that conception cannot occur "the first time you have it", "without an orgasm", "if you have it standing up", and if "you go to the toilet straight afterwards". Certainly few boys and girls realize that introduction of sperms onto the external genitalia, or premature small discharges before withdrawal, may result in pregnancy.' I have found that many *adults* did not know about these last dangers as well. Sex education really is often a case of the blind leading the blind.

Mr Barnard added: 'The symptoms of pregnancy, other than stopping periods, and then getting fat, are largely unknown, except for morning sickness. People do not realize that six weeks after conception (or thereabouts) is the earliest that the best current pregnancy tests can be arranged other than through one's parents, or even family doctor . . . It is on the physical side of sex that factual ignorance is so woefully common among teenagers.'

Then he touches on one of the central facts about our education system – the majority of teachers are middle-class and the majority of pupils are working-class. Much of the lack of communication between teachers and taught results from this class-division. Mr Barnard says: 'The middle-class teacher is least equipped by his background to initiate, *and enter into*, frank discussions in the "public" atmosphere of the classroom. Here also, the teacher must often "heal himself" before he can hope to ease the wounds of the succeeding generation.'

He then explains: 'Most teachers are born, or become, middle-class and this can be a fundamental barrier to communicating with children, particularly working-class children. Yesterday's middle-class *mores*, inhibitions and language do not necessarily cut any ice with youngsters today of *any* social class. . . Four-letter words and scientific terms represent the black and white of vocabulary: the unacceptable to middle-class society and the incomprehensible to working-class teenagers. But between "fuck" and "fornication" there are a host of phrases containing no swearwords, sexual or otherwise, and having clearly understood colloquial meanings.'

Mr Barnard rightly describes how working-class pupils

are often embarrassed by using the 'correct' terms when they know them. This can be part of their general hostility to correct English and sounding 'posh'. He adds: 'In contrast the more intelligent child will often be proud to show it knows the correct term, the long medical word. A workable compromise has been to use these non-obscene colloquial phrases linked to their more formal synonyms. The dangers of "having it away" with every boy in the street can be discussed while one explains that promiscuity is the proper word for this behaviour.'

He then explains: 'Parents are generally agreed to be the best people to impart knowledge about sex, because of their special relationship with their own children. But in many cases, we all know that parents do not always do this. Some teachers still have girls coming to them in tears, frightened because they are bleeding. *No one has explained to them about periods.*'

I was amazed to find (during my investigations) how poor the standard of sex instruction was. For example, the highly praised Nuffield 'O' level biology course has been of little use in teaching sex. In the five-year course, with five pupils' texts and five teachers' guides, human sexuality gets very little mention. Year 1 pupils' text contains only seven slides of material, including front-view diagrams of male and female genital systems. The appropriate section of the teachers' guide blandly states: 'It is not possible to anticipate the many questions this section may provoke, but there may be opportunity for making comparisons between human birth and the birth of domestic or farm animals with which some children may be familiar'. But, as Mr Barnard comments: 'Nowhere in the entire course is there a useful mention of venereal disease, contraception, or a number of other topics of great interest to teenagers.'

Mr Barnard's estimate of the shocking extent of ignorance among pupils, and adults, is supported by the known facts – based on nation-wide surveys. At the last count 56 per cent of boys, and 13 per cent of girls, said they had *received no sex instruction of any kind in school.*

An opinion poll in 1971 (carried out by NOP) showed that nearly 70 per cent of Britain's *adults* think they were given too little sex education at school. Even among people aged 21 and 34, 67 per cent (roughly two out of three) believe they were not told enough. Fifty-three per cent of all those interviewed said no one had taught this vital subject.

An earlier Harris poll confirmed that the vast majority of adults picked up their sex education in the most casual and off-hand way. Over half the men had no sex instruction, while 41 per cent of the women were left ignorant. The pollsters interviewed 2,255 people, all over 16, and those they spoke to were representative of the population as a whole. Once again girls were better off than boys. Three out of ten got certain facts explained by their mothers and one in four learned from books and pamphlets. As one would expect, fathers tended to talk to their sons, and mothers to their daughters, about 'the facts of life', but more fathers than mothers shirked this duty. This inquiry revealed that more parents are doing their duty today than ever before. Among those questioned over 65, only *one in sixteen* had learned anything about sex from a father. Only one in six were taught a little by their mothers. Among those 16 to 24 today, one in six learned from fathers, and one in three from mothers.

The majority of those interviewed thought sex was best taught in the home, in conjunction with schools. Only one in ten thought schools *alone* should handle the task. Dr Robert Kind has taken regular surveys every five years of teenage opinion. His findings tally with those of the opinion polls. He says far too many parents tend to rely on the schools to give their children the basic facts about sex.

More specific inquiries have further disclosed the appalling extent of ignorance – and the human consequences of this neglect by parents and teachers of the needs of pupils. A senior lecturer in Health Education at the University of London Institute of Education, Mrs Mary Holmes, revealed, in November 1968, that six out of ten boys, and four out of ten girls, suffering from venereal infection, *had received no sex education at all.* Her study of 152 youngsters caused her to comment: 'It is certainly not the adequacy of the sex education they have had at school that prevented the majority of average pupils from contracting venereal disease.'

She confirmed that children were leaving primary school knowing all about the life cycles of various creatures – but little about their own biology. Mrs Holmes, a school inspector, commented: 'Many of the existing biology and general-science courses hardly mention man at all. Preference is given to the rabbit as the example of a mammal. Few children leave our schools without an intimate knowledge of the tadpole. We would have our children learn about space and space machines, but not about the marvellously intricate human mechanism, upon the limits of whose ability to adapt, survival ultimately depends.'

Another investigation in April 1971 showed that youngsters leaving the 3,100 Catholic schools (which have a total of about 800,000 pupils) were often unprepared for the difficulties of courtship and marriage. The report blamed this on the reluctance of the schools to give pupils any form of sex education. These teenagers were socially immature – especially in relationships with the opposite sex. This investigation also made other criticisms of these schools (which one child in ten attends). They said they often weakened faith and 'dulled moral awareness'. They accused the schools of employing teachers who showed an excessive inclination to use the cane. They also said some of the schools were overconservative, demanded docility rather than inquiry, and conformity rather than creativity. By their preoccupation with religious education they had often neglected *moral* education. There were also allegations that the young products of Catholic schools were: 'Less honest, less truthful, less trustworthy, less hardworking, less reliable and less thrifty.'

I quote these findings to show that even schools more dedicated to the moral welfare of their pupils than most are failing the children in their care. I am also concerned to emphasize to parents that you *cannot* leave the sex education of your children to teachers. Many schools are carrying out their responsibilities, but far too many are not.

It is also important to remember that education is not just a question of passing exams, getting top marks, or obtaining paper qualifications. No one has perfected a satisfactory definition of education, but everyone agrees (except the Jehovah's Witnesses, the Nazis, and some Communist regimes) that schools should inculcate a spirit of inquiry. We must teach children to ask questions, to challenge authority when authority expects them to believe something *merely because they are told it is true*. As Milton said: 'Let Truth and Falsehood grapple. Who ever heard of Truth put to the Worse in a Fair Fight?' Those Catholic schools (and any other similar institution) which try to produce docile, conformist teenagers, are failing on educational, as well as on moral and intellectual grounds.

I must quote another survey to show the connexion between the kind of schooling a child receives, and his, or her, attitude to sex. John Peel, a sociologist at York University, studied 350 couples in Hull and found that girls leaving school at 15 (as fast as the law allowed) are twice as likely to be pregnant as their brighter classmates. He told me: 'Our research explodes a number of widely held ideas about the immorality of students. It is quite clear girl undergraduates are not as permissive as everyone seems to think they are.' Mr Peel (a married man with two daughters 'both planned for') questioned one in five brides and bridegrooms who got married in Hull between March 1965 and April 1966. He said: 'Birth control expertise as well as attitudes to family planning are clearly influenced by length of education. There are, of course, some obvious commonsense reasons why girls who leave school as fast as possible are more likely to be pregnant brides. Girls who do more homework, swot for exams and so on, are less able to lead a social life or meet new boy friends.' A NUT spokesman commented on this research: 'We have always said there should be more education for more pupils. It is quite clear the more education children get the less likely they are to have unwanted babies.'

Mr Peel's findings may appear to contradict the opinion of men, such as Dr Nicolas Malleson, who emphasize the rising amount of promiscuity and pregnancies among the well-educated young. I am sure however that the contradiction is only apparent. Mr Peel is right to state that well-educated teenagers are more likely than their slower-learning contemporaries to avoid unwanted babies. Dr Malleson is right to emphasize the growing tendency of educated youngsters to scoff at the old taboos ('masturbation makes you blind', 'men only want to marry virgins', 'bad girls go to hell') and to believe that it is healthier to have orgasms than to indulge in the frustrating practice of 'heavy petting'. The trend among girls to lose their virginity earlier, and to have more affairs before getting married, is connected with the growing popularity of Women's Lib ideas. As more girls take the birth-control Pill they are able to say: 'Why should there be one law for men and one for women? Why does society approve of the sexually experienced bachelor and frown on the fun-loving spinster who thinks it unfair to tease men sexually when she also enjoys intercourse?'

These questions of behaviour and morality are each individual's private concern. It is our task as parents and teachers to enable children to have the *freedom* to choose their way of life. A child of eleven with a baby, a 12-year-old seducer on the run from the law, a teenager with incurable VD, and a young wife who 'had to get married' to a man she hardly knew, do not have that freedom. We can only give the young freedom of choice by giving them *the right kind of sex* education.

There is clear evidence that sex education is the cure for, and not the cause of, abortions, VD, and unwanted babies. In March 1971 it was disclosed in *The Times* that the number of girl students at Aberdeen College of Education who had sought abortions had dropped from a 'quite high' figure to zero after lectures on sex education were started there.

But too few teachers, local-authority chiefs and heads of schools have learned this simple lesson. By May 1971 it was revealed by the School Broadcasting Council that most schools buying the BBC Sex Education films *were not showing them to children*. Over 1,680 primary schools bought film-strips but only one in three used them. About one in four said they 'expected' to use them, and the rest (about half) admit to having wasted their money. The Council said: 'These schools preferred not to enter a situation of which they were as yet unsure, or which in their judgement would embarrass their relations with parents.' Some of the schools were not showing the films because they thought they were: 'Contrary to their educational, moral or religious principles.' Some heads said they were worried that if they used the film they would be 'usurping the right of parents'. Others were concerned that the proposed ages of the audience of children were 'too young', and some were upset that there was no mention of 'love and marriage'. Others insisted that unless 100 per cent of parents approved of the films being shown no child could see them.

This report also said that out of a total of 11,200 schools using the programmes 'Merry-Go-Round', 8,600 (77 per cent) *did not* continue with the three programmes contributing to sex education. It explained: 'Two-thirds of these did not consult the parents. A basic reason for not taking the programme was *the absence of sex education in their schools*.' The heads explained the lack of sex education by saying that primary-school children were 'too young'. They also said: 'The classroom was not the place for sex instruction – bearing in mind that children become curious about sex at different ages.'

These attitudes are opposed by Albert Chanter, one of the pioneers of frank, useful sex education in this country. Head of Ladysmith Junior Mixed School, Exeter, Devon, he started these lessons because his experiences as a marriage-guidance counsellor left him dismayed by the ignorance of most adults. He never shirks from using necessary helpful words such as penis, vagina and sperms. He gives weekly lessons to 10- and

11-year olds, and uses diagrams to show how a baby comes into the world at the moment of birth. He says: 'The primary school age is *ideal* for teaching facts about sex. Children are ready to learn – but are not old enough to be affected by emotional feelings.'

Those schools which were sensible enough to use the BBC's film-strips confirmed the benefits of providing sex education in this way. The Council's report says children were relieved to be able to discuss the meaning of words and to contrast them with 'rude' playground words – without shame. They add: 'Parents commented it was now much easier to talk to their children, and teachers said the programmes had alleviated embarrassment – instead of causing it.'

There is much evidence to support those who believe teachers are wrong to deprive young children of these films. In June 1969, for example, a report by a working party on Science Education in Scotland said the subject of human reproduction was an essential part of every child's education, and should be dealt with early in the child's school career. One member of the working party, David Ritchie of Kircaldy, said: 'With the increasing maturity of school children earlier, it is important that they be given some knowledge of this in their first year. It is something teachers have to face up to because parents often do not have the knowledge.'

One fact stands out from all others in my investigations. It was quite clear that once adults understand or become acquainted with the best sex education, *they usually approve of it*. For example Dr John Daines of Nottingham University questioned 452 students and occupational therapists about their reaction to a colour film on contraceptive methods called: 'Every Baby a Wanted Baby'. Only five said they were 'embarrassed', and only three considered it 'offensive'. Seventeen said they had seen a film like this when they were at school – and 369 said they *wished they had*. No student of any age found the film embarrassing, and only two students said it was 'offensive'. Out of a further 178 parents who were shown the film only six had seen a contraceptive film at school themselves. *More than 80 per cent wished they had done so*. Only one parent was embarrassed by the film, and none were offended. One in three admitted they had learned something from viewing the film. *Most agreed their child should see it*. The report commented: 'Perhaps the most encouraging feature of the whole exercise was the smallness of the number who thought the film would encourage promiscuity or experimentation. Only one headteacher, sixteen parents, ten students, and "a few" occupational therapists, said it would encourage promiscuity.'

The campaign to provide adequate sex information for adults as well as children has recently received some powerful official backing. Sir Keith Joseph, Minister in charge of the Social Services, has authorized councils to treble the amount spent on family planning to a total of two and a quarter million pounds by 1973. However, the poor record of local authorities in the past in this field does not make one optimistic. Far too few councils are brave and wise enough to expand and advertise their family-planning services properly. It is time they realized the practical arguments (curbing the population explosion) and stopped worrying about accusations that they are encouraging 'Sex on the Rates'.

The other official encouragement came from Lord Belstead, the Under Secretary for Education responsible for the country's 28,000 schools. He has said: 'If young girls have sexual relationships it is surely better that they should have proper contraceptive advice.'

The Government have further shown their awareness of the *real* needs of young people by rejecting a plea by Baroness Summerskill that the birth-control Pill should be banned to girls under 18, unless they had their parents' permission. But there are some people, such as Dr Louise Eickhoff, the Birmingham psychiatrist, who still allege sex education is harmful and wrong.

Such critics have little, or no, factual evidence to support their case. Men such as Dr Robert Bluglass, who has a regional clinic, the Midlands Centre for Forensic Psychiatry at All Saints Hospital, Birmingham, welcome the spread of sex education. He says: 'There are *no* indications it increases delinquency – the signs are rather to the contrary. Pregnancies result from errors of judgement, poor home backgrounds, or ignorance. As many as 90 per cent of all pregnancies before the 19th birthday are unplanned, and conceived before marriage. In my view contraceptive advice should be readily available wherever there is a risk of pregnancy. It is a common finding among all delinquents who present themselves for my examination that sexual education has been poor, or absent in the past. Some adolescents are very ignorant in relation to 1971.'

Such views are powerfully supported by Sir John Peel, the president of the British Medical Association. In July 1971 he pleaded for contraceptive advice to be made more freely available for the young, to reduce the need for abortions. Sir John, a former president of the Royal College of Obstetricians and Gynaecologists, said gynaecologists and general practitioners were getting more and more angry, incensed by the increasing demand that they should recommend and carry out abortions. He said they resented not being able to make contraceptive advice freely available. He also said it was extraordinary that so many women were concerned about the risks of oral contraceptives, and were so utterly unconcerned about the risks of driving a car or heavy smoking, or *that the mortality rate from pregnancy was some four times the risk involved in taking the Pill.*

This last fact is the sort of information that parents, doctors, priests and teachers need at their fingertips when advising a young girl. It is clear, as we have seen, that few adults possess such knowledge. It is obvious that public opinion must persuade local authorities, headteachers and doctors to cooperate to help the campaign to improve and increase the provision of sex education.

But it is much easier to advocate sex education than it is to provide it. It is time to examine the questions: 'Who is going to advise?', 'When should they tell?' and 'How should they tell?'.

Sex Education: Who, When, How?

Now that we have answered the question: 'Why is sex education necessary?' it is clear that parents and teachers need to acquire sufficient knowledge to help children. I have added a list of books at the end of this chapter which should enable you to cope with any questions your child might ask. You should never be afraid to say you do not know the answer. It will help your relationship with the child if you seek out the answer together. This basic rule of education applies to sex instruction as to every other lesson.

Dr Robert Kind has studied the question: 'How to teach sex?' for thirty years. He says: 'There can be no *one* exclusive method in practice. But there are several generalizations which can be made. The subject should be as freely discussed in the home as the result of a football match. Some teachers who have not yet come to terms with their own sexuality can be worse than shy parents. I do not agree with the widely held view that sex education should be placed in the context of learning about health, mental health, hygiene and religion. I agree with the theoretical need to place sex information in perspective, but I feel many people use this idea to obscure and to dilute the sexual content. There must be an adequate, uniform vocabulary for teaching this subject. Absence of this is an important barrier to communication.'

This last point causes controversy among educationists. You remember David Barnard's comments on this. He suggested that it was wrong to use a word such as promiscuity with children who were unused to hearing it. He suggested we allowed the class, or pupil, to say 'Having it away with all the boys in the street', and then gradually introduced the word promiscuity. Children will appreciate that it is easier to use one word instead of ten. They spend a great deal of time using slang, or 'in-talk', to shorten expressions, and they will respond if you use precise words casually, and without pomposity.

It is vital to be consistent in your vocabulary in order to get children speaking about the subject fluently, accurately, and without blushing. I noticed in the controversial part of *The Little Red School Book* that the translators had been rather inconsistent. They began by talking about 'prick' and 'cunt', and then referred to 'vagina' when it would seem to have been more appropriate to use the word 'cunt'. Dr Caroline Deys, a family doctor, mother of a three-year-old daughter and wife of Dr Malcolm Potts, the director of the International Planned Parenthood Association, agrees with David Barnard about the difficulties middle-class teachers have with most of their pupils. She says: 'There is a perfectly good four-letter word for intercourse which children hear every day in the playground, and they find it easy to say. Why not use it? Children find words like intercourse and coitus difficult to say. So forget them.'

I think Dr Deys gives a misleading impression here. The whole question of vocabulary is related to the question: 'When should sex education be carried out?' All the experts agree we should start as early as possible. If we take their advice children in secondary schools would not need to be told the meaning of words like 'vagina', 'penis' and 'umbilical cord'. They would have acquired these words in their junior school. Dr Kind says however that we should begin even earlier. He says: 'Start around the age of three and a half. This is when a child asks: "Where did I come from?" The answer should be: "You grew in Mum's tummy." The child will forget it because he isn't that interested. But the fact that *he did get an answer will encourage him later to ask more questions.*'

Dr Deys says: 'We should take the heat off sex education and regard it as just another lesson. It should start at school around the age of seven when children are unembarrassed and soon lose interest. If you wait until ten, many of the girls will be starting their periods, and the boys will begin stirring. The whole thing at this age becomes an emotional subject.'

Dr Deys says sensibly: 'Don't bring morals into the factual sex side. Leave that until 11 or 12 when you can start talking about the responsibility of having children. Then a bit later you can tackle birth control, at the same time *talking about testing the temperature of a baby's bath*'.

It is important to relate her stress on bringing up explosive topics in a natural, casual way to Dr Kind's remark about making the subject as freely discussed 'as the result of the football match'. Mature, secure adults who have come to terms with their own sexuality can carry this off, but neurotic, insecure, immature, or even just plain shy, inhibited adults have difficulties here.

If teachers received proper training they could probably overcome personality weaknesses and give sex-education lessons better than untrained, insecure parents. Even if they do not have the training it looks as though teachers are going to have to fill the gap in children's education here. As Dr Kind says: 'Parents have fallen down so badly on sex education that the teacher must take over. Up to the age of 8 or 9 the average child will happily accept all information on the mechanics of sex.' Like Dr Deys he points out: 'It isn't until the child reaches puberty that he has any emotional feelings. It is essential that by that time *the basics are out of the way.*' In this way, as we have noted, the adolescent is equipped to discuss sex with an adequate, functional vocabulary instead of the emotional, associative language of the playground and 'behind the bike sheds'.

Dr Kind and the other experts I spoke to insist that we must convey the idea that 'sex is fun'. He says: 'It is essential to make it clear that if you engage in sex you do so to enjoy it – not just to have babies. The bright child of 9 will ask: "How do you avoid making a baby every time?" Think how many people would raise their hands in horror at the thought of telling this child about contraception. But I believe you should because it is a fact of life. Some people are hesitant about teaching sex in class because of the different stages of development among children. At 9 you have no problem *because they are all more or less the same*. If you leave it until 13 – then you are in trouble.'

Throughout the whole field of sex education one dominant theme occurs when you question those who teach pupils best. The theme is that we must try to avoid making children frightened or guilty. The organized religions have for centuries attempted to reduce the amount of pleasant sexual activity for its own sake. Children have been reared for far too long on the idea that women do not, and should not, enjoy sex. Now this notion is dying. It is however taking far too long to disappear. It has, for example, been said that it was *not* the four-letter words in *Lady Chatterley's Lover* which offended the middle-aged, middle-class males who run our society. They knew these words, and were not really worried that 'servants might be corrupted by them' (as was said at the trial!). The aspect of the book which angered them was the attitude that as Lady C. could not be satisfied and delighted by her husband, she was morally right to seek her orgasms with the gamekeeper.

The spread of more liberal ideas in the past twenty years has, however, resulted in more people sympathizing with her Ladyship – and even approving of her action. One example of the more humane attitude prevalent today is the approach to masturbation in women's magazines. The magazine *You*, in a Summer issue in 1971, dealt with this thus: 'It is important for parents to realize that, in itself, masturbation is a completely normal and harmless activity. It does not indicate that the child is over-sexed, or has "dirty thoughts", and it is not the foreshadowing of a promiscuous future or anything of that sort at all. It is simply a perfectly normal part of sexual behaviour and development. It needs, however, to be distinguished from irritation of the genital organs, which may lead to scratching or rubbing . . . Parents who come across their child in the act of masturbation should do nothing about it at all, and should carry on with what they proposed to do without comment of any kind. If it is being done in a public place then it is reasonable for them to attempt gently to distract the child. Any expression of disapproval of the child for masturbating or any suggestion that this is in some way *an unnatural or unclean or abnormal activity can cause untold damage in later years*' (my italics).

It is significant that the tone and content of this advice is similar to the following : 'If anyone tells you it's harmful to masturbate, they're lying. If anybody tells you you mustn't do it too much they're lying too, because you cannot do it too much. Ask them how often you ought to do it. They'll usually shut up then.' This comes from *The Little Red School Book* which is thought to be very 'permissive' and extremely shocking.

Another controversial piece of work, Dr Martin Cole's film *Growing Up*, tried to approach the question of masturbation in such a way that children would be able to masturbate without fear of going blind or feeling guilty. Although I thought the overall effect of this film was disappointing (the commentary contained at least one factual error and two highly arguable opinions) I recognized that the showing of a young man and woman masturbating was perhaps a valid way of diminishing fears and guilt. Children watching the film with adults are more likely to get the message that there is nothing wrong with masturbation than those who are *just told this is so*.

I approve of the sensible approach of the quotation from *You* magazine. Their comments on the connexion between over-strict toilet training and sexual prudery are also apt. They warn that over-strict toilet training and too much concern about the child messing himself or showing an interest in his excretory products, does seem to be related to an excessive degree of sexual inhibition in later years. They point out that the sort of parent who is likely to be fastidious about toilet training is also *likely to adopt a prudish attitude to sexual upbringing*.

This magazine (which is backed and published by the British Medical Association) adds : 'Parents often attach far too much importance to their children being "clean" at an early age – as though this were some kind of competition in which the child had to excel to prove his worth. Certainly many parents still feel that a child who is late in developing what are regarded as civilized toilet habits is, in some way, backward, and that this bodes ill for his subsequent intellectual development. Yet, except in extreme cases, *there is no evidence that this is so at all.*'

The best thing for mothers to remember is that a child usually becomes clean when he gets tired of being unclean. You should also aim to stop the pot being associated with punishment or an endurance test. Parents can applaud a successful session on the pot, but you should avoid showing so much pleasure at success that the child feels guilty or deeply unhappy when he fails. It is sometimes difficult for mothers to stop showing disgust at a child's performance on the pot. You should bear in mind that children associate their urine and faeces with their sexual organs. Damage can be caused by making him or her feel something produced by, or near, these organs is disgusting.

It is understandably difficult for parents to bear all this advice in mind amid the rough-and-tumble of a happy, noisy home. It is hard to be casual and spontaneous if you have had a formal upbringing which made you feel that sex was something shameful, 'dirty', painful and unmentionable. However, one principle must be remembered. *Always answer questions as they arise.* We have noted that the answer to the question 'When should children receive sex education?' is 'As early as possible' as far as the teaching of vocabulary and the mechanics of the act of love are concerned. The useful principle behind this approach is that it is better to be years early – than a second too late! These are the answers which explain why we advocate sex lessons in the primary school and a general effort to relate the rabbits and hamsters to 'Where do babies come from?' But there is another aspect of 'When should we teach sex?' which is often left unexplained. Parents are told to answer questions when they arise – but they are often not made to appreciate what this means. It is easy to understand that you can answer a question like 'Where did I come from?' by saying 'You started in Mum's tum.' But parents are not usually prepared for much more difficult situations. If you are not warned about these pitfalls you may harm a child by acting in a thoughtless way. The sort of situation I have in mind is when a child charges into a bathroom on a morning when Dad may have an erection. The child might have approached quietly in fun or because the landing carpet is thick. Dad must realize that such an incident could be embarrassing if he has not anticipated (as soon as his first child started walking) it could happen. He must make no attempt to shoo the children away. There is no need for him to explain why his penis is erect, as the question has not been asked. If and when it is asked he should explain an erection in the words he knows the child understands.

This is of course asking a lot of a father who may be a shy or inarticulate man, but he should realize the reaction of the child who has been shooed away or told to mind his own business. You can comfort yourself when anticipating this question by estimating most children will not pursue their inquiries – if the initial explanation is casual and comprehensive enough (for their stage of development). If you *are* shy or inarticulate you can always avoid such incidents by using the lock on the bathroom door!

So far I have urged parents to adopt the informal, liberal, humane, unembarrassed approach. This will cause some of you to wonder : 'Just how far does this progressive attitude go? Are there no limits at all? Can children, for example, watch their parents making love?' The answers to these questions are simple. I say to parents : 'Yes, there are limits. Yes, I certainly draw the line at the idea of allowing children to watch their parents having intercourse. Among the many obvious reasons why this is wrong is the fact that most children will get the idea "Daddy is attacking Mummy". The effect of such a scene is likely to be alarming, deeply disturbing and quite traumatic' – but some teachers disagree with me!

I would also draw the line at advocating, as some teachers and so-called 'experts' do, that children should have a special 'loving room' at school where *they can practise what they have learned in sex-education lessons.* This idea was first publicized in Germany. In recent months it has been urged by British teachers. I do not want to publicize such a ridiculous notion by naming its advocates. I merely mention this suggestion to show how out-of-touch with reality and commonsense some adults can get when considering this subject.

It is an extremely complex and difficult matter to give advice on. We are dealing with an explosive topic. We are dealing with human beings at their most sensitive stage. We cannot be too careful how we discuss the subject. It is as wrong to wrap children in cotton wool – protecting them from the reality of intercourse, periods, VD, and abortions – as it is to put forward suggestions which mean they encounter experiences before they are ready for them. One useful example of the delicate balance that must be struck is the suggestion by Dr Kind that we should tell children that they came 'from Mum's tum'. This is sound advice if you are quite confident that the child is not brooding on the question, and will not brood on the answer. If the question came out as though it had just been thought of, and if the answer sends him racing off to play football, then Dr Kind's advice is sound.

But the child who has been pondering the question, and lingers, looking worried, after you have given this brief answer, needs something more. He may believe that babies burst open Mum's tum causing her pain, as well as a bloody mess. He may get the idea that the baby is put inside the stomach – after it has been cut open. Some children get the idea that they are 'born' when mother vomits them into life through the mouth. For children, especially for girls, such nightmarish imaginings cause unnecessary anguish. It is always wrong to leave children in painful ignorance. I cannot describe in detail *precisely* how you must judge whether the answer 'from Mum's tum' is good enough for *your* child. I am confident however that you will sense whether your child is going to be harmed by receiving such a brief answer.

Throughout this book I have tried (where possible) to put forward a form of words, some suggested sentences, instead of giving vague advice. I want to give you some idea of *what* to say to your child, instead of merely telling you 'Talk to your child.' Here is an example of an answer to a vital ques tion from a six-year-old. The answer is approved by doctors and sex educationists. It will help you form your own answers to similar questions.

Question: Why do boys have a thing between their legs?

Answer: 'It is called a penis. It has two jobs. It lets the wee-wee, or urine, out of the body when a boy goes to the toilet. When he is a man, and both he and his wife want to make a baby, he puts it into his wife between her legs. It carries the sperms that are needed to make a baby. The sperms are made in those two little balls just beneath it. They are called testicles. The bag they are in is called the scrotum. In this part of the body girls are different from boys. They do not have a penis. They have an opening for the man to put his penis into. Their wee-wee or urine gets out through a smaller hole just above this.'

Such an answer provides the vocabulary which the child will need later on in his, or her, life. It also avoids creating misconceptions and spells out the information in such a way that the child, at this age, is unlikely to have many follow-up queries. If you follow the guide-lines I have given in this chapter your child should be able to avoid most of the guilt and fear which my generation experienced.

You may ask why I have not written anything about love and marriage. This is not the duty of the sex educationist. He is *first* of all concerned with preventing VD and unwanted babies. I believe that when we have knocked the mystique out of this subject, when we have got rid of the fear, guilt and taboos, we shall be surprised how *moral* our children are. Dr James Hemming, the 61-year-old psychologist who has been studying sexual problems for over twenty-five years, agrees with me. He says: 'Marriage will not disappear. If young people do not get "married" in the traditional way, they will still seek an enduring relationship. Adults will gradually realize that if you free young people from the old taboos – you *do not* get mass promiscuity.'

Dr Hemming believes that we can get some idea of the morality of the future by looking at the attitudes today of the nonconformist section of the middle classes. 'Here you will discover the pace-setters', he says. 'These are the young people who are forging new values.' He blames those pre-War-born parents, who passed on a confused attitude to morals, for the formation of the Permissive Society. He says: 'We just used to bustle youngsters off to the altar. We did not give them a real chance to select a mate. They used to get married on the basis of infatuation, or simply because they were sexually starved. Now they try to get "married" on the basis of real selection, which will give them a much better chance of building up an enduring relationship'.

One young woman I came across during my investigations, a Cambridge graduate called Helena, typifies the kind of new 'morality' in the 1970s. She is one of the nonconformist, professional classes who refuses to be bustled off to the altar. She lives with her boyfriend, and his widowed mother, above a pie-and-eel shop in North London. She has no intention of getting married, and, although she is 25, she does not yearn to have children. She concentrates on her career and is very good at it – she writes for magazines. She told me: 'Many people think I'm immoral or promiscuous just because I refuse to get married. I think I'm more moral than many "married" people, blessed by the Church. I slept with my boyfriend the first time we went out. I wasn't a virgin at the time. I would never, never be unfaithful to him. I don't think you have to be in love with someone to go to bed with them. Who knows whether they are "in love" or not? Who knows what love is? But once you have "committed" yourself to someone you should stay true to them in every sense.'

She is horrified by the degree of adultery she learns of in her office. 'The married men end up despising the girls they lay', she says. 'Much adultery is between people who don't really like each other. The relationship is inferior to the one they have with their wives – but they cannot see it.'

Although many will frown at her attitudes to white weddings and legal marriage, it has to be recognized that her view is less irresponsible than it might appear to be. She takes the birth-control pill. If she did not, she would be running the risk of pregnancy. This would seem to most adults to be reckless and immoral. Yet she, unlike many wives, is loyal, loving and faithful to her boyfriend. If our children are as 'moral', no one could claim their generation have created a new Sodom, and another Gomorrah.

My finding (that the pill is not to blame for an apparent increase in promiscuity) was confirmed in April 1971 by Dr Leon Tec, who runs a child-guidance clinic in Connecticut. He told a London Congress: 'I have never been asked by a virgin to be given a prescription for the pill. Promiscuous girls would be promiscuous whether they were on the pill or not'. But he did have a serious warning about the popularity of the pill. He said: 'Contraceptives are being used less and less by young men. Therefore venereal disease is spreading by leaps and bounds. When young men know a girl is using the pill they are much less likely to have contraceptives ready.'

This warning should be widely publicized. The popularity of the pill is indeed increasing. By August 1971 an Opinion Research Centre Poll showed that eight out of ten adults approved of the pill for married women, and four out of ten for single teenage girls. Nearly 60 per cent thought unmarried women in their twenties should be able to be on the pill, and nearly 70 per cent thought engaged women could use this contraceptive.

But, two days before these results were published, another survey revealed that *one person in every 200 is going to a VD clinic*. Dr Catterall, Director of the Department of Venerology at the Middlesex Hospital, commented: 'You'd be surprised how many men and women who come to us have no idea of the *names* of the people they have slept with.' These facts about VD cause me to come to two conclusions. I am concerned that all youngsters should know the truth about VD, and I am anxious parents should attempt to provide children with the kind of moral values which would prevent them sleeping with anonymous partners.

The first point was well made by Michael Scholfield of

the Health Education Council when he told the Family Planning Association, at this time, that nine out of ten boys and girls leaving school today would fail any exam on the symptoms of VD, and yet the great spread of the disease is in these young age groups – 15 to 21 for girls, and 19 to 28 for boys. Some adults encourage myths about VD by saying: 'It doesn't matter if you get it, you just go along for a few jabs and you're OK.' People who talk like this have not seen women made sterile by VD, and men with chronic arthritis, heart disease and eye infections. Children need to be told there are *twelve to fourteen different kinds of VD*. Some strains are becoming more difficult to cure. Girls need to be warned that over half the women with VD do not know they are infected because they have no symptoms. If they think there is the remotest chance they may be infected, they should be urged to contact the local GP, or hospital, and in this way they can discover the location of the nearest VD clinic. Mothers should mention this kind of information to daughters when they leave home for the first time. In Sweden there are massive posters which say: 'Tonight 107 Swedes Will Get Gonorrhoea'. We should publicize the information about clinics, and a similar warning, in cinemas, newspapers and magazines.

But when all the factual information we know has been given to all the children and young adults we know, our task is not finished. All lessons should be taught with, and because of, love. If your children admire, respect, and trust *you*, it will be easier for you to encourage them to restrict their love-making to people with whom they are having lengthy relationships. It will be easier for you to advocate marriage if you have demonstrated with your partner that it is an institution worth preserving. Most young people look blank when you ask them if they know any happily-married couples.

SUGGESTED READING

Homan, William E., *Child Sense*. Nelson: London, 1970.

Demarest, R. J., and Ciarra, John J., *Conception, Birth, Contraception*. Hodder & Stoughton: London, 1969.

Kind, D. R., Leedham, John, and Kind, Anne, *Programmes in Sex Education*. Longman: London, 1969.

Claësson, B. H., *Boy, Girl, Man, Woman*. Calder & Boyars: London, 1971.

Vaughan, Gerard, *A Pictorial Guide to Common Childhood Illnesses, 'Mummy, I don't feel well'*. Arcade Publishing: London, 1970.

CHAPTER EIGHT

Some School Questions Answered

We have examined many of the problems which arise while your child is at school, but there are several more which still cause difficulty. Before going on to the issues which crop up when your child leaves school, I will deal with some questions which puzzle most parents.

Question: What is the CSE exam? Is it a better qualification than the GCE 'O' level? Is it recognized by employers and colleges of further and higher education?

Answer: The CSE (Certificate of Secondary Education) was launched in 1965. (It seems to take about twenty years for the public to understand the significance and relevance of a new exam in this country, for I still meet people who refer to the General Certificate of Education as the 'School Cert', the 'Matric' – or even the GEC.) The CSE is not yet sufficiently well known or understood by all employers and parents. At the last count well over a quarter of a million candidates sat this exam. It is therefore important that it should be fully explained and appreciated. Many people believe that, in time, the CSE will replace the 'O' level of the GCE. In 1967 Edward Heath, the leader of the Conservative Party, told an education conference:

> It seems extraordinary that we have *two* national examinations at the age of sixteen – the GCE and the CSE – whereas most countries get on perfectly well without any. If we study this matter, we might well find we could make do with the CSE, and declare 'O' levels redundant.

Most educationists and teachers with experience of the CSE would agree with this. They welcome the CSE as a more flexible way of examining pupils, and they appreciate the efforts being made with this exam to assess what a teenager has learned, instead of merely testing his ability to write against the clock, and to compete with children of his own age.

The CSE was suggested by the Beloe Committee, which reported to the Minister of Education in July 1960. It was recommended that candidates should be in the range of ability just below those taking the 'O' level of the GCE. The next 20 per cent of pupils below the 'O' level candidates should take a range of CSE subjects, and a further 20 per cent below this group might take individual subjects. The Beloe Committee stressed that the CSE should not be allowed to become a sort of replica of the 'O' level, and that it should be designed to fit the needs of the children in the ability range described above. It also proposed that the new exam should be firmly controlled by the teachers in the schools which entered candidates for it.

As a result, there are *three* kinds of CSE exam, they are known as Mode 1, Mode 2, and Mode 3. The first is based on a syllabus devised outside the schools, and the papers are marked *externally*. Mode 2 is based on a syllabus drawn up by one school, or by a group of schools, who choose to have their candidates examined and marked *externally*. But Mode 3 is based on a sylabus devised by a school, or group of schools, who examine *their own* candidates and mark *their own* pupils' papers. There are, of course, safeguards to preserve standards when Mode 3 is used, in order to prevent some exams being too easy and some too tough.

Eight candidates out of ten at present take Mode 1. Only 8 per cent take Mode 3, and only 5 per cent take Mode 2. The reason for the popularity of Mode 1 with teachers is quite clear. Modes 2 and 3 involve teachers with a great deal of unpaid extra work on top of their normal teaching load.

The candidates are placed in five grades when their papers are marked. Grade 1 represents a standard comparable to that which the pupil would have needed to attain a pass in the 'O' level of the GCE. Grade 2 represents a slightly lower standard, though much above average as an achievement. Grade 3 indicates a level just above average for a sixteen-year-old (remember six out of ten school-leavers do not have a single 'O' level pass). Grade 4 is the average level a sixteen-year-old can reasonably be expected to attain. Grade 5 normally means the candidate is informed of his or her performance, but is not awarded a certificate.

Roughly 95 per cent of candidates achieve one of the top four grades. Bear in mind that, although Grade 1 is considered by employers and teachers to equal the standard of a pass at 'O' level, it is not the *same* type of exam. It is a more flexible test designed to arouse in a child a more exploratory and creative approach to learning. It aims to relate education to living. It tries to bring out less of an academic, bookish attitude to study than the more rigid 'O' level test.

Most CSE courses last two years, and it is not wise to allow pupils to try sitting both the GCE and CSE exams. In one large area 37 per cent of the candidates who tried *both*, passed the 'O' level, but *failed* to get a Grade 1 in the CSE. This is probably because of the obvious difficulties of attempting two syllabuses at the same time.

As for the question of whether the CSE is accepted by employers as a recognized qualification, I can say only that well over 100 professional bodies *have* approved it at the time of writing. More and more are stating that Grade 1 of the CSE is an acceptable, and often superior, alternative to the 'O' level of the GCE.

Supporters of this new exam point out that some CSE subjects are assessed, not on the candidate's written achievement in a three-hour exam, but on his work in a course spread over two years. They claim this approach is sounder educationally and fairer to the candidate. My feeling is that, once all employers and college principals are well versed in the procedure and merits of this exam, there will be no need for the 'O' level. If I were an employer, I would rather know an employee had covered a wide-ranging course in a subject vital to his work, than be told he had passed an 'O' level test, which may only mean he was lucky enough to be asked just those questions he knew something about.

Question: Can parents appeal to an examining board if they think their child has been unfairly marked in the GCE or CSE?

Answer: Most examining boards (there are eight GCE boards in this country) do not give any clue in their regulations as to how an appeal is lodged. This is, of course, quite deliberate. If the appeals procedure were properly publicized, they would be swamped with queries every year from parents who refuse to believe their child has been lazy, slow-learning or unlucky with his exam questions.

As a general rule, a board will only consider appeals against failure or low gradings if the plea for reconsideration is put forward by the headteacher or the candidate's tutor. So if you wish to take the matter further, you must first consult your child's headteacher. If he thinks a mistake has been made, you should then get either an explanation or a re-assesment from the board. In case you want to be well-briefed when you approach the school, here are the addresses of the eight GCE boards.

1. Associated Examining Board: Secretary, Wellington House, Station Road, Aldershot, Hants. Tel 25551.

2. University of Cambridge, Local Examinations Syndicate: Secretary, Syndicate Buildings, 17 Harvey Road, Cambridge. Tel 54223.

3. Joint Matriculation Board: Secretary, Manchester 15. Tel 061-273 2565.

4. University Entrance and School Examinations Council, University of London: Secretary, 66–72 Gower Street, London WC1. Tel 01-636 8000.

5. Oxford and Cambridge Schools Examinations Board: Secretaries, 10 Trumpington Street, Cambridge. Tel 50658; and Elsfield Way, Oxford. Tel 54421.

6. Oxford Local Examinations: Secretary, Delegacy of Local Examinations, Summertown, Oxford. Tel 54291.

7 Southern Universities Joint Board: Secretary, 22 Berkeley Square, Bristol 8.

8 Welsh Joint Education Committee: Secretary, 30 Cathedral Road, Cardiff. Tel 41253.

The full list of these boards (in case the address has changed by the time you read this), the list of the CSE boards, City and Guilds of London Institute, Regional Examining Boards, and the Scottish examining boards, can all be found in the *Education Committees Year Book* in your local library.

Bear in mind that the Southern Universities GCE Board charges a fee in return for giving details of marks, and for a higher fee will provide a special report on a script by the chief examiner.

Question: If a parent does not approve of corporal punishment, can he stop his child being caned by teachers?

Answer: A teacher's rights in matters of discipline derive from a parent's. While the child is in his care in the classroom, he is considered to be able to punish in the same way as the child's father. Parents' rights were laid down in 1888, when the principle was stated that it was the duty of a parent to take whatever steps he considered necessary for the correction of the child. But he must act 'honestly'. A father must be reasonable. The crime, or childish offence, must merit the degree of punishment inflicted. If the father uses excessive punishment he loses his rights in this matter.

But, although parents delegate part of their duty to correct their own children to the teacher, they do *not* have the right to instruct the teacher as to the form or the extent of punishment. Equally a teacher could not plead in defence against a charge of assault, that he had received clear or implied instructions from a parent. The teacher, therefore, must make up his own mind on this issue.

The limits to which a teacher can go in inflicting pain were laid down in 1908. They are that the punishment should be moderate, that it should conform to the recognized practice in the school, that it should be such that a *reasonable* parent might expect the child to receive if it did wrong, and that it should not be irresponsible and dictated by bad motives.

> If it be administered for the gratification of passion or rage, or if it be immoderate and excessive in its nature or degree, or if it be protracted beyond the child's power of endurance, or with an instrument unsuited for the purpose and calculated to produce danger to life or limb – *in all such cases the punishment is excessive, the violence is unlawful*, and if evil consequences ensue the person inflicting it is answerable to the law, and if death ensue it will be manslaughter.

If the punishment is unreasonable or unlawful, no teacher can plead that his action came within the letter of the local authority regulations. But if the punishment was within the above definition, the teacher would not be liable for any accidental injury arising in consequence.

This last point is important. A twelve-year-old girl was struck by a teacher and, as a result, one of her thumbs became paralysed. But the courts decided the punishment was in accordance with the practice of the school, and was not vindictive or severe, and so neither the teacher nor his employer was liable.

It is up to the magistrates, in the first instance, to determine where the amount of force used was unreasonable. The law, however, offers little support to parents who oppose corporal punishment. You may avoid hitting a child at home, but you cannot insist that teachers exercise the same degree of restraint and humanity.

If you consider your child has been punished harshly for a trivial offence which the school believes sufficient cause for the pain inflicted you are unlikely to get very far with a legal action. You may be disturbed and distressed by the amount of caning that goes on in schools, but magistrates are unlikely to regard it as 'unreasonable'.

The vast majority of teachers favour the retention of corporal punishment, and most parents agree with its occasional use. Only one local education authority has forbidden it in primary schools, although most of them have regulations to control it and prevent its abuse.

This massive support among parents and teachers is unique in the Western world. Poland banned the cane in 1790, Sweden in 1958, Denmark in 1967 (after a well-organized campaign by *parents*), Norway in 1935, and Finland in 1914. Neither the West Germans nor the Americans allow caning. But one survey of 724 British teachers showed that 89 per cent valued it for use in the last resort, while 78 per cent strongly favoured it being used with discretion. Only one teacher in 12 (8·8 per cent) declared it did more harm than good, and only 5·6 per cent favoured abolition. One teacher in three agreed, however, it should not be used in infant schools.

Only three per cent of the primary school teachers questioned for the Plowden report on primary schools *admitted* that they caned regularly; but this still means that 3,000 teachers, in charge of about 120,000 children under the age of eleven, are still using the cane.

I think all parents and teachers should consider the evidence against corporal punishment. Two persuasive facts have convinced me that there is no reason why we should not copy other civilized countries and ban the cane. The first concerns the notorious London comprehensive – Risinghill school. In 1960 this school, full of eleven-plus failures and situated in an area of crime, prostitution and squalor, had only five passes at 'O' level and 98 boys on probation. In 1964, after the headmaster, Michael Duane, had banned the cane, there were only nine children on probation, two children went to University, and 42 pupils passed 'O' levels – one child being successful in six subjects. It was by then a happy school. A visiting diplomat said: 'It has succeeded in doing something the United Nations cannot do. The headmaster has children of all nationalities, living together in harmony.' The school was tragically closed in 1965, amid great controversy, and despite strong pressure from parents to keep it open.

The other fact which shows how powerful the case for removing fear from the classroom is, appeared in a survey of schools in Yorkshire's West Riding. One of the authors was Sir Alec Clegg, who studied many schools in the area, where he has been Education Officer for twenty-four years. He concluded:

'Our investigations have shown fairly clearly that schools serving the poorest of backgrounds can *dispense* with the cane, and yet achieve a standard of behaviour as high as any in the county.'

His research also showed that beating children has no effect on their behaviour – except possibly to make them even more delinquent. He told of a school where the behaviour of the pupils was generally depraved and deplorable. Caning them had no effect. But a new enlightened headmaster was appointed. He banned the cane and soon the school had one of the *lowest* delinquency rates in the county – where before it had one of the highest. The number of indictable offences committed by pupils in another school in the West Riding, dropped dramatically by 20 per cent when corporal punishment was abolished. This school was in a tough mining area.

I am supported by the Plowden Committee in my view that caning is often associated with psychological perversion, affecting both beater and beaten, and that it is ineffective in precisely those cases where it is most hotly defended. The Plowden Committee concluded: 'We think the time has come to drop it. After full consideration, we recommend that the infliction of pain as a recognized method of punishment in primary schools should be forbidden.'

But, if you agree with me, bear in mind the legal rights of teachers and parents, as they exist at present, before you complain to a headteacher.

Unless the teacher who caned has been particularly vicious, your only hope is a long-term one. In 1969 a new organization was launched called STOPP (Society of

Teachers Opposed to Physical Punishment). Its members are both teachers and parents. It is campaigning to arouse public opinion to the point where no Government can avoid banning the cane. If you wish to help STOPP, you should write to the Secretary, 12 Lawn Road, London NW3, or, if you live in the North, you should contact David Graham, 58 High Lane, Manchester 21.

Question: Has a parent any redress if a child loses property at school?

Answer: The two important things to remember in this issue are that the article lost must be something which a child might *reasonably* require while at school, and it must, if possible, be *marked* with the child's name, so as to be easily identifiable. No local authority is going to compensate a parent who sends a child to school with an expensive gold watch, or a brand new raincoat without a name-tag in it.

You should also bear in mind that if a teacher confiscates an article (again which is considered to be necessary during school hours) she has a responsibility to look after it. The courts, and the local education authority, expect her to look after it as well as she would her own property. If by gross negligence or by failure to observe the school-rules she lost the article, the parent would have cause for legal action.

But it is very difficult to *prove* a teacher has been grossly negligent, or had acted in breach of the school rules. One judge said :

> If a scholar loses his coat while it is in the cloakroom of a school, his parent is not entitled to compensation from the education committee concerned unless he can prove gross negligence, breach of orders or fraud.

Question: What is the legal position about school uniforms? Does a teacher have the right to send a child home for wearing the wrong clothes? Why do we have school uniforms?

Answer: The enforcement of school uniforms is based on a mixture of social pressure and blackmail. *In State schools, it has no legal basis.* If a parent, when his child goes to secondary school, signs a form promising to observe the rules of the school (which implicitly or explicitly includes the wearing of uniform) *he is not accepting a legally binding commitment.* If he chooses to object to uniform, it is extremely unlikely that the school could do anything about it *by formal means.* The social pressures in favour of your child conforming in this matter are so strong that any dispute is unlikely to reach the courts. Headteachers manage to avoid annoying their employers, the local authority, by settling the matter before it gets to this stage.

But, if a parent objects when a child attending a 'non-uniform' school is sent home for wearing unconventional clothes, he may be in a more difficult position legally than if he refuses to send the child in uniform to a school which uses uniforms. Section 39 of the 1944 Education Act points out that parents have a duty to send their children to school. The authorities usually back a teacher who objects to a child's clothing. If the parent keeps his child at home because he wants the school to relent in their opposition to jeans or mini-skirts, he is not fulfilling his duty under the Act. The only court case on this point (*Speirs* v *Warrington Corporation*, 1954) went against the parent.

The position is therefore that a teacher, perhaps for eccentric or capricious reasons, can exclude a child from a school, and thereby put parents in danger of committing an offence they had no intention of committing. Until parents are well briefed and sufficiently well organized to take a number of teachers to court, the law is likely to continue to be weighted against parents.

The arguments in favour of uniforms are that they obscure the difference between rich and poor, they develop a sense of group loyalty in pupils, they help to maintain discipline, and generally maintain the standard of appearance among pupils in the school.

The case against these arguments is, for me, quite overwhelming. Although one child in six among State-school pupils suffers from poverty, our standard of living has risen markedly since the 1930s. Not only are most of our children decently dressed, but it is quite possible for a child to use hard-wearing clothes which cause no offence, and are just as functional as uniforms. My wife, who is Norwegian, finds the whole question of school uniforms quite comic – when she is not feeling heartbroken at the sight of small boys in short trousers with blue knees on a cold winter day. I tried to defend our uniforms with all the stock arguments, and I asked: 'What happens if a girl comes to school wearing outlandish make-up, long dangling beads, and a micro-mini-skirt?' My wife, who went to her neighbourhood comprehensive in Oslo along with the King's son, just laughed and replied that if anyone did turn up dressed like that, the rest of the girls would pull her leg so much that she'd soon come dressed more suitably next day.

The arguments about uniform improving school loyalty, and discipline, are both invalid. In most British primary schools, and in all types of school abroad, discipline and morale are maintained – without uniforms.

The real basis for the arguments in favour of uniforms is, as usual in our status-crazy society, snobbery. The private schools have had uniforms for as long as anyone can remember. The grammar schools think they need uniforms so that their pupils can be distinguished from the 80 per cent of teenagers who are unlucky enough not to be able to get a proper secondary-school education. The secondary moderns have tried adopting uniforms – so their schools are not quite so left out of the academic status-stakes.

But the real inequalities remain, and it is stupid to think we can remove the tragic inequalities of our system by using the appearance of uniforms to hide the reality of wastage of talent.

Although the issue of uniforms may seem to be a trivial matter, the compulsory wearing of uniforms has evil side-effects. As we noted in the last chapter many girls leave school too early, and regret it, because they feel, as young women, they should not be dressed as children for seven hours a day. There is a more important matter, which is rarely discussed. One of the main purposes of education is to encourage independence of mind, and creative thought. New methods of teaching in our primary schools are the envy of the world. But the docility, conventionality, and uniformity of thought, which is bred by uniforms in secondary schools, militates against originality of thought, and individuality of expression.

Parents must ask themselves whether teachers have the *right* to ban long hair, black tights, duffel-coats, certain petticoats, and headgear. What have these restrictions got to do with learning? As Nevil Johnson wrote in *Where* magazine in 1964:

> Whilst guidance and advice on many of these matters may be needed, what is disturbing and objectionable is the arbitrary manner in which action is usually taken, and the motives of snobbery which sometimes inspire it, revealing a complete ignorance of changing social habits.

It is worth remembering that the only other civilized country in the world which is almost as keen on uniforms as Britain is the Soviet Union. The world's oldest democracy should not be proud of being emulated by a totalitarian state bent on crushing vestiges of individuality among its citizens. The quasi-military uniforms seen in Russian schools are as much a symbol of conformity, docility, and undemocratic tendencies as the blazers and straw hats of our private-school system – which, unfortunately, many State schools try to copy.

Question: What can parents do if their child is bright but fails to win a grammar-school place in the eleven-plus?

Answer: The simple, short answer is: 'Not very much.' Only three-quarters of a million pupils are able to go to comprehensives at the present time. There are only about 1,000 comprehensive schools. In seventeen out of the 165 local education authorities, no effort has been made, since 1944, to give *all* children a chance of the best education by introducing non-selective secondary schools. In Surrey, four out of every ten eleven-year-olds are bright enough to benefit from a grammar-school education (either in a grammar school or in a comprehensive) but there are places for *only one child in ten*. In areas such as this the parents have only themselves to blame. If they keep re-electing a Council dedicated to depriving the majority of pupils of a chance to be educated properly, it is no wonder they and their children are suffering heartbreak.

Until all secondary schools are non-selective comprehensives, parents will not have the choice of education for their children. Parents often forget that there will be *more* choice, *more* opportunities, and *more* freedom when all secondary schools are comprehensive. At present, choice depends on geographical accident, and eight out of ten parents have no choice – their children *have* to go to secondary modern schools.

If you have a bright child, whose headteacher was confident before the exam he would win a grammar-school place, and yet you are told he has to go to a secondary modern, you may ask yourself why other children living near you have been admitted to a comprehensive some distance away, while you are told your child cannot go there. In such a case it is again the question of a 'catchment' area. Because you still have grammar schools in your district, the comprehensive has to admit bright children over a wide area in order to have a balanced intake. Every comprehensive, which tries to be truly *comprehensive*, should secure its fair share of pupils from each range of ability. It is impossible to get a fair share while authorities insist on preserving grammar schools, which cream off the brightest pupils in the area. In such a situation many parents cannot understand why *their* bright child is unable to get either a grammar-school place or an academic education (and a chance of a university place) at a comprehensive.

Sometimes parents who are told their able child has to go to a secondary modern can persuade the local education authority to think again by getting the child tested by an educational psychologist. If he thinks your child is ten IQ points brighter than the assessment of teachers, or the results of the eleven-plus, you may get them to change their minds.

You should also remember, when arguing about the distance between home and school with the local authority, that the rules (of the Ministry of Education) about travelling limit the distance between classroom and home to ten miles, or an hour-and-a-quarter's journey.

But the best advice in cases of unjust selection for secondary schools is: 'Write to the Education Minister direct.' He or she has the power, under section 68 of the 1944 Education Act, to 'prevent unreasonable exercise of functions' on the part of a local authority. Since no part of this Act gives you the right to insist on a grammar- or comprehensive-school education, you can only claim the authority has been 'unreasonable'. The Minister is unlikely to interfere unless the authority has been 'grossly unjust'. If he or she does intervene, it will be only behind the scenes.

But if all parents wrote to the Minister when told that their children *with an IQ over 120* must go to a secondary modern school the Minister's hand would be greatly strengthened in fighting stubborn authorities. You must, however, do some homework before writing to the Minister. Thus, if you are complaining about equally able children in your area being selected, while your child is rejected, you *must* send their addresses in your letter, for the central issue is often one of geography (catchment areas).

Question: How can a poor parent avoid making a child leave school at fifteen, if the *only* reason for leaving is to supplement the family income?

Answer: You can apply to your local education authority for an Educational Maintenance Allowance (an EMA) to help you keep your child at school. You may find the application form difficult, or you may be timid about inquiring at the Town Hall, and so I suggest you contact either the Citizens' Advice Bureau or a local Councillor for help with your application.

The amount of money you are awarded will, like so many other things in our varied education service, depend on where you live. The most paid to parents of sixteen- and eighteen-year-olds is, respectively, £115 and £140 a year. But only *one* of the 165 authorities was paying as much as this at the time of the last investigation.

Not only are too few authorities paying enough, but too few parents are claiming these allowances. It has been estimated that nine out of ten families either do not know these grants exist, or have no idea what they are worth. Until local authorities do their duty, and tell parents exactly what an EMA is, and how much they might get, thousands of bright children will leave school at fifteen when they could have stayed on. It was estimated in 1953 in a Government report that one boy in ten, and one girl in six, left school too early because of financial hardship. As we noted earlier, it has been shown that 30,000 working-class children (who could have been doctors, teachers or lawyers) leave school each year to take up manual work. In 1967 a research worker at the University of Essex, Dennis Marsden, said: 'It seems unlikely that the 1953 figures have been reduced.' He added: 'In general, deprived at home, poorer children get an *inferior, shorter* education, and emerge from school with relatively lower, and more insecure earning power.' Poverty, even today, twenty-seven years after the end of the war, is still a major problem in our society. Fourteen per cent of the population, *including two million children*, live in poverty. Another survey in 1962 showed that one child in three had diets which lacked calcium, protein, and energy-giving foods.

Teachers should make sure they see the parents of all children from low-income homes, at least a year before the child is fifteen, to inform them about their right to an EMA. They can also help by visiting parents in their homes to discuss mutual problems. They can also make some arrangements for children whose home circumstances are cramped to do homework at school. Politicians should press the Government and the local authorities to cooperate in setting a national, uniform scale of allowances for staying-on at school. This would remove the anomalies and injustices caused by the wide variation of payment throughout the country.

If *you* would like to act unselfishly, you should urge in your local newspaper, in your PTA, in your Council or with your MP, for some action in this matter. You should press the politicians and teachers to do their duty by one in seven of the electorate.

Question: What can parents do if their child cannot spell?

Answer: You must make sure that your child *really is* backward in spelling. If you pick up some schoolwork he leaves lying about the house, you may misinterpret what you see. If you see a vast number of spelling mistakes crossed out by the teacher, or if they have been apparently ignored by the teacher, you still may have nothing to worry about : it may well be only a temporary phase. Go and chat to his teacher before you start worrying. Many teachers today encourage very young children to write down their thoughts as soon as they show both sufficient interest and skill. If their spelling is atrocious by adult standards, the teachers do not want to inhibit them by constant corrections at this stage. If your child's work is uncorrected it *may* mean the teacher is lazy, overworked or incompetent, but it is much more likely to indicate a deliberate policy to give a growing child confidence.

Adults have to be very careful about criticizing errors in an infant's writing. If a child writes 'yot' for 'yacht', you can see what he meant but you know the spelling is wrong. Even if the child writes 'szhp' for 'yacht', there is usually no need to get disturbed. He is probably trying to remember a word he saw under a picture of a sailing vessel. It was, of course, 'ship'.

Teachers have a pretty good idea of how well a child should be spelling words at each age. An eight-year-old may have a 'spelling age' of a seven-year-old. This would not be cause for worry. But if a junior-school pupil is *two* years behind then both parents and teachers need to take action. The child may be encouraged to make his own 'dictionary' of words he has misspelled, or he may 'collect' new words which interest him and keep them in a special box-file.

Parents need to realize that highly specific disabilities are extremely rare. Poor spelling may not be the worst of his disabilities: he may need a speech therapist, or more help with his reading. A child may have *slightly* defective sight, or hearing, which does not stop him reading or talking but which handicaps him when he tries to write words down for himself. You can after all guess at a word you are reading from the context, even though you can see it only hazily. In case your child is defective in this way, you could suggest to the school that he needs a thorough medical check-up with special attention to his vision, hearing and speech. You could be amazed at the improvement in his *spelling* when he is given a suitable hearing-aid.

There are two other points to remember when you see poor spelling in a child's schoolwork. Some children can see the words from 'left to right', but, when they write them down, they do so from right to left'. In this way 'was' becomes 'saw', and 'on' becomes 'no'. This fault can be cured by remedial teaching. The second factor to bear in mind is the effect on some children of a stern teacher who overstresses the importance of spelling. We all know how children can react against someone they dislike, and refuse to do the one thing they insist on. Again, a talk with the teacher (be as tactful as possible) should produce results.

Most cases of spelling difficulty need never arise. If all parents followed the advice given in the early chapters of this book, and if all teachers were careful not to teach spelling too soon or too formally, very few pupils would need special attention. If there are plenty of books, journals and newspapers in your home, your child will not need nagging to make him realize how exciting and useful reading and writing properly can be.

But if your child does need special treatment you should be prepared to assist either the remedial teacher, educational psychologist or child-guidance clinic in any way you can. They may ask you to help him at home. Keep in mind that lessons should be frequent (at least three times a week), short (twenty minutes at the most) and that the words practised should be the words the child uses, *not* difficult or unusual ones. Try not to practise words, such as 'there' and 'their', which might be confused, during the same lesson.

Finally try not to get over-anxious. Many adults achieve great success in life without being able to spell perfectly. You must beware of making a poor speller's life a misery.

If you are asked by the school, or the psychologist, to help at home, there are two books which you may find useful: *Backwardness In The Basic Subjects* by F. J. Schonell (Oliver & Boyd), and *Remedial Techniques In Basic School Subjects*, by Grace Fernald (McGraw-Hill).

Question: How can I help my child at home during the time he or she is taking an exam, such as 'O' level?

Answer: Exams are often the cause of emotional problems. Try to adopt a balanced attitude towards this tense period, and give your child a sense of proportion. You both know the exam is a very important matter. Try to keep up the candidate's morale without giving him either the impression you are indifferent whether he fails or succeeds, or the idea it will be a family tragedy if he does not pass.

I do not advise you to try bribery. Any attempt to create incentives by promising new bicycles or gold watches, as a reward for success, would upset the atmosphere of 'determined calm' I have outlined above. But by all means do what you can to give a child a surprise after the exams are over (and before the results are known), as you will both deserve the pleasure of giving and receiving.

Some parents are so keen on their child's success that they enrol with an adult-education college to take the same exam, at the same time, so they can work together. This is an excellent idea, but I cannot imagine many mothers having the time, the inclination, or the opportunity to take such a course.

But all parents can do *something* to make life easier, more productive and happier while a candidate is preparing for a crucial exam. As a parent, you are responsible for providing the room in which work outside school is to be done. If you are one of the lucky few who can give your child a study-bedroom of his own, he will be helped enormously. If this is out of the question, you can try to see he has at least a corner of his own, equipped with his own desk, comfortable working chair and ample shelf space for books. One way to avoid rows at such a tense time is to accept that it is best if he tidies his own desk and corner of the room. What looks like a mess to *you*, may well be a carefully-organized system of notes, papers, books and revision reminders.

Meal-times are another source of dissent and bad feeling. It is as well to have a full family discussion over this question so that there is the minimum of misunderstanding about arrangements at week-ends, or the evening routine. You do not want to interrupt him, when he is not hungry, and when he is working well, with some meal which cannot be kept in the oven. Casserole dishes are useful here, as they can be warmed up when they are needed, and they are not wasted if your child cannot eat with the rest of the family.

If your home conditions are really cramped and grossly unsuitable for study, you should consider encouraging your child to use the space available in the local library. He may agree it is far better to work there (in the company of others engaged in similar work) than to suffer the distractions of the television or radio at home. You can also consider adapting meal-times to match the closing time of the library.

A major factor which deters many parents from giving children a chance to work on their own at home is the cost of heating both a bedroom and a living-room at the same time. You may get the family to agree that the exam is so important to the candidate's whole future that it is worthwhile the rest of you sitting in silence – reading, writing letters, playing chess, doing the football pools, knitting, examining recipes, or filling up scrapbooks – while he gets on with his study. Some children insist, however, that they can work better with the radio or gramophone on. I have some sympathy with this, as I spend most of my working life typing in a noisy atmosphere, with five telephones ringing and hoots of laughter erupting from colleagues and secretaries. I am so used to noise while I write that I feel a bit unsettled if I try working in complete silence. But most children can be persuaded that their concentration on differential calculus is not improved by having the latest pop record going at full blast.

Try to ensure that your child's desk or work-table is not more than a foot higher than the seat of his chair. For long periods of work, chairs with plastic seats and backs are usually more comfortable than wooden chairs or tubular steel chairs with padded seats. It is also vital to examine the lighting in the room where he studies and to make sure it is not a cause of eye-strain. Some parents might consider installing fluorescent lighting. Although this is initially expensive, it is relatively cheaper to run and is far less liable to produce glare than the ordinary bulb.

Even if you were unhappy and unsuccessful at school, you can help your child with some of his subjects. Preparation for the English-language paper, for example, can be made more productive if you make a point of encouraging him to take an interest in articles in newspapers or talking points on television. Visits to theatres, museums and art galleries (where, incidentally, you can study the guide or catalogue together) can provide him with a rich experience which will help to provide ideas for essays and to broaden his vocabulary. Some parents may be able to go and see a play which he has seen on a school outing, and which is one of his set-books in the literature paper. By casually discussing the plot and the characters, and the impression they made on you, you can help him get his own ideas on the work in better order. I remember my father stimulating me in this way when we saw Laurence Olivier in the film *Richard III*. He sat quietly through the film, as the rest of the audience roared with laughter at the villainous king. As we came out he said : 'I don't see how a murderer can be amusing.' This remark made me consider how much of Olivier's performance was in the text of the play, and how much he should be faulted for making evil look too attractive.

You can also help your child by discussing with him his revision time-table. But you must make sure he does not waste valuable time compiling elaborate plans about what he is *going* to do, when he should be getting on with his studies. If his time-table is both realistic and approved by his teacher, he will be better able to cope with the tension of the last three days before the exam. If the time-table has been completed by this stage you will be better able to reassure him as the vital day approaches.

During the two weeks when he is sitting his papers, your main role is to ensure that he gets his favourite foods (within the limits of health and economy), and a constant supply of clean clothes so that he does not get uncomfortable in the sticky atmosphere of the exam room. It is *unwise* to give him a new fountain pen the day the exam starts. Pens take at least a fortnight's getting used to, and a strange new pen may well distract him in the exam.

Above all try to reduce tension in the home while the revision period and the exam are in progress. Family rows cannot be organized or delayed, but many of them can occur while a child is at the library or at school. No great effort is needed to avoid letting the candidate know about some family issue or domestic squabble until the exam is over, if at all.

Finally, a word about coaching. No outside tutors should be employed without the agreement of the child's teacher. There are cases where a harassed teacher with a class of forty would welcome a borderline child getting some individual, *expert* tuition. But consult the school about how much you should pay, and make some effort to check whether the coach is telling the truth about his qualifications. Much harm can be done by some of the so-called tutors who offer their expensive services to unsuspecting mothers.

Question: What can be done about school reports? Why are

they so difficult to understand? Why do they tell us so little that is really useful about our child's work?

Answer: Britain's 350,000 teachers write about twenty million reports a year, most of which are misleading, unfair, or inaccurate. Some are worse than useless, others are downright harmful. Parents should urge teachers either to make reports more detailed, or else to scrap them altogether. If they tell you Sammy's conduct is 'fair', or Janet is 'not interested in the subject', or Brian's work has been 'satisfactory' – what do they mean? Has Sammy been swearing, late for school or bullying? Why is Janet 'not interested' now, when last term, with a different teacher, she was top of the class? Is Brian 'satisfactory' at French because he smiles at the teacher and is polite? Or is the teacher thinking 'The boy comes from a deprived home – he is doing as well as I thought he would'.

Some private schools do not tell the truth about a child's achievement. They play down a pupil's failure, because his parents are paying large fees. They understate a pupil's success because they do not want the child to get complacent, and their income depends on their exam record.

But parents need the truth told in a tolerant, humane, tactful manner. We have seen elsewhere how children can live *down* to a poor reputation, by being depressed at being put in a 'C' stream or in a secondary modern school; it is important to recognize that children can be equally dispirited by an inaccurate, unfair, carelessly-written report from a teacher, who dashed it off just to get the 'blasted thing' over with. Leslie Keating, a teacher with thirty-seven years' experience, claimed, in his book *The School Report* (Kenneth Mason), that many teachers cannot even remember the face of the pupil they are writing about.

Some enlightened headteachers are experimenting in this field. They are inviting parents to put *their* comments on the reports before signing them and returning them to the school – to show they have been seen. These teachers realize parents can reveal many vital aspects of a child's personality and background that a teacher may miss. They also welcome the parents whose children have the worst reports to come and see them, to talk things over. You could bring this idea up at the next meeting of your PTA.

Question: What can parents do if children acquire ugly accents or bad language from their schoolmates?

Answer: Many parents pay a great deal of money to send their children to private schools so that they will learn to speak with an 'acceptable' accent. Many of these schools are no better academically than State schools, and some are inferior. You must make up your mind about priorities in this matter. A good school is not a finishing school. A good school teaches a pupil how to live in a community, and how to understand people from different walks of life. Most children are 'bi-lingual'. They have one language for the playground and one for their homes. If parents speak consistently in the way they wish their children to speak there is little chance of a child picking up permanent bad habits.

It is worth remembering that parents with children at day schools spend enough time with their children to be able to counter-balance the effect of their schoolmates' bad or ungrammatical speech. You should also realize that the posh accent (which is thought of as BBC English) is really a regional accent found in South-East England and spoken by Oxbridge graduates or their imitators. Anyone who thinks that a rich Somerset or broad Newcastle accent is ugly, or a handicap, should consider the number of successful men who have regional accents.

Parents and teachers should aim to get children to respect the spelling and the grammatical order of words. Any attempt to have elocution classes for Cockney pupils is a mistake. We do not want a nation of people who speak with grey, uniform voices.

If your child is spending too much time in the company of pupils who use four-lettered words you should have a quiet word with his headteacher or class-teacher. When your child gets older he will soon spot that most of the people he respects can manage to express themselves without such language.

In any good school debates will be organized in class or in societies and children will get plenty of practice at speaking in front of an audience. This will show them the importance of speaking clearly and effectively. Such activities are far more useful than asking forty children to chant 'How now brown cow'.

Question: What can a parent do if a child is bullied or bullies others?

Answer: Some children are bullies because they have bullying parents. Others are working off their frustrations at being less intelligent than their brothers and sisters, or slower than their classmates. Some who fear their own homosexuality react by persecuting the most effeminate boy in the class.

All parents should make certain that the incident of bullying, or of being bullied, has really taken place. Even the most honest children can get things out of perspective. They may feel some child is 'picking on' them, but it could just be part of the usual, harmless rough-and-tumble of the playground.

Once you are convinced that the situation is serious, you should see the headteacher as quickly as possible. If he is indifferent, and appears to believe that enduring bullying is a part of character-building, or always trivial 'ragging', you should be firm and point out that good schools are happy schools, where violence has no place.

If the headteacher does not end the bullying you should contact ACE who will put their legal department at your disposal.

Glossary of Educational Terms

The aim of this glossary is to enable you to approach teachers more confidently. The education system is very confusing unless you are aware of what initials and terms stand for. Your child may miss an opportunity if you do not know, for example, the meaning of 'HNC' or 'CNAA' or 'day release'.

AGREED SYLLABUS : A syllabus of religious instruction agreed between the local education authority, religious denominations, and teachers.

AIDED SCHOOL : Voluntary school whose governors or managers are responsible for the provision and maintenance of the premises, and can appoint and dismiss staff, and decide the religious teaching.

ALL-AGE SCHOOL : A school which takes children from five to fifteen. Many village schools were of this type : they are fast disappearing.

BILATERAL SCHOOL : A secondary school which is in effect a combination of two schools, eg, a grammar/technical or a technical/modern.

BURNHAM COMMITTEE : The committee which agrees teachers' salaries. Representatives of the seven teachers' unions and the local authorities all have a place on this body.

CENTRAL ADVISORY COUNCILS : Two bodies, one for England and one for Wales, set up to advise the Minister of Education on theory and practice.

CHIEF EDUCATION OFFICER : The chief, permanent, paid official of a local education authority. He may also be known as the director of education, or secretary for education, or simply the education officer.

CITY AND GUILDS OF LONDON INSTITUTE : The largest of the independent examining bodies in technical education. Its address is : 76 Portland Place, London W1. Tel : 01-580 3050.

COLLEGE-BASED STUDENT : A student doing a 'sandwich' course, an advanced course involving alternate periods (usually of six months) of theoretical training in a technical college, and practical training in industry, and who is enrolled by the college.

COMMONER : A student at Oxford or Cambridge who has not won a scholarship or exhibition.

COMPREHENSIVE SCHOOL : A non-selective secondary school

which admits children from the whole range of ability in an area, and gives them a wide variety of courses.

CONTROLLED SCHOOL : A voluntary school (a school built by a voluntary body, eg, the Church, but maintained by the local education authority) in which the managers or governors have the right to appoint a limited number of teachers, who will give special religious instruction. They are nearly all C of E.

COUNCIL FOR NATIONAL ACADEMIC AWARDS (see Chapter Nine) : A body which awards degrees (of university standard) to non-university students.

COUNTY AWARD : An award to a student by the local education authority. It may be a scholarship, exhibition or bursary.

CURRICULUM : The plan of lessons and subjects taken by a class or a school.

DALTON PLAN : A way of arranging school work so that pupils can spend much time in private study.

DAY CONTINUATION SCHOOL : An institution giving continued education for young workers released for the purpose by their employers.

DAY NURSERY (see Chapter Three) : A place where babies and young children may be left while the parents are at work. Not to be confused with a nursery school. A day nursery is organized by the *health*, not the education, authority.

DAY RELEASE (see Chapter Nine) : A system whereby employers allow days off for education without loss of pay.

DIRECT GRANT SCHOOL : One of the 177 grammar schools which, although independent, receive a grant direct from the Ministry on condition that 25 per cent of the places each year shall be offered, either directly or through the local education authority, to pupils who have at any time previously attended a State school for not less than two years. Some places are available for fee-payers.

DIRECT METHOD : A way of teaching languages by concentrating on using them in conversation rather than on formal grammar.

EDUCATION WELFARE OFFICER : Originally a school attendance officer, whose main duty was to help to ensure school attendance. He is now much more engaged with the welfare problems of children.

EVENING INSTITUTE : An establishment for further education having no day sessions, and perhaps housed in school premises used during day for normal school instruction.

EXTRA-MURAL DEPARTMENT : A university department which organizes courses for students who are not full members of the university.

FORM ENTRY : A method of describing the size of the school by the number of forms (or classes) admitted each year. Thus a two-form entry school will have sixty or eighty new pupils each year – divided into two forms.

FROEBEL METHOD : A system of education pioneered by F. W. A. Froebel (1782–1852), emphasizing educational play for young children.

FURTHER EDUCATION : Education (full-time or part-time) after leaving school for young people and adults; the term should be distinguished from 'higher education', which means the universities and teachers' training colleges.

GIRLS' PUBLIC DAY SCHOOL TRUST : A trust set up to give secondary education for girls. It has about twenty-five schools.

GOVERNORS, BOARD OF : The body to whom the headteacher of a school is responsible. In independent schools they are self-appointing, or are appointed by the terms of a trust. In State schools they are appointed by the local education authority in accordance with an instrument of government approved by the Minister of Education. The members of a governing body of a primary school are called managers.

HER MAJESTY'S INSPECTOR (HMI) : Ministry officials who inspect schools and make reports. There are about 550 in England and Wales.

INTELLIGENCE QUOTIENT (IQ) : The percentage that the mental age is of the chronological age (eg, a child of eight with a mental age of ten has an IQ of $10/8 \times 100$, which is 125). The IQ is the measure of intelligence. A university student has an IQ of at least 120, and an average pupil one of about 100.

MAINTAINED SCHOOL : One maintained by the local education authority. The term includes voluntary aided, and voluntary controlled schools.

MONTESSORI METHOD : A system of education pioneered by Maria Montessori which lays emphasis on freedom, self-education, and sense and muscle training.

MULTILATERAL SCHOOL : A secondary school which provides grammar, technical and secondary modern education in separately organized divisions.

NATIONAL CERTIFICATE (see Chapter Nine): Includes the HNC and ONC.

NATIONAL DIPLOMA (see Chapter Nine) : Includes the HND and OND.

NON-VOCATIONAL EDUCATION : Education not directed towards a job or career.

PAEDIATRICIAN : Person who specializes in the study of children.

PART III OF THE EDUCATION ACT, 1944 : The section which deals with the registration and inspection of independent schools.

PROJECT : A study undertaken by a class (or, on occasion, by the whole school) on one broad subject (eg, the local neighbourhood) through which the normal school subjects are studied.

QUALIFIED TEACHER : A teacher who has successfully taken a course at a training college or university department of education, and been awarded the Teacher's Certificate and granted qualified-teacher status by the Ministry. After 1973 no graduate will be able to enter the profession until he has been trained.

RELIGIOUS INSTRUCTION : The only subject which schools are obliged to teach by law. In county and controlled schools it is given in accordance with an 'agreed syllabus', and parents may withdraw their children from it if they wish. In voluntary aided schools the faith taught is determined by the denomination of the organization which founded the school. There is a strong movement gathering momentum which is pressing for reforms in religious education. Many church leaders and teachers believe children should learn more about the lives of good men (such as Socrates, Jesus and Gandhi), and less about specific religious doctrines. The next Education Act will take account of this view and of the decline in church-going since the last war.

SETTING : The division of an age-group which is already divided into forms into different 'sets', according to their ability in some subjects (eg, a boy could be in the top 'set' for French, and the bottom 'set' for Maths). Many experts think this is the best way to divide children, as a child is not condemned as a total 'failure' by his overall performance. He gains confidence from shining in those subjects he is good at. (See also 'Streaming'.)

SPECIAL SCHOOL : A primary or secondary school for pupils who need special treatment because of some mental or physical handicap, or some maladjustment.

SPECIALIZATION (see Chapter Nine) : Concentration at school or university on one or a few subjects, usually to the exclusion of others.

STREAMING : The grouping of children on the basis of their overall ability. This practice is under strong attack from critics who say it should be abolished in primary schools. The Plowden report condemned it on the grounds that children live *down* to the reputation they are given. Nine out of ten pupils never move out of a 'stream' once they have been condemned to it, often as early as the age of seven.

TRIPARTITE SYSTEM : The division (now completely discredited) of secondary schools into grammar, technical and secondary modern. It was based on the iniquitous eleven-plus exam which misplaced one child in every six (a total of 70,000 mistakes *every year*). This system will be replaced by a nation-wide system of non-selective schools which will give parents *real* freedom of choice, and *all* children a chance of a proper education.

TRIPOS : A final exam at Cambridge, for undergraduates,

taken in two parts, the first of which is taken at the end of a student's second year. Name taken from three-legged stool used by students in medieval times.

UNIVERSITY GRANTS COMMITTEE: Body which distributes grants of money from the Treasury to the forty-five universities.

YOUTH EMPLOYMENT SERVICE (see Chapter Nine): Service run by either the local education authority or the Department of Employment and Productivity, to help teenagers find jobs or careers.

SUGGESTED READING

Fernald, Grace, *Remedial Techniques in Basic School Subjects*. McGraw-Hill: London, 1943.

Jackson, Brian, and Marsden, Dennis, *Education and the Working Class*. Routledge & Kegan Paul: London, 1962.

Keating, Leslie, *The School Report*. Kenneth Mason: Havant, Hants., 1969.

Larsson, Lena, *Your Child's Room*. Penguin Books: London, 1965.

CHAPTER NINE

Education After School— Job Prospects

Too often parents assume that when their child leaves school, unless he has done well enough to gain a university place or to enter a teacher-training college, his education is at an end. Teachers themselves are not usually in a position to offer much advice to the parents of an average child, who is likely to have few if any passes at 'O' level. This chapter is about the opportunities that the network of further-education colleges offers to such young people, not just to learn a trade but also to catch up on the education that their schooling did not give them. You probably regard these colleges as 'techs', full of rough engineering apprentices and little else. If so, you could not be further from the truth, for they are a whole range of institutions that cater for many subjects at many levels, and they are unique to this country.

As an illustration of how the system works, take the case of Linda. She left school when she was sixteen, without a single 'O' level. But ten years later she began a degree course in history and economics at the London School of Economics. She had achieved her entrance requirements by going to evening classes at Wandsworth Technical College.

Linda was very fortunate. When she decided to continue her education she was twenty-three years old and had, by this time, already passed two 'O' levels at night school. Her good luck came when her mother suggested contacting the Inner London Education Authority's office to find out what was available for someone of Linda's age. This ILEA put her in touch with the college at Wandsworth, and there she had her second piece of good fortune. The head of the business-studies department was so impressed with Linda that he recommended her for an 'A' level course, although she was not strictly eligible. She did brilliantly in her exams, and won her place at the LSE.

This true story teaches us three lessons. First, it shows how the network of further-education colleges provides a second chance for thousands of school-leavers who have 'failed' at school. Secondly, it indicates the importance of knowing the right person, in the right place, who can help you find out the opportunities available. Thirdly, it demonstrates the value of imaginative teachers, and local-authority officials, willing to bend the rules to help someone who deserves a second chance.

Further Education

But the above case is very unusual. Very few of the 350,000 children who leave school each year without a single 'O' level pass manage to get the second chance Linda had. The reason is simply that far too few parents, and teachers, realize what is available in the technical colleges, and even fewer encourage pupils in Linda's position to search them out. One of the causes of this ignorance is the complexity of the further-education system. Too few people outside the colleges understand the language used in further education, and teachers make little effort to do enough homework on the subject to advise pupils or parents. Even in the further-education department of the Ministry of Education there is nobody who has either taught, or studied, in a technical college. This widespread public ignorance extends to newspapers, where many editors assume the public want to read about the public schools, the universities, and the State-school system. They think, for the most part, there is little glamour, interest, or excitement in the 'local techs'.

But *whatever* your interests, the chances are that a further-education college, or a university extra-mural department, the Workers' Education Association (WEA), or some similar body, will be able to provide a course. If you live in a large city you will probably not have to travel far to find it. More than *three million* people with ages ranging from fifteen to eighty-nine* benefit from these courses at present. I hope that this chapter will aid many more, either to get a second chance to gain qualifications, or to enrich their leisure by pursuing some study that interests them.

You must first understand the terms used in the technical-college field. Once you have grasped their meaning, you will be able to choose which course suits you, or your child, best. It is important to realize at the outset that further education is the poor relation of the universities. When we talk of 'further education' we mean the provision, for people who have left school, in colleges run by local authorities. These colleges have various names: College of Technology, Polytechnic, College of Commerce, Technical College, College of Further Education, College of Art, Farm Institute or College of Agriculture.

In some cases the name may indicate the level to which subjects are taught: a college of technology is often a large institution, drawing students from a wide area, and offering a wide range of courses up to degree level. A polytechnic is a centre for advanced studies, usually of degree level. The Labour Government began after 1965 to start a national system of thirty new polytechnics. Some of the degree courses at these new colleges are superior to those in any of the universities. Polytechnics will be smaller than most universities; they will have about 2,000 students, whereas the average university has around 3,500. But the biggest polytechnics will have 5,000 students, and the smallest about 500. A college of further education serves a smaller area, and specializes in work of a less advanced level. Other titles, eg, College of Commerce, may show more clearly the main subjects taught without indicating their level.

The main characteristic of all these colleges is that they cater for both full-time and part-time students. Most of the

* There was a student of this age at Southgate Tecnical College, at the time of writing.

full-time students come straight from school, or are sent to the college by their employers to improve their qualifications. Most of the part-time students are sent by their employers either for one day a week ('day release'), or for periods of a few weeks at a time ('block release'). Other part-time students study in the evenings only, on their own initiative.

Day-release and Sandwich Courses

The opportunities for 'day release' vary enormously from job to job. It is important that your child asks about this *before* starting work with a firm. A boy going into a bank or an insurance company has a one in 11 chance of being allowed day release. His brother, who works in the gas, electrical, or water-supply industries, can be virtually certain of being given time off to study in this way. Roughly 16 out of 17 boys starting work in shops are forced to study at night if they want to earn new qualifications.

The situation for girls is as usual even worse. If your daughter works in public administration or defence establishments she has a very good chance of being given time off to study, but if she goes into a bank her chances drop to about one in 66. In no job, apart from public administration or defence departments, are her chances better than one in five. Only two per cent of girls in the leather-goods and fur trades are given this opportunity.

The extension of this idea is what is called the 'sandwich' course, on which the student alternates between studying in college and working in industry or commerce. These 'sandwich' students can go straight to the college from school, and not be committed to any one employer, or else they can be sent to the college by their employer who realizes the value of training for young people. Many degree courses are organized on a sandwich basis.

An advantage of the system is its close links with business and industry. It is one of its great strengths that students mix with people who are working outside the college. The teachers have often been in industry, and know all about handling a wage packet, overtime, and 'clocking-in', so they cannot be accused of adopting 'ivory-tower' attitudes.

As a consequence, sandwich-course students usually take a more responsible view of their studies than many undergraduates at, say, Oxford or Cambridge or the LSE. They mix with mature students, are under a job discipline, and get many opportunities to see what life is like for other people ranging from apprentices to retired bank clerks. It could be significant that there have been more student mutinies and rebellions in universities and art colleges than there have in further-education colleges. The presence of more mature students, and the experience of life outside the college and the classroom, could be the factors which make technical-college students less impatient to change the world in a week-end sit-down.

Nothing is hard and fast in the further-education system. An opportunity missed at one point can be retrieved at another, and it is seldom too late. Those who left school too soon get an opportunity to renew their academic studies. The colleges offer a way from part-time to full-time study for those at work to gain higher qualifications. They run courses at a number of levels in any given subject so that students without any qualifications can come in at the bottom and work their way up, while those with 'O' levels, or whatever, can enter at some intermediate point.

Who pays for these courses? Further education is incredibly cheap. Students do not normally have to pay fees up to, and during, the session in which they reach the age of eighteen. After that they may be liable for nominal fees, but grants may be given by local education authorities to both full- and part-time students, and to 'sandwich-course' students. The best account of the grants available is in the *Grants Yearbook*, published by the National Union of Students (3 Endsleigh Street, London WC1). If you want additional information you should contact your local education authority, or the further-education department at the Ministry of Education (Curzon Street, London W1).

After School

The decision to raise the school-leaving age to sixteen may well affect *where* your child is educated during that year. The Government is sympathetic to the idea that many fifteen-year-olds could spend it partly in school, and partly in a further-education college. Teachers are not keen to lose the extra money which they get for having pupils who stay on beyond the normal leaving age. But a compromise is likely to be worked out so that pupils stay on the school register, but spend most of their time in the local college. The law would have to be changed to allow this, but the advantages are considerable. Pupils at this age, especially girls, may not like the restrictions of being at school, and, as we noted earlier, many leave school just to get away from being treated as a child. They would find the idea of going to college far more appealing than the prospect of wearing the school uniform for another year.

Such a compulsory year at a technical college could open up new horizons, and ambitions, for your children. Mixing with a variety of students would give them a chance to rethink their ideas about the future. The connexion between social class and the classroom is strong, and social-class factors affect a child's whole academic career. Many one-class 'neighbourhood' schools fail to give pupils an idea of the way in which other people, in other social classes, live and behave. A year in a technical college, with its wide-ranging facilities, would also introduce the student to subjects that are unknown in the schools. Indeed, some parents persuade their children to complete their education in this way for this very reason.

Higher Levels

At the other end of the scale, the high-level colleges offer excellent degree courses in imaginative combinations. The Council for National Academic Awards (CNAA) provides its own degrees for students studying outside the universities. The number of students on CNAA courses has risen from

3,000 to 25,000 in seven years. If your child is a talented school-leaver, perhaps with three or four 'A' levels, or has failed to gain a place or to find the right kind of course at one of the forty-five universities, you should write to the CNAA, at 3 Devonshire Street, London W1N 2BA, for full details of the courses offered. These CNAA degrees are by no means inferior to university degrees. Indeed it is quite clear that many of them are of a *higher* standard and *more* difficult to pass than university degrees. By 1971, the Council was able to point to many courses which were superior to anything in the universities. Similar information is also available in the 'Compendium of Advanced Courses in Technical Colleges', obtainable from the Council for Technological Education, Tavistock House (South), Tavistock Square, London WC1.

Four national qualifications can be obtained through these colleges: the Higher National Certificate, the Higher National Diploma, the Ordinary National Certificate and the Ordinary National Diploma. The HNC is gained by part-time study, and is recognized in fields such as building, engineering, science and business studies as a high-level technical qualification. The HND can be achieved by full-time or sandwich-course studies, and is recognized as the equivalent of a pass degree at university. The ONC is obtained by part-time studies. It is recognized, depending on the level of pass, as an entrance qualification for degree-level work. The OND is a similar full-time course.

Careers Advice

The courses offered in the colleges all contain a vocational element that will aid your child in his, or her, chosen career. Be it 'O' level or degree work, the student has often by this time made a choice of what job he or she would like in the future. That choice will depend on the advice given to the child during the last year or so at school, advice that *may be grossly inadequate*. Most schools delegate the work of careers guidance to a particular teacher, who may have a special interest in the topic, or who may just be the one member of staff with some free time. In the last year, time is set aside for talks, lectures, etc., during the school day on the matter of future jobs. As *you* will not be attending these, it is imperative that you find out from your child just what is said, and done, in such periods. What you *will* be invited to attend, is a series of careers conventions where local employers and people from the nationalized industries will explain to you, and the child, what their particular industry has to offer.

The time available to discuss your child's future will be extremely limited, and it will help considerably if you are fore-armed with the facts as to *what* colleges offer *what* courses in your area. Ideally you should acquire the prospectuses of the colleges, and go through them with your child, *before* the careers convention. Then you can devote your attention to topics which will help your child the most.

For the vast majority of children leaving school, deciding on a future career, and the education to accompany it, is the most crucial decision that they will have to make. It is one *you* should help them make. But, as we have seen, it is never too late to start a course leading to qualifications if you, and your child, realize the full potential of, say, the polytechnics, and the rich opportunities in further education generally. Follow my advice and you have every chance of helping your child find a job or a career he or she will enjoy.

Into Work

If your child feels he has finished studying, and wants to find the best available job, he can do one of three things : (*a*) contact the local youth-employment officer (whose address is in the telephone book) or (*b*) if he has high qualifications he can contact the Careers Research and Advisory Centre (Bateman Street, Cambridge); or (*c*) in *all* cases contact the Careers Service, The *Daily Express*, Fleet Street, London EC4. If you use the *Daily Express* service you should tell your son to write stating his name, age and sex (to avoid confusion over Christian names which are the same for both sexes), giving his qualifications, if any, and his state of health. The service is organized in conjunction with the Cornmarket Careers Centre (42 Conduit Street, London W1).

Such new services are a *supplement* to, not a substitute for, the work of careers teachers and youth-employment officers. Senior officials of the Youth Employment Service realize their local officers are grossly underpaid and overworked but they would like to hear of any complaints about them. They assure me that your local officer will do his best to help you.

You may be forced to depend on the help given by the independent organizations and by careers teachers. But the majority of teachers do not, as we have noted, provide the best available advice. Paul Gillett, principal careers officer for the Inner London Education Authority, says:

> The secondary-school child usually has to decide on courses at the age of thirteen. This is much too young to specialize. But, as they *have to* under the current system, we must do all we can to help them make the right choice. As soon as pupils have to make this decision, they should understand what is likely to happen to them as a result in their adult life. Children cannot make up their minds about a career until they have the facts and available information. This is a long-term process which requires more school participation.

Men like Paul Gillett urge schools to make careers guidance an integral part of the curriculum for all pupils. (Any teacher anxious to improve his skills and knowledge about careers should contact the National Association of Careers Teachers at the NUT headquarters, Hamilton House, Mabledon Place, London WC1.) They point out that undergraduates who fail to finish their courses have in many cases been badly advised much earlier in their lives, and are studying the *wrong* subject. He also recognizes that reforms are needed in the youth-employment service. Every youth-employment officer should have had full-time training. And, with more and more graduates coming into the service, we must have salaries commensurate with those of graduates in other fields. At present the youth-employment officer earns less than many school-teachers.

Parents will spot the main conclusion to be drawn from these diagnoses. We have untrained and poorly-paid employment officers trying to help children who come to them too late, perhaps without the qualifications necessary and probably without the information they should have received from teachers. In Hertfordshire, for example, only *half* the secondary schools work closely with the local-authority service, and very few schools invite the employment officers to come to speak to children at the age when they need advice the most – *before* they start specializing in some subjects and dropping others. It is pointless for a group of sixth-formers to hear a talk about the attractions of working for ICI, say, if they dropped the studies such a job requires four years before. Clearly we need a national careers advisory service for people of *all* ages. It should be staffed by fully-trained, well-paid men who are capable of conveying to thirteen-year-olds some idea of the variety of opportunities before them, and who are able to advise middle-aged workers, axed after a merger, how to start in a new field.

Of course some teenagers do have unusual ambitions which are not always practicable. One boy wanted to be a game warden on a reserve in central Africa. This was almost certainly out of the question, but there seems little excuse for the employment officer who suggested he ought to be a butcher. Similarly, a successful national-newspaper journalist was originally asked by his youth-employment officer to give up such fancy thoughts as being a reporter, and to become a lathe operator. Do not allow your child to be slotted into the same inadequate trap. The girl who is offered a job in a hardware shop is the girl who could become a teacher – if she is left with other alternatives.

Your Responsibilities

Parents must find out what they can do to help their children choose the right job. In any event you should persuade your child to keep studying and gaining qualifications for as long as possible, even while working. When children seem determined to leave school they are, as we noted earlier, often merely showing their natural desire to be treated as adults. If you find out all the facts, and explain to your child how he *can* leave school *and* still keep studying, this may well be the solution to the problem.

Unfortunately, as we have seen, far too few schools have thriving, effective parent–teacher associations, and there is far too little contact between home and school. If you are not on close terms with the staff at *your* child's school, it is hard to see how you can get a true picture of his ability, and prospects if he were to stay on.

Parents can give their own, and other children, 'a chance' by pressing for better relations with secondary schools. If, individually or together, parents take the initiative and show the headteacher that there *is* a powerful demand for fruitful relations and frequent contact with the staff, they will probably succeed. *Without* adequate information, the parent can be the last person who should proffer advice. Father who has made a career in a particular field may speak from his own practical experience about that field, but even this information may no longer be valid in our rapidly changing society. *With* adequate information, you can be your child's greatest ally.

The best single source of information on the full range of courses, outside schools and universities, is the invaluable *Directory of Further Education* (Cornmarket Press Ltd, 42 Conduit Street, London W1). From the same publishers you can also obtain the *Dictionary of Opportunities for School-Leavers*, and a paperback called *Careers for School-Leavers*.

But many parents find such reference books difficult to cope with, and admittedly these large volumes can look formidable to a tired housewife or an exhausted father. It is much easier, for those of you who are daunted by such books, to understand a kindly, experienced adult's explanation of the opportunities open to your child. I do, therefore, urge you to drop in at your local technical college and ask when you might see some member of staff about your child's future. If, as is likely, he is getting little detailed information about further education or careers from his school, and if, as is possible, the local youth-employment officer is more concerned with filling vacancies on his books than with finding something to suit your unique child's needs, your best hope is to approach the technical college.

But in order to get the most out of such an interview you should spend some time with your child trying to find out whether he has the resolution to pursue further education, or what kind of employment would match his personality best. As neither of you will have much idea of the enormous range of jobs and studies available, there is no need to be too precise in these discussions. My father wanted me to be a lawyer (most policemen harbour this ambition), and I talked vaguely about wanting 'irregular hours, a chance to travel and live by my wits'. I thought briefly about trying to be a detective, but my father spoke persuasively against this idea. It was not until I'd been at Cambridge for two years that I realized journalism was the only profession for me.

Although you may find the reference books confusing and time-consuming, they will be useful for both you and your child in at least one important way; the lists of studies and jobs in them will spark off thoughts, and enable you to strive for a wider range of choice among the 80,000 jobs and careers.

If you read of some possible career, or hear one mentioned, make a note of it and also write down your child's response to it. Take the list with you when you go to see the man at the technical college so that you can avoid wasting his time with an incoherent verbal report.

Remember, above all, that the child who comes to a decision earliest may be at a great advantage over other children. Early decisions about courses or careers mean that the child can move in the right direction more quickly. But this does *not* mean you should nag a child to make up his mind before he is ready. As we have seen, the further-education system in all its glorious variety is capable of catering for people who change their minds or make them up long after others have been settled in employment or training.

One of the best examples of the wide range of opportunities available in our age for those who make late decisions is the popularity of correspondence courses. Over 500,000 people (including housewives, policemen, nuns, prisoners, midwives, factory workers, and missionaries) take advantage of these studies, and some of the students who are enriching their leisure are well over eighty. Education, as we have seen, is *not* something which ends when you accept your first wage-packet, or stand at the altar as a bride.

In 1969 the Correspondence Accreditation Council was launched to preserve standards in these studies. I advise any parents (possibly thinking of taking an 'O' level to give a child moral support) to check with, say, the National Extension College in Cambridge, one of the leading correspondence colleges, before they embark on a course. Some of the studies offered in the past, by *some* colleges, have had dubious value, so it is wise to ensure you are getting your money's worth.

Another example of the chances provided by our rich education system is the 'Open University' which used to be known as the 'University of the Air'. This institution gives even more opportunities to adults (*including those without any qualifications at all*) who have missed satisfying educational ambitions earlier in life. At the time of writing the Government is considering changing the nature of the Open University by allowing some 18-year-olds who cannot get into other universities to take its courses. This is likely to happen unless more adults wake up to the fact that the Open University could be for *them*. Far too few have realized that *unqualified* applicants are welcomed at this institution. Many manual workers and housewives are studying for degrees on the courses which are provided through radio and television. Not all the studying is done at long distance, however; each year students get a chance to attend three-week-long courses where they meet tutors and other would-be graduates. I urge everyone in education to publicize this unique university which has confounded its critics so far.

It is difficult to imagine a determined adult who could not

be helped either by this university or by the National Extension College in Cambridge. Their addresses can be found on pages 246 and 247.

For far too long the majority of people have accepted the fact that education was for the lucky few. They have created the myth that education stops when the school-gates close for the last time, and that all that matters afterwards is getting a wage-packet. They have tolerated the idea that a minority of citizens have careers which are financially rewarding, while the rest of society do boring jobs. Now, however, more and more people are beginning to realize the spiritual *and* financial rewards of learning and re-training.

I know a man who regretted not working in films for most of his adult life. Then, at the age of forty-five, he met a television producer who encouraged him to write a script for a film. Both the script and the film won awards, and the man now has a new lease of life, and a vastly higher income, working as head of a large office in the biggest British film studio.

With determination, imagination and good luck, you and your children can learn the vital lesson – it is *never too late*.

Suggested Further Reading

1   Your local education officials have a special service designed to tell you of degree courses at further-education colleges. The Ministry of Education will supply you with the name of your local advisory officer. I suggest you discover his name and address as soon as your child is sixteen. The Ministry also publishes pamphlets such as *On Course* and *What Next After 'A' Level?*

2   Two other publications containing a great deal of useful information are *Into Further Education*, published by the Association of Teachers in Technical Institutions, Hamilton House, Mabledon Place, London WC1, and *Going Places* by Willem Van Der Eyken, published by Macdonald.

3   You may also be able to arouse your child's interest in an unusual subject which is not often taught at school, and

which may be suitable for a further or higher education course, if you contact the Advisory Centre in Cambridge. Remember that there are 80,000 different jobs and careers – *every* parent, teacher and child needs hours of help before making decisions.

4 Pamphlets about CNAA degrees are provided free by the Council. Your child should have five GCE passes, including two appropriate subjects at 'A' level, or four GCE passes, with three appropriate subjects at 'A' level, or on certain courses an OND or ONC at a good standard. (Remember that good passes at CSE are counted as equivalent to 'O' level passes.)

5 The ACE also provides a supplement called *From School to University*, containing a list of thirty-six different subjects your child could study at CNAA degree level. It gives the names of the technical colleges and polytechnics which provide these top-level courses. ACE has another pamphlet with similar advice called *Taking a Degree at a Technical College*.

7 Some of the books listed at the end of Chapter Ten are also relevant to this one. I specially recommend the books and pamphlets dealing with individual careers and subjects.

SUGGESTED READING

Careers for School Leavers. Cornmarket: London, 1969.
Directory of Further Education. Cornmarket: London, 1969.
Grants Year Book. National Union of Students: London, 1969.
Hartley, Kathleen, *Careers for the Unqualified*. Wolfe: London, 1970.
Heap, Brian, *A Guide to Careers and Courses*. Ward Lock Educational: London, 1968.
Inside Information Series. Careers and Education Advice, The Dickens Press: London, 1969.
Van Der Eyken, Willem, *Going Places*. Macdonald: London, 1968.

CHAPTER TEN

Could Your Child Go to University?

It is becoming increasingly difficult to gain a place at university. In the past twelve years the proportion of successful candidates with the minimum qualifications (two 'A' level passes) has fallen considerably. Children with sympathetic parents, and a go-ahead school behind them, have a much better chance of getting to university than those whose parents are inexperienced, or apathetic, or whose school does not keep up with the quickly changing situation in this field.

The all-important decision of choosing the *right* subject to specialize in, at the age of fourteen or so, determines a child's field of choice when he tries for a university place. You may feel that the day your child comes home and says: 'They say at school I ought to try for a place at Salford University to study engineering', is the big moment in the whole process of gaining entry. But the day, years earlier, when he sits down to tea and mutters: 'Old Jones says I can't do French next year', may be much more crucial. It means he *may* have lost all chance of reading French, or any other foreign language, or any course requiring these subjects, at university. If you want to help your child in the annual scramble for places, remember that the *time* factor is vital.

Specialization

I cannot stress too strongly how foolish it is for teachers and parents to relax their interest and energies when children reach secondary schools. You may feel relieved, or resigned, when they leave their primary school, but you cannot allow these emotions to blunt your alertness. Teachers usually try to do their best, and many of them will make the wisest judgements on the best subjects for your child to pursue, but you cannot allow a decision to *drop* a subject, such as French or Maths, to go unchallenged. Many such decisions are reversible, and it is quite possible that your child has not made clear at school his wish to pursue a career which cannot be approached without a particular subject as a qualification.

Of course it is rare for a child of thirteen or fourteen to know what job he wants to do after leaving school. It is even rarer for a child to have parents willing to search out the right books and pamphlets so that he can discover, before it is too late, the subjects needed for a course of study leading to a particular career. But a child can keep certain options open by being given a chance to stick at certain subjects in his early teens. It is far better for teachers to persevere with a pupil at this stage, than for the child to try taking a subject at night-school or on a full-time technical-college course years later.

Time-table of Approach to University

Roughly *half* the applicants for university this year will *fail*. This fact dominates all discussion about university entrance, and puts the whole problem in perspective; it shows the urgency of making decisions at *the right time*, in the most effective way.

At the last count, 116,735 school-leavers tried for university places, but only 62,519 were successful. There are signs that the situation at some universities is getting worse. A popular university, such as Sussex, receives about 12,000 applicants for a thousand places. Many of those who fail to get in have three, or even four, good passes at 'A' level.

The first point to bear in mind is that these applicants began their search, and put in their completed form to the

Universities Central Council on Admissions, in the autumn of the year before they wanted to enter. A candidate wanting to go to a university in October 1973, for example, should send off his form by the first week in October 1972. You *must* appreciate this time-table. The last stage of the process starts twelve months *before* your child actually enters a university.

The 1968 report of the Universities Central Council on Admissions (known as UCCA) showed that, by the middle of June of that year, 14,450 pupils had received an unconditional offer of a place, and had accepted it. More than 16,000 applicants had been told they were unsuccessful in *all* their applications. We can see, therefore, that about 30,000 out of 100,000 candidates had received a firm decision three and a half months before the start of the university term in October. Most of the remaining pupils could not be told, even as late as this, because *their* fate depended on their performance at 'A' level that summer. The results of these GCE exams come out between August 12th and August 22nd. Then the big scramble begins in earnest. By August 30th, 1968, all but 2,560 candidates, whose application depended on exam results, had received final decisions. By September 6th, a further 1,560 had heard their fate. Throughout September about 20,000 candidates asked to be reconsidered by any university which still had vacancies in their subject.

This tight schedule is obviously unsatisfactory. The UCCA does a magnificent job, but is severely handicapped by the dates of the 'A' level exams, and by the timing of the start of the university year. Until 'A' levels are brought forward, or until the beginning of the academic year is delayed, this worrying, last-minute September scramble will continue.

This analysis of the UCCA operation emphasizes the need to apply as quickly as possible. It also shows the importance of keeping degree options open in polytechnics and technical colleges, in case *your* child's application to a university is unsuccessful. I do not mean to imply here that a degree course at a polytechnic or a technical college is inferior to a university degree, indeed some courses outside the forty-five universities are *superior* to any inside these more famous institutions, as we have noted. My point is that if you want your child to go to a university as a first choice, rather than to a polytechnic, you should not forget the opportunities, outlined in Chapter Nine, outside the universities, in case your child cannot win a university place.

It is also essential for parents to realize that only about one applicant in five, of those 20,000-odd still trying for a place in *September*, are successful. In 1967, for example, the number of lucky last-minute acceptances was 4,160 – of which nearly two-thirds were students wanting to read either pure science or technology. These are, as we shall see, the two faculties which often end up with vacancies after all possible applicants have been considered. School-leavers with two mediocre 'A' level passes can often get a place in these subjects, while applicants with three or four 'A' levels can fail to get any sort of a place in the most popular arts subjects.

It is also very important for parents, teachers and pupils to heed a powerful warning in the UCCA report for 1967. In that year 23,000 applicants were considered in the September scramble, and 1,585 of these were candidates who had applied *too late* to be considered in the earlier stages. This means, of course, that over 1,500 applicants might have got a place, or won a place more suited to their needs, if only they had sent off their form at the correct time. The right time is the autumn of the year before your child wishes to start at university. Timing is so important a factor in this matter that I make no apology for repeating this fact. You will be greatly helped in your efforts to assist your child in this difficult field if you have copies of the booklets *How to Apply for Admission to University*, the *Compendium of University Entrance Requirements*, and *University and College Entrance – the Basic Facts* (see p. 245).

Armed with these publications you should start thinking about the problem when your child is about fourteen. You should be able to discuss the future with your child's teachers at this stage. Such discussions when your child is about to specialize in some subjects, and drop others, are the first steps towards a university place. The next stages are further discussions at the time of the GCE 'O' level and just before decisions are made about entering the sixth form. The tight time-table twelve months before university entrance will not catch either you, or your child's teachers, unawares, if you have prepared the ground in this way.

Choice of Subject

The other crucial factor, apart from sending in forms at the right time, is the bewildering variety of choice of subjects taught in the forty-five universities. There are at least 130 different courses, including at least seventeen *different* types of engineering. The average sixth form teaches only about twelve subjects, and the greatest number taught in the sixth form of any school is thirty-five subjects. So you can see how important it is to be aware of these possibilities at the time your child is dropping some subjects and concentrating on others.

Although it is true in general that a candidate stands a better chance of getting a place to study a science subject than an arts subject, this maxim needs to be qualified. Even in the sciences an applicant's chances are better in some studies than in others. Your child will have a better chance if he opts for automobile, aeronautical, municipal, control, production or structural engineering, than if he goes for a course in the more popular civil, mechanical or electrical engineering.

It is at this stage in the process that an imaginative decision to try something unusual, but *suited to your child's personality and talents*, could pay off. There are, for example, courses in brewing and malting at Birmingham and Strathclyde; there are studies in hotel and catering administration at Surrey and London; your child could read domestic science at Bristol or London; there are courses in ceramics at Leeds, Sheffield and Strathclyde; poultry husbandry is taught at Reading; and paper science is a course at the Manchester Institute of Science and Technology.

You will have discovered already that choosing a subject

is not just a matter of deciding between English at Cambridge, history at Oxford or economics at the LSE. Most parents find to their surprise, when their children reach their early teens, that there are forty-five universities, including many they have never heard of.

When your child has decided on a course for which he has obtained adequate 'A' level passes, or for which he hopes to get passes, he must then select five universities offering such a course. At this point another vital decision has to be made which affects chances of success considerably: does one put the five universities down in order of preference or state them without preference?

It is possible to say: 'My first choice is Loughborough; here are four other universities which are equally attractive to me'. It is also possible to refuse to indicate your preference. This second approach may *seem* the most sensible thing to do, as it avoids offending any one university whose staff feel slighted at being placed low in your list. University dons are just as human as anyone else, and they do seem to be affected adversely by such decisions. Each learned institution is bound to be pleased if your child rates them higher than others.

The reactions of individual tutors speak for themselves:

Applicants who put no preference order arouse two conflicting reactions in me : (*a*) surely he could have had the guts to prefer *something*; (*b*) well, none of the candidates can possibly have the basis to express genuine preferences yet – and at least this one is honest enough to say so. I think (*a*) weighs heavier.

We postpone decisions on students who give us a preference below third. In effect this means that any candidate who indicates a preference for three or more universities will in fact have his application considered only by the first three. If, on the other hand, he indicates no preference, or only one, his application will be considered by all five universities.

There is no easy answer to increasing your chances at some universities by putting them high on the list, and prejudicing your chances with others by putting them towards the bottom.

Other tutors comment:

> The order of preference seems to influence the applicant's decision rather than mine. My offers are quite independent of preference, but the likelihood of their being firmly accepted decreases as one goes down the list. Experience shows that if we accept candidates who put us low in the order of preference – they seldom materialize.

> Decisions are, in general, made *earlier* when our university is high on the list. There is little point in spending time considering students who will probably go elsewhere.

> Candidates who place us higher than third tend to be dealt with first as an arbitrary means of dealing with the large number of candidates. Offers to highly qualified candidates are made regardless of their preference. Average candidates stand more chance of being offered a place, if we appear above third preference.

It is clear the case against putting preferences is not very convincing – in spite of the powerful point (*b*) made by the first tutor above. But, on the other hand, candidates who do not express preferences *are* considered by all five universities. I advise your child to state preferences – especially if he can back up his beliefs at an interview with intelligent reasons. 'Having the guts to prefer something' is an important and, I suspect, widespread academic reaction.

The question still remains: 'How does anybody decide which university is more attractive than another?' It is, at best, a hit-or-miss affair, influenced by rumour, prejudice, opinion, good public relations, a fine campus, and a host of other factors. Some candidates make up their minds after studying about twenty prospectuses. If your child began thinking of going to university at the age of fourteen, if he was forced to specialize in certain subjects at this age, part of the question 'Which university?' is answered for him. The range of choice is reduced by the subjects he *cannot* study at university. Many of the 130 courses will not be open to him. Your task at this stage is to find out which are the best universities for the subjects your child may like to read. Reputations rise and fall, and a university faculty which was once famed for its work in a particular subject may be less attractive now that its leading professor is no longer the force he was, or because of some staff changes.

It is important to remember that the teachers at your child's school may well be giving advice based on *their memories* of their days as an undergraduate. While the quality of a university department does not soar up and shoot down all that dramatically, reputations can be based on memories which are irrelevant to the situation at the time your child applies for a place.

The following advice is a shade difficult to carry out, but it could well be a decisive factor in whether your child gets a coveted place in the face of strong competition. When you have chosen, with your child and his teacher, some likely courses at a few universities, you could check with an organization (such as ACE) on the latest news about the quality of the departments at these universities or colleges. The headteacher at your child's school should cooperate in these investigations. A discreet telephone call to another head, or to an old graduate friend now working in the particular university, could reveal the information you want. Of course if you approach all these questions *in good time* you have a better chance of finding out the necessary answers. Headteachers will not be pleased to get forty or fifty such inquiries during the 'A' level exams.

This crucial question of choosing a university also involves a little piece of gamesmanship. The ploy is to check on the key teacher in the department at the university of your choice. You may be able to find out quite easily, say from *Who's Who* in your library, what his interests are, or what books he has had published. If, for example, your child is trying in a highly competitive subject such as English or history, the knowledge of a professor's pet theories, or favourite period in history, could help a great deal. I know candidates who have quite subtly praised an examiner's favourite poem, or alluded to a theory of how the First World War began; and such references have been noticed when the candidate reached the interview. In many cases the entrance exams at Oxford and Cambridge are marked by dons who will not be present at the interview, but the head of the department will, at some time or other, be involved in the final choice of successful applicants.

Even if such detective work cannot be useful in an entrance exam at Oxford or Cambridge, it will help you make up your mind about choosing a university. If you have a choice between two universities with departments of equally-high repute, the personal details about the professors in charge could sway you one way or the other. Similar investigations would also be in order to help your child make up his mind on questions such as 'Do I live at home or go to a university so far away that I come home only once a term?', or 'Is an urban university better than a rural one?'

The forty-five universities fall into several groups. There are the newer, beautifully-placed ones such as York, Kent and Sussex. There are the older, urban universities (usually known as 'red-brick') such as Leicester, Birmingham and Liverpool. There are the universities which are converted in the 1960s from the old Colleges of Advanced Technology, such as Loughborough, Salford and Bradford.

When making choices between Keele and Sheffield, between Southampton and Lancaster, and so on, you and your child will need to take non-academic factors into account. Will the rival attractions of the town be a distraction? (This could be true at Sussex with its proximity to Brighton, but it is not so true at Kent which is close to the more sedate Canterbury.) Will the fact that there are nine boys to every girl be an attraction or a distraction to my daughter? Will living in lodgings in London be depressing for my son who has always lived in a small country town? These are typical of the questions which must be faced and examined before final choices are made. In any case, the more you know about the staff, studies, location and reputation of a university, the easier advising your child will be. Such information will also, as we have noted, give him confidence at the interview.

Interviews

The question of interviews and interview-technique deserves close attention by parents, teachers and candidates. Most universities still interview applicants. They defend this part of the selection process convincingly. A boy who claims he desperately wants to go to a particular university, but reveals at an interview that he has not bothered to read its prospectus and clearly knows little about its special character, is not likely to impress those in charge of the interview. Such a candidate would appear at best irresponsible, and at worst slightly dishonest.

The UCCA application form contains a section on 'personal interests', as well as the usual formal queries. An intelligent, able candidate can notch up a few pluses by taking advantage of these personal questions and giving a good account of himself. Universities are searching for signs of an inquiring mind; they are looking for evidence or breadth of personality and interests. It would be foolish to allow your child to fill in this part of the form hastily.

Again, the views of tutors are revealing. They comment that:

> This section is often very badly done. One gets the impression of schoolchildren sat down in rows, and their efforts scrutinized to see if anything unconventional has been said, before a fair copy is allowed. If *only* they would write this with imagination. It is really the top qualification – and so *rare*.

> One is not terribly interested in information on minor

good works. It is after all primarily an academic competition, and anything the candidate can tell us about his or her intellectual interests, is worth more than titbits about philanthropic endeavours.

I take little note of games skills. Positions of responsibility weigh a bit – but I'm not naturally in favour of 'joiners'. I look for an interesting and educable mind, evidence of strength of purpose, and ability to stay the course.

The information on 'interests' clearly helps the university to decide whether to interview the candidate or not. The importance of the interview can be seen in this comment from another tutor:

Anything the candidate writes may well have to be defended at an interview. Since some universities only interview *20 to 25 per cent of applicants, and probably accept only a fifth of these*, anything a candidate says on the form which can make us decide to interview him is extremely important.

You should advise your child not to sell himself short by being excessively cautious. It would be silly for him to appear less knowledgeable, or less sensitive, because he kept something to himself unnecessarily. He might omit a topic of interest because he was only eighty per cent sure of being able to discuss it at an interview. But the dons will forgive uncertainty caused by poor memory or nerves. They will also accept a candidate's frankness if he says: 'It's a long time since I read that book, but I'm fairly sure my reaction was . . .' You cannot encourage your child too much to be honest at the interview, and thorough in his preparation for it. University tutors are looking for students who will be painstaking, imaginative and responsible. If your child has 'flair', if he has neglected part of his 'A' level studies because of a passionate interest in one or two aspects of the course, do not try to persuade him to cover *all* the gaps in his revision just before an interview. Tutors will often respond favourably to a candidate who appears a touch eccentric – he may be a genius. They do not want plodders, and so a boy who speaks with real feeling and insight about a particular part of his studies may be preferred to others who, while knowing the basic fundamentals of the whole course, appear listless or unimaginative.

Alex Evans, the former general secretary of the association in charge of teacher-training colleges, once told me of a candidate who came for the interview and talked fervently about jazz for at least 15 minutes: 'I could see we need not discuss anything else. I accepted him right away. He was alert and alive – we don't want grey teachers.'

You should warn your child against answering too promptly at his interview. Today's candidates are usually younger than those of a few years ago, and consequently they are less mature and more nervous. The successful candidate will be conscious that his immaturity could lead to his giving a poor account of himself, and he will take steps to avoid this. Tutors, as we have noted, will be sympathetic towards a very young, nervous applicant, but it is hard for them to be objective about someone whose nervousness leads to muttering and incoherence. Girls should also be warned against wearing too much make-up or excessively short skirts. There are well-authenticated stories of dons who have a weakness for a well-shaped leg or a large bust, but there are also some signs that a significant number of professors dislike women. Moderation is the watch-word here.

Not all universities and colleges interview candidates. The practice of interviewing has declined in recent years as the number of applicants has risen. Reading University, for example, has decided it would be unfair to try to see all the candidates, and still ensure a just criterion of selection.

If At First You Don't Succeed

Even if your child does not drop vital subjects at the age of fourteen, even if he gets good passes at 'A' level, even if he sends off his application promptly and acquits himself well at the interview, he may still be among the unlucky 50,000-odd candidates who *fail*. What should a parent do if a child does not win a place at the first attempt?

The first thing for a parent to bear in mind is that one in six of the successful candidates in any year *failed the year before*. In 1965, for example, 5,532 unlucky applicants returned to school, 6,284 went to technical colleges, and 3,931 continued their education part-time while working. Parents who realize these facts will be better able to cope with the understandable disappointment, and often tears, which result from a first-attempt 'failure'.

It is vital to get the whole question of 'success' and 'failure' into perspective. So much depends on luck rather than ability that, providing you have followed the advice given earlier in this chapter, you will probably have no need to blame yourself or your child if at first he does not succeed.

When the postman brings the bad news your child has four options open to him : he can give up and go out to work; he can go back to school; he can try for a place at a technical college; or he can decide to study part-time, while working.

Unless, after consultation with his headteacher, you all decide the first course is the wisest, I do not advise it. Perhaps your child is in no state to continue his studies, in any form, but only a very few students will be in this position. Just as four out of ten children who leave school as fast as they can, at the age of fifteen, regret it later in life, so a substantial number of those who give up and go out to work after missing a university place will wish they had decided differently.

If your child goes to a polytechnic or technical college after an unsuccessful atempt at a university place, there is no need for you to feel he has had to be content with 'second-best'. In fact, as we saw earlier, many courses in these colleges are *superior* to anything comparable in the universities.

Parents of the one child in four (among the first-time 'failures') who stops studying and starts work, should make sure there is no course available in further education before allowing him to take such a defeatist step. I must warn you again, however, that you will have to be pretty persistent when investigating the chances available in technical colleges, for careers teachers and headteachers can be amazingly ignorant about non-university degree courses. As the vice-principal of a college of technology told me:

> Many schools look no further than the universities when placing their pupils. A technical college may send out fifty to 100 letters to nearby schools with information on vital new professional courses, and offer to give up-to-date careers advice – but these will not produce more than a handful of replies. Education authorities could help by recognizing that careers teachers in schools need far more time for their job than they are given at present. In the meantime parents, or their children, would be *welcomed* if they turned to the 'Tech' for help.

This essential message was also given to all parents by a spokesman for ACE, which pioneered the idea that unsuccessful university candidates should be informed of vacancies on degree courses at technical colleges. Its success in this field was so great that the scheme was eventually taken over by the Ministry of Education. The ACE spokesman said:

> University entrance is held out as the pinnacle of achievement in schools, and many schools never tell pupils of non-university opportunities for taking a degree. At one co-educational grammar school there was always praise at assembly for anyone who got to university – underlined by a sermon from the headmaster on the virtues of this achievement. A girl who went to public school told me her headmistress was absolutely *appalled* to hear one of her pupils would be going to a technical college. The element of chance in seeking entry to a university is so great, it is often Lady Luck who should be praised at morning assembly.

Once again I make no apology for repeating this vital piece of advice. Ignorance of the opportunities which abound in the technical colleges may hinder your child's efforts to get a second chance of a degree.

Some parents, perhaps a majority, will be concerned about the financial difficulties resulting from a decision to allow an unsuccessful applicant to return to school. It may be more expensive to provide uniforms and pocket money for a school-pupil than to help out a grant-aided undergraduate – although grants do not go far these days. If you are worried in this way, allowing your child to take a part-time course at technical college (to try and improve an 'A' level pass) could be the answer. Your son, or daughter, can then help out the family income by getting a job.

So we can see once again how the facilities in further education can help people with a variety of needs. Consult your child's headteacher about them. If he shows the kind of hostility to the 'Techs' described above, get the necessary information from your local college, confront him with it tactfully, and, if he is still unhelpful, ask him what alternative course he suggests.

Bear in mind, if your child does combine part-time study with a job, some employers will allow part-time students time off to study with full-time students. This is the first of two reasons why you should help your child to select a job with the greatest of care. The second reason is that it is sensible to choose a job which has some bearing on one's future career or degree subject. The prospective medical student might, for example, consider working as an orderly or hospital porter.

It may be some comfort to you, if your child has to take a job and study part-time after a first-attempt 'failure' for a university place, to consider the psychological, social, and *educational* benefits of this period. Many children go straight from a single-sex, single-social-class school to a university which is dominated by men and middle-class attitudes. If your child has some experience of mixing in a working-class atmosphere, and handling a wage-packet, he will probably be more mature, more socially-aware and certainly more knowledgeable about the 'university of *life*', when a university place is finally secured.

But let us return to the sad moment when a child hears the bad news about his unsuccessful application. We have considered the arguments against giving up, and the benefits of part-time studies. Your responsibilities as a parent are considerable at this time when the bad news is received. Consider the story of Shelia :

> When I heard I hadn't got a university place – I didn't say anything to my parents for two days, and they kept nagging at me constantly because I was so snappy with them, and with my little brother. A girl I knew at school had a place, and she was always ringing me up to tell me about the fencing gloves and college scarves she was buying. We were supposed to be friends, but I couldn't help being jealous. Eventually I told my parents, and they tried to hide their disappointment, but I kept thinking I'd let them down, and of how humiliated they'd be when they told the rest of the family. I went round hating everybody for weeks, and though I must admit my parents were pretty patient with me, my mother couldn't resist telling me off about my hair being untidy. I admit it was, but I couldn't have cared less about my appearance, particularly as my face suddenly erupted into horrible great spots. I cheered up a bit after I'd decided to brazen it out, go back to school, and retake one 'A' level. I had my hair cut, the teachers were sympathetic, and by December I had already been interviewed by my first-choice university, and had accepted their conditional offer.

Her story reminds us of the human distress behind the cold fact that *half* the applicants fail. It also shows how important it is for a child to have sympathetic parents and teachers, who realize there is no disgrace in being unlucky. The attitude of teachers is an important factor to consider when you are trying to answer the question of whether your child should return to school or study part-time at the 'Tech'. Teachers may find it embarrassing to have pupils in class who are hearing it all for a second time, and may even dismiss the child as a 'failure'. The views of your child are often decisive in this issue. Some pupils feel school is a far less attractive place when most of their closest friends have left. Others find that school rules, uniform and atmosphere, which were only just bearable before, are now intolerable.

The attitude of parents may be more sympathetic if they realize how narrow the margin is between 'success' and 'failure' in the GCE 'A' level. Shelia said she returned to school to retake one subject at 'A' level. We can assume perhaps she had previously been given a 'D' grade pass in this subject. Her parents, and even her teachers, may feel this is a poor performance. But consider what such a grading really means. She could have been given a 'D' grade pass by getting 54 per cent, while her friend with the passion for fencing may have scraped a 'B' grade with 60 per cent. In other words, *a mere six marks* separates the bottom of 'B' grade from the top of 'D' grade. Once you appreciate how small these differences are, you will be far less likely to nag your child, and far more likely to encourage him to retake the subject, either at school or technical college.

But, apart from retaking the same exam to improve a low grade, the child has the option of attempting a completely new subject to increase his chances of acceptance the following year. If all your child's energies are concentrated on one subject, the course can easily be managed in a year. It is important at this stage to reconsider the relative popularity of the different subjects. If your child has been trying in a highly competitive field such as geography, he might profitably change to some subject (eg, biology) which is less popular with candidates.

As we noted earlier, it is vital for parents, pupils and teachers to know which are the most difficult subjects to win a place in. For some reason (it may be stricter marking, poorer teaching, or weaker candidates) geography is something of a jinx subject. Candidates who include geography among their three subjects face huge odds against winning a place. They are much less likely than other candidates to obtain three 'C' grade passes. If your child had been studying history, a language and geography, or two languages and geography, you could advise him to study something other than geography for a year. He could, for example, try for a combination of history and two languages. This group of subjects gives a candidate almost as much chance of success as the combinations of science subjects, which are the best subjects to offer. It is also necessary to understand that two 'B' passes are a better passport to university than three 'C's.

The facts speak for themselves. 80 per cent of applicants with two good 'A' levels (but only 60 per cent if one of the subjects was geography!) got places at the last count, but only 25–40 per cent of the non-science candidates with *three* poor 'A' levels were accepted.

It is worth considering the success-rate of candidates with three passes below 'C' grade. Of those with maths, physics and chemistry; or two maths and chemistry; or two maths and physics; or physics, chemistry and biology – *more than three-quarters still got places*. Of those with chemistry, botany and zoology; or history and two languages – *over a half were accepted*. But of those offering three languages; or English, history and a language; or two languages and geography; or English and two languages; or history, a language and geography; or English, history and geography; or English, a language and geography – *only 25–41 per cent were successful*. Only 21 per cent of the applicants with economics, history and geography managed to get in.

The figures show that a girl with poor 'A' levels has less chance than a boy. Although 62 per cent of girls had grades above three 'C's, compared with only 57 per cent of boys, the same proportion of boys and girls were accepted. This is a difficult point to grasp, so I will put it another way. If only 38 per cent of girls compared with 43 per cent of boys had grades below three 'C's, it seems odd that equal percentages of boys (55 per cent) and girls (56 per cent) were awarded places. In short, although the brightest girls suffer no discrimination, when it comes to a choice between an *unpromising* girl and an unpromising boy, the boy tends to be favoured.

When you are examining the alternative subjects your child might take at 'A' level, after one unsuccessful attempt at a university place, you should consider the following report from UCCA:

> As in previous years there was a notable *shortage* of candidates for pure science and technology with suitable examination qualifications, and a considerable *surplus* of such candidates for arts, social studies, law and the medical group – although in the medical group there was rather less competition for dentistry and the medical sciences (physiology, biochemistry, etc) than for the MB and ChB (Bachelor of Medicine and Bachelor of Surgery). In pure science and technology the exam qualifications required for admission were again *considerably lower* than in the non-scientific subjects. Only in the biological sciences was the supply of qualified candidates nearly adequate to fill the available places. In the social studies group (which includes accountancy, anthropology, business and management studies, economics, geography, law, politics, psychology, and sociology) *all courses were again highly competitive*, and for some candidates with high advanced-level grades, *it was impossible to find a place*. Geography in particular had a high ratio of applications to places. In arts, English was particularly difficult. Candidates who found it difficult to secure a place in English could be more easily accommodated in a combined course. Classics and theology were not so heavily over-subscribed as English, history or Arts General.

Note how it is admitted that many highly qualified candidates, often with three or four good 'A' level passes, have to be turned away. I advise you to consider all the above information when you discuss the choice of a fresh 'A' level with your child and his teachers.

But apart from resitting an 'A' level, or attempting a new subject, the unlucky applicant who misses a place at a first attempt has other alternatives for further studies. Universities which do not demand a pass at 'O' level in a language receive an unusually large number of applicants. Many candidates find their choices of a university diminished by poor 'O' level qualifications. Your child could spend his extra year working for another pass at 'O' level. One girl, who had never done any French, and who was certainly no linguist, spent five hours a week at an evening class, and passed her 'O' level in this subject easily. She then added a pass in 'O' level Latin by using a teaching machine.

But all parents with children thinking of a second attempt at university will wonder whether the universities are prejudiced against those who have been rejected already. Although, as we noted earlier, one in six of the successful candidates in any one year was trying for the second time, it is worth looking at this question in more detail. I know it bothers both parents and teachers. The answer seems to depend on whether the student had applied for the same university previously. If he had, and been offered a place, but had failed to obtain high enough grades at 'A' level, the prospect of another offer looks quite hopeful; and in this case it might be worth breaking the general rule of not making a second application to the same place. Universities have a rather naïve faith in their own judgement, and the reasoning here seems to be that if a candidate was thought promising one year, then he will still be promising the next, *though he must be a good boy and improve his grades*. Many university dons prefer third-year sixth-formers to the others because they are not so arrogant, and have realized they are going to university to learn something rather than to show how much they know.

But if a candidate was rejected the previous year, and only obtained mediocre grades, then the university has been proved right, and, as one tutor put it, 'There is nothing in his "A" level performances to recommend him to us, or to convince us he's going to do better next time.' Most tutors agree that if a candidate had obtained a poor 'A' level grade in a subject he wished to study at degree level, he would be unlikely to be offered a place anywhere. If, for example, a student with grade 'E' in economics, a 'C' in economic history and a 'B' in sociology was unlucky first time round, he should not apply for a degree course in economics at his second attempt. If he does, he is likely to be rejected by all five universities. But if he seeks a course in sociology his chance will be improved, although the competition in this subject is very severe.

All tutors concerned with admissions insist that each case is judged on its merits. We can be sure they do try to be fair, but a great deal depends on the relations between a candidate's school and his parents, and on the 'know-how' of parents and teachers.

Consider the case of an average boy with three 'C' passes at 'A' level, who comes from a home which has never had any experience of the problems of university entrance, and who attends a school with a small sixth-form and no tradition of sending pupils on to the universities or to those technical colleges which offer degrees. Such a boy *could* get a place (especially if his 'A' levels were in science subjects), but if his subjects were the most popular ones, if he filled in his UCCA form carelessly or too late, or if he was not well briefed about his interview – he might well fail to get in. Any one of these 'if's could mean the difference between success and 'failure'. Your child's chances will be greatly improved if you make sure you consult his teachers at each stage, and if you take great care to provide a place in your home for him to study in peace and comfort.

Wastage

If your child does obtain a place, what are his chances of getting a degree? Undergraduates often complain that some universities admit more first-year students than they can transfer to the second-year course. The students allege this practice is the method used to cover errors in selection : the university admits too many students so that it can weed out those who later prove to be below par. They also allege that even if *all* the first-year students are able, some are *still* expelled because of the shortage of second-year places.

Such allegations are difficult to prove, but the newer universities such as York and Lancaster do have a better reputation for exam justice than some older ones. If your child's headteacher is really on the ball, he should be able to keep up with such tendencies in certain universities and colleges through the headteacher's grape-vine.

If your child stays the course, he has a good chance of getting a degree. The pass-rate in our universities is the highest in the world. At the last count only 17 per cent of male students, and only 13 per cent of female students, left universities without a degree. This success-rate is much higher than it is in the technical colleges, where a third of the men and a quarter of the women do not complete their courses.

If, however, your child is the unlucky one in seven who fails to get a degree, the outlook for him is not bright. He may even be worse off than someone with three 'A' levels who left school and went straight out to work. An employer looks warily at a man who confesses he is a 'drop-out'.

Half the students who fail to get degrees at their first try eventually manage to graduate, but only after considerable delay, distress and financial hardship. Local authorities are obliged to provide a grant only for the school-leaver's first degree course. If your child fails, he can try for an external degree of the University of London through part-time studies, or he can approach the Open University which we mentioned earlier.

Parents should warn children, when making the choice of a university and when deciding on a subject to study, to consider the factor of high and low 'wastage' rates. The failure rate varies widely throughout the universities and colleges. The figures given above are the national average picture. The highest pass-rate in the country is at Cambridge, where 97 per cent of students get their degrees first time. The lowest pass-rate is at universities such as Loughborough, where one student in four fails. Standards, and the difficulty of staying on through the three-year course, vary considerably from subject to subject. In arts subjects the drop-out rate varies from three to 20 per cent, in science from three to 28 per cent, and in technology from five to 36 per cent. You should press your child's headteacher to find out the precise figures for your child's selected subject at the university of his choice. Although some of the universities with high failure-rates are very attractive for other reasons, you should consider the dangers of struggling to help an average child through his course, only to hear at the end he has not got a degree.

If your child is one of the 3,500 students each year who fail to get a degree, and if he appears to have little hope of a second chance, you might ask ACE to put you in touch with the service for 'drop-outs' which is organized by the Inner London Education Authority in conjunction with the University of London.

Grants

Parents should contact their local education authority about his maintenance grant as soon as possible in the year *before* a child goes to university, and before the UCCA form is completed. If you tell them your income and personal circumstances, they will give you some idea how much your child will be given to cover his books, living accommodation, travel, food and so on. The amount may affect your child's choice of university, for it may be more economical for him to go to the nearest university so that he can live at home.

The size of the grant is based on a 'means test' of the father's income, but there are many anomalies. My father earned £20 a week and received £16 after tax. I was given a grant of £330 a year, and my father was expected to pay £50 a year towards maintaining me. Yet a friend of mine with a £4,000-a-year father got a full grant.

Detailed advice on the latest level of grants can be obtained from the National Union of Students (Endsleigh Street, London WC1). The Ministry of Education also produce a handbook called *Grants for Students*, which should answer most of your questions.

Further Sources of Subject Information

Your child may find some of the following publications helpful with his choice of study and career:

ACCOUNTANCY : *The Universities and the Accountancy Profession*. Institute of Chartered Accountants, 56–66 Goswell Road, London EC1.

AGRICULTURE : *Full-time Agricultural Education in England and Wales*. Ministry of Education.

BIOLOGY : *Biology as a Career*. Institute of Biology, 41 Queen's Gate, London SW7.

COMPUTER SCIENCE : *A List of Courses* and *Careers with Computers*. The British Computer Society, 23 Dorset Square, London NW1.

ECONOMICS : *Courses in Economics*. The Economics Association, Banstead Road South, Sutton, Surrey.

ENGINEERING : Hutchings, Donald (ed), *Engineering Science at the University*. University of Oxford Department of Education, in cooperation with the Association of Professors of Engineering.

ENGLISH : Arnold, Eric, *A Guide to English Courses*. The English Association, 8 Cromwell Place, South Kensington, London SW7. (Published by John Murray.)

GEOGRAPHY : Jackson, C., *Degrees in Geography*. Royal Geographical Society, 1 Kensington Gore, London SW7.

HISTORY : Barlow, G., and Harrison, B., *History at the Universities*. Historical Association, Kennington Park Road, London SE11.

MANAGEMENT STUDIES : *A Conspectus of Management Courses*. British Institute of Management, 80 Fetter Lane, London EC4.

MATHEMATICS : Rollett, A. P., *Honours Courses in Maths*.

Incorporated Association of Headmasters, 29 Gordon Square, London WC1.

MODERN LANGUAGES : Stern, H. H., *Modern Languages in the Universities*. Macmillan : London, 1965.

PHYSICS : Redman, L. A. (ed), *The Physics Teacher's Handbook*. Spectrum Books : London, 1966.
The Scientific Education of Physicists. Institute of Physics and the Physical Society, 47 Belgrave Square, London SW1.

SOCIOLOGY : Tropp, A., and Banks, J., *A Guide to Social Studies*. British Sociological Association, 13 Endsleigh Street, London WC1.

For students who may be nervous about their ability to last the course at university, I recommend : Maddox, Harry, *How to Study*. Pan Books : London, 1963.

The following will help in the choice of university :

Beloff, Michael, *The Plateglass Universities*. Secker & Warburg : London, 1968.

Boehm, Klaus, *University Choice*. Penguin Books : London, 1966.

Association of Commonwealth Universities Yearbook (in your local library).

The three books mentioned in the text in connexion with university entrance are :

How to Apply for Admission to University. Universities Central Council on Admissions : PO Box 28, Cheltenham, Gloucestershire.

Compendium of University Entrance Requirements. Percy Lund, Humphries & Co : Priestman Street, Bradford 8.

University and College Entrance – The Basic Facts. National Union of Teachers : Hamilton House, Mabledon Place, London WC1.

Organizations Mentioned Throughout the Book

Advisory Centre for Education, 32 Trumpington Street, Cambridge.

Association for All Speech-impaired Children, 63 Alicia Avenue, Kenton, Harrow, Middlesex.

Association for Headmistresses in Preparatory Schools, Mrs Cecilia Leigh, Meadowbrook, Abbot's Drive, Virginia Water, Surrey.

Association of Teachers in Technical Institutions, Hamilton House, Mabledon Place, London WC1.

Careers Research and Advisory Centre, Bateman Street, Cambridge.

Catholic Education Council, 147 Cromwell Road, London SW7.

Common Entrance Exam for Girls' Schools Ltd, Secretary, Miss Helen Garnett, 2 Bankfield, Kendal, Westmoreland.

Confederation for the Advancement of State Education, General Secretary, Mrs B. Bullivant, 81 Rustlings Road, Sheffield.

Cornmarket Careers Centre, 42 Conduit Street, London W1.

Council for National Academic Awards, 3 Devonshire Street, London W1N 2BA.

Council for Technological Education, Tavistock House (South), Tavistock Square, London WC1.

Educational Explorers Ltd, 40 Silver Street, Reading, Berkshire.

Elfrida Rathbone Society, Toynbee Hall, 28 Commercial Road, London E1.

Friends Educational Council, Friends' House, Euston Road, London NW1.

Home and School Council, 1 White Avenue, Northfleet, Kent.

I.t.a. Foundation, 154 Southampton Row, London WC1.

Incorporated Association of Preparatory Schools, 138 Kensington Church Street, London W8.

Ministry of Education (Department of Education and Science), Curzon Street, London W1.

National Association for Autistic Children, 1a Golders Green Road, London NW11.

National Association of Careers Teachers, 31 Lamplugh Road, Bridlington, Yorks.

National Association for Gifted Children, 27 John Adam Street, London WC2.

National Extension College, Shaftesbury Road, Cambridge.

National Federation of Parent–Teacher Associations, Mrs May Swinson, 1 White Avenue, Northfleet, Kent.

National Institute for Adult Education, 35 Queen Anne Street, London W1.

National Society for Mentally Handicapped Children, 86 Newman Street, London W1.

National Union of Students, Endsleigh Street, London WC1.

National Union of Teachers, Hamilton House, Mabledon Place, London WC1.

Nursery School Association of Great Britain and Northern Ireland, 89 Stamford Street, London SE1.

Nursery 3-4-5, 92a Old Street, London EC1.

Open University, PO Box 48, Bletchley, Bucks.

Pre-School Playgroup Association, 87a Borough High Street, London SE1.

Scottish Institute of Adult Education, Education Office, Alloa.

Society of Teachers Opposed to Physical Punishment, The Secretary, 12 Lawn Road, London NW3.

Universities Central Council on Admissions, PO Box 28, Cheltenham, Gloucestershire.

Word-blind Centre, 93 Guilford Street, London WC1.

Index

Abortions, teenage, 145–6, 147–9, 158
Accent, acquired, 198
Accountancy as a career, 244
ACE, 1, 10, 28, 64, 65, 71, 94, 110, 117, 121, 125, 199, 220, 228, 234, 243, 246
Admission to grammar school, 116, 187–9
to primary school, 110–12, 123–5
to secondary school, 125
to university, 221–44
Adult education, 218
Advisory Centre for Education, 1, 10, 28, 64, 65, 71, 94, 110, 117, 121, 125, 199, 220, 228, 234, 243, 246
Age and learning to read, 77–80
Agreed syllabus, 200, 203
Agriculture, education in, 244
Aided school, 200
All-age school, 200
Allen, Anne, book-list for children, 97–108
Allocation of pupils to schools, 110–15
Apprenticeship, 209
Association for All Speech-impaired Children, 72, 246
Autistic children, 72, 246

Baby talk, dangers of, 19
Backward children, 4, 17, 72, 93
Bad language, 198

Barnard, David, 152–4, 163
BBC sex education films, 159
Bedtime stories, value of, 28
Behaviour problems, 38–9
Belstead, Lord, 161
Berg, Leila, 28, 36
Bernstein, Basil, 1
Bilateral school, 200
Biology as a career, 244
Birth factor in schooling, 4, 5, 128
Blackstone, Tessa, 69n
Blind children, 71
Bloom, Benjamin S., 3, 17
Bluglass, Robert, 161
Board of Governors, 202
Boarding schools, 112, 128, 139
Bookbinder, G. E., 4
Books,
choosing and buying, 28, 95–6
for children, 28–30, 97–108
home-made, 24–6, 89
importance of in the home, 85
on careers, 219
on choosing a university, 245
on further education, 216
on university entrance, 224
Bramall, Margaret, 148, 150
Bullying, 199
Burnham Committee, 200

Cane, Brian, 10
Caning, 118, 180

249

Careers, 211–20, 244
  advice on, 212–19
  for girls, 137–8
Careers Research and Advisory Centre, 213, 220, 246
CASE, 6–8, 117, 125, 246
Catchment areas, 112, 188
Catholic education, 132, 156, 246
Catterall, Dr, 173
Central Advisory Council, 200
Certificate of Secondary Education, 176–9
Chanter, Albert, 159
Child Education magazine, 24
Chief Education Officer, 200
Child-guidance clinic, 93
Children's books, 28–30
Choice of university course, 225, 237
City and Guilds of London Institute, 200
Class, social, xiv
Clegg, Sir Alec, 183
CNAA, 201, 212, 220, 246
Co-education, 127, 138–40
Cole, Martin, 167
College-based student, 200
Colleges,
  Agriculture, 208
  Art, 208
  Commerce, 208
  Further Education, 208
  Technical, 208
Comics, educational value of, 94
Common Entrance, 130–31
Commoner, 200
Comprehensive schools, 187, 200
Computer science as a career, 244
Confederation for the Advancement of State Education, 6–8, 117, 125, 246
Contraceptives, 148, 149, 151, 161, 162, 173–4
Controlled school, 201
Corporal punishment, 7, 70, 118, 180–84
Correspondence courses, 218
Council for National Academic Awards, 201, 212, 220, 246
County award, 201
CSE examination, 176–9
Curriculum, 201

Daily Express Careers Service, 213
Daines, John, 160
Dainton Report, 134
Dale, Reginald, 127, 138
Dalton Plan, 201
Day-continuation school, 201
Day nurseries, 65, 201
Day release, 201, 209
Deaf children, 71
Degree,
  chances of obtaining, 241
  courses outside university, 233–4
  external, 242
Deprived children, 9–10, 13, 17, 62
Devlin, Tim, 148
Deys, Caroline, 164, 165
Diack, Hunter, 81–2
Direct-grant schools,
  definition, 201
  quality of, 114
Direct method of language teaching, 201
Directory of Further Education, 216
Discipline, 118, 180
  in nursery school, 69
  problems of, 10
Doman, Glenn, 15, 27, 35–6, 86
Douglas, J. W. B., xiii, 139
Downing, John, 77, 82, 90, 91

Duane, Michael, 182
Dyslexia, 94, 96-7

Early leaving in girls' schools, 136-7
Early reading, related to academic success, 88
Eastman School, New York, 12, 13
Economics, courses in, 244
Education,
   after school, 206-20, 233
   Ministry of, 61, 73, 112-14, 129, 148, 189, 202, 207, 219, 234, 244, 246
   non-vocational, 203
   of girls, 133-44
Education Act (1944), 60, 109-10, 185, 189, 203
Education Committees Year Book, 64, 180
Education Welfare Officer, 201
Educational Explorers Ltd, 94, 246
Educational Maintenance Allowance, 189-90
Educationally subnormal children, 131
Eickhoff, Louise, 161
Eleven-plus examination, 187
Elfrida Rathbone Society, 72, 246
EMA, 189-90
Engelmann, Siegfried and Thérèse, 8, 18
Engineering, university courses in, 244
English, courses in, 244
Evans, Alex, 232
Evening institutes, 202
Examinations,
   coaching for, 196
   CSE, 176-9
   eleven-plus, 187
   emotional problems of, 193
   GCE, 179
   parental help in preparing for, 193-6
Examining boards for GCE, 179
Exam neurosis, 136
Excursions, importance in learning, 21
External degree, 242
Extra-mural university department, 202
Eyesight defects, symptoms of, 94

Failure rates at universities, 242-3
Family, influence of, xi-xiv
Family outings, role in increasing vocabulary, 21
Family Planning Association, 145, 174
Farm institutes, 208
Fee-paying schools, 111
Fees,
   nursery school, 66
   secondary school, 111
Fernald, Grace, 193
Flash cards, 27, 81, 86
Form entry, 202
Froebel method, 202
Full-time students, 208
Further education, 202, 206-20, 233-4

Games, role of in home-learning, 33-4
Gandhi, on women's education, 133
Gardner, Keith, 74, 75, 76
GCE, 176-9
General Certificate of Education, 176-9
Geography, university courses in, 244
Gifted children, 71, 246

251

Gillett, Paul, 214
Girls,
    education of, 133-44
    university entrance, 134-5
Girls' Public Day School Trust, 202
Girls School Year Book, 128
Glynn, Dorothy, 87-8, 93
Good Schools Guide, 121, 122
Governors, Board of, 202
Grammar schools, 116, 187-9
Grants for Students, 244
Grants, maintenance, 189, 210, 243
Grants Year Book, 210
Grender, Iris, 69

Handicapped children, 33, 246
Headmasters' Conference, 114, 131
Headteachers,
    interviews with, 116
    qualifications of, 129-30
Heath, Edward, 176
Hemming, James, 171-2
Her Majesty's Inspectors, 202
Higher National Certificate, 203, 212
Higher National Diploma, 203, 212
History, university courses in, 244
HMI, 202
HNC, 203, 212
HND, 203, 212
Holmes, Mary, 155
Holt, John, 121
Home, influence on learning, 1-10
Home and School Council, 5, 246
Homework (private study), 193-6
Howell, David, 65

IAPS, 128, 246

Illiteracy, 73-5
Incorporated Association of Preparatory Schools, 128, 246
Initial teaching alphabet, 90-91
Intelligence, 17, 131, 189, 202
Interview at university, techniques of, 230-2
IQ, 17, 131, 189, 202
ITA, 90-91, 246

Jackson, Brian, 116, 118
Jenkinson, Amelia, 121*n*
Job prospects, 206-20
Johnson, Nevil, 187
Johnston, Stanley, 83
Joseph, Sir Keith, 161

Keable, Sue, 137
Keating, Leslie, 197
Kind, Robert, 152, 155, 163, 164, 165, 170
Kirk, Samuel A., 17

'Ladybird' reading scheme, 78, 82, 93, 95
Language, as factor in choice of school, 113
Larsson, Lena, 41
Learning to read, 24, 73-95
    age for starting, 77-80
Learning to talk, 22-3
Leaving school, 206-11
Letters, forming correctly, 83
Libraries, 30, 93
Linguistic ability, role in education, 13
Literacy, standards of, 73-6
Little Red School Book, 164, 167
Local education authorities, 64

Maintained school, 203
Maintenance grants for students, 243

Malleson, Nicolas, 150, 158
Management studies, courses in, 244
Marsden, Dennis, 190
Masters, Philip, 131
Masturbation, 166-7
Mathematics, honours courses in, 244
Medical factor in choice of schools, 113
Menstruation, 141, 145, 154
Mentally handicapped children, 72
Mill, John Stuart, 15
Miller, Ernest, 147
Modern languages, university courses in, 245
Modern teaching methods, 119
Montessori method, 203
Morris, Joyce, 74, 75, 91
Mothers,
  schoolgirl, 145-6, 147-50
  working, 58
Moyle, Donald, 79
Multilateral school, 203
Music, role in home-learning, 30-32

National Association of Careers Teachers, 214
National Certificate, 203, 212
National Council for the Unmarried Mother and her Child, 148
National Diploma, 203, 212
National Extension College, 218, 219, 246
National Foundation for Educational Research, 10, 23
National Union of Teachers, 118, 148, 157, 247
Neill, A. S., 69
New mathematics, 119
'New morality', 171-3
Newsom Report, 9

Non-university degree courses, 234
Non-vocational education, 203
Numbers, awareness of, 87
Nurseries, distinguished from nursery schools, 65
'Nursery 3-4-5' postal service, 64, 69, 247
Nursery School Association, 65, 247
Nursery schools, 58-72
  choosing, 66
  discipline in, 69
  need for, 3
  size of classes, 66

ONC, 203, 213
OND, 203, 213
Open days, use of in choosing a school, 117
Open University, 218, 242, 247
Opportunities for unsuccessful university applicants, 237
Ordinary National Certificate, 203, 213
Ordinary National Diploma, 203, 213

Paediatrician, 203
Parents,
  as teachers, 1-11, 15, 18-24
  attitude to education, 2
  cooperation with teachers, 5-8, 14, 54, 80
  help of in choosing career, 215-19
  preference of in choice of school, 126
  rights of appeal to examining boards, 179
  rights of in choice of school, 109-10
  rights relating to corporal punishment, 180-84
  rights relating to property lost at school, 184

Parents—*continued*
   role in education, 3, 5, 8, 137
   role in expanding vocabulary, 27
   sex instruction by, 154–7, 168–9
   views of in assessing a school, 122
Parent–teacher associations, 6–10, 61, 117, 125, 141, 216
Part-time students, 208, 235
Peaker, Gilbert, 75
Peel, Sir John, 162
Peel, John, 157
Pets, value in home-learning, 53
Phonic spelling, 82
Physical proximity, importance in learning, 28
Physics, courses in, 245
Pill, contraceptive, 151, 161, 173–4
Pines, Maya, 16, 17
Pitman, Sir James, 90, 91
Play,
   educational value of, 1, 2
   need for direction in, 39–40
   need for space, 56, 58
   with other children, 56, 58
Play-groups, 58–72
   Acts governing, 64
   cost of setting up, 63
   fees, 63
   independent, 63
   training for work in, 71
Playgroup Book, The, 64
Play-pens, 35
Plowden Committee, 4, 182, 183, 204
Plowden, Lady, 65
Polytechnics, 208
PPA, 63, 70, 246
Preparatory Schools Association, 114
Pre-school education, 3, 12, 18–34

Pre-School Playgroup Association, 63, 70
Preston, Peter, 130
Printed word, awareness of, 85–8
Private education, cost of, 111
Private schools, choice of, 128
Private study, 193–6
Project, 203
Property lost at school, 184
Psychologist, educational, 93
PTA, 6–10, 61, 117, 125, 141, 216
Public and Preparatory Schools Year Book, 128
Public schools,
   admission to, 130
   criticism of, 111
Public Schools Commission, 111

Quaker education, 132, 246
Qualified teacher, 203

Reading,
   age for starting to learn, 77–80
   backwardness in, 93–4
   importance of, 73
   preparation for, 80
   readiness for, 78, 79, 82
Reading ability,
   of girls, 142
   of the pre-school child, 142
Reading schemes, 82, 90, 95, 96
Registered schools, distinguished from recognized schools, 129
Reich, Wilhelm, 69–70
Religion, as factor in choice of school, 113
Religious instruction, 203
Reports, school, 196
Rights of parents, 109–10, 179, 180–4
Risinghill School, 182

Ritchie, David, 160
Roman Catholic education, 132, 156, 246
Ross, Jean, 139

Sandwich courses, 209–10
Scholfield, Michael, 173
Schonell, F. J., 73, 193
School,
  assessing the character of, 115
  choice of, and parents' rights, 109
  fees, 111
  how to choose, 109–32
  leaving age, 149, 211
  reports, 196
  starting age, 9, 110, 123
  uniforms, 116, 184–7
School Broadcasting Council, 259, 260
Schoolgirl mothers, 145–6, 147–50
School-leavers, xiii
  opportunities for, 207
Schools,
  aided, 200
  all-age, 200
  bilateral, 200
  boarding, 128, 139
  co-educational, 138
  comprehensive, 187, 200
  controlled, 201
  direct-grant, 201
  fee-paying, 111
  grammar, 116, 187–9
  maintained, 203
  mixed, 138
  multilateral, 203
  nursery, 58–72
  secondary modern, 113
  segregated, 139
  special, 204
Science,
  in girls' schools, 134–5
  in the home, 51–4

Secondary modern schools, 113
Secondary schools,
  admission to, 125
  fees, 111
Setting, definition of, 204
Sex education, 141, 145–75
  films, 152, 159–61
  need for, 145–52
  parents and, 152, 154–7, 168–9
  poor standards of, 154–7
  provision of, 152–3
  starting age, 164, 168
  teaching methods, 163–74
  vocabulary of, 134, 160, 163–4, 171
Sheridan, Mary, 51
Short, Edward, 3, 63, 75
Singing, role in home-learning, 31–2
Slome, John, 146
Society of Teachers Opposed to Physical Punishment, 183, 247
Sociology, courses in, 245
Southgate, Vera, 91, 92
Specialization, 204, 221
Special schools, 204
Speech-impaired children, 72, 93
Spelling, backwardness in, 191–3
Spock, Benjamin, 38, 79
Starting school,
  primary, 123–5
  under-fives, 67–9
Stonar, Winifred Sackville, 16
Streaming, 9–10, 117, 204
Students,
  day-release, 209
  full-time, 208
  maintenance grants for, 243
  part-time, 208
Study, home facilities for, 193–6
Subnormal children, 131
Summer-born children,
  handicaps of, 4, 5, 128

Summerhill School, 69
Summerskill, Baroness, 161
Suzuki, Shinichi, 12–13

Teachers,
  attitude to girls, 135
  attitude to home-learning, 54
  attitude to parents, 5–6
  attitude to reading, 91, 92
  cooperation with parents, 5–8
  legal rights of, 180
  middle-class, 153, 164
  qualified, 203
  status defined, 129
  training of, 92
Teaching methods,
  Froebel, 202
  modern, 119
  Montessori, 203
Tec, Leon, 173
Technical colleges, 206–20, 233
Thatcher, Margaret, 114, 129, 148
Thomson, James, 14, 15
Toilet training, over-strict, 167–8
Toys, 34–51
  choosing and buying, 34, 36, 39, 42–3
  for infants up to 18 months, 43
  for toddlers, 44
  for 2¼–4-year-olds, 44
  for 4–6-year-olds, 45
  home-made, 49–51
  household objects as, 51, 54
  inexpensive, 48
  organizations welcoming gifts of, 72
  purpose of, 1
  storage of, 40–41
Toy-shops and suppliers, 46–8
Training in basic skills, 32
Travelling, as factor in choice of school, 113
Tripartite system, 204

Tripos, 204

UCCA, 223–4, 230, 239, 247
Uniforms, 116, 184–7
Universities,
  admission to, 221–44
  applicant's interview, 230–2
  choice of courses at, 221, 225, 237
  factors influencing applicant's choice, 227–30
  failure rates, 242–3
  intake of girls, 134
  order of preference in applying to, 226–7
  student maintenance grants, 243
  wastage at, 241–3
Universities Central Council on Admissions, 223–4, 230, 239, 247
University Grants Committee, 205
Unrecognized schools, 129

Venereal disease, 145–6, 173–4
Vocabulary, increasing, 20, 22, 27, 28
Vocational guidance, 212–19

Walker, Patrick Gordon, 129
Wall, William, 23
Warburton, Frank, 91
Wastage at universities, 241–3
Wastnedge, Ronald, 53
WEA, 207
Webb, Lesley, 33
Where? magazine, 3, 121, 187
Witte, Karl, 14–15
Women,
  careers for, 137–8
  educational opportunities for, 133
Word-blind Centre, 94, 247
Word-blindness, 94
Word-recognition, 80–82

256

Words, stimulating interest in, 24–5
Workers' Educational Association, 207
Working mothers, 58
Wright, Helena, 145, 147
Writing, starting to learn, 83

You magazine, 166, 167
Youth-employment officer, 214
Youth-employment service, 205, 214

Zoning of primary schools, 112

Popular Reading

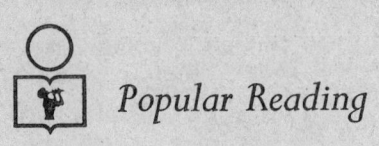

GOLDMINE Wilbur Smith	35p
LOUIS THE WELL-BELOVED Jean Plaidy	30p
GRAB Zeno	30p
BELLE CATHERINE Juliette Benzoni	35p
CARTHERINE AND ARNAUD Juliette Benzoni	35p
THE BIG FISHERMAN Lloyd C. Douglas	40p
THE ROBE Lloyd C. Douglas	40p
THE UNKNOWN AJAX Georgette Heyer	35p
REGENCY BUCK Georgette Heyer	35p
THESE OLD SHADES Georgette Heyer	35p
THIS PERFECT DAY Ira Levin	35p
HIGHLAND YEAR (illus) Lea MacNally	45p